ANJA MEULENBELT

The Shame Is Over

A political life story

Translated by Ann Oosthuizen

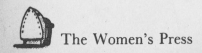

The Women's Press

Published by The Women's Press Limited 1980
A member of the Namara Group
124 Shoreditch High Street, London E1 6JE

The title of this book is from an article by Kate Millett,
published in *Ms* magazine: 'The Shame is Over'.

'Time wounds all heals' and 'All women are lesbian
except those who don't know it yet' are from Jill Johnston,
Lesbian Nation: The Feminist Solution, Simon & Schuster,
New York, 1973.

'The Angel in the House' is from Virginia Woolf, 'Professions for
Women', *The Death of the Moth*, Hogarth Press, London, 1932 and
reprinted in Virginia Woolf, *Women and Writing*, The Women's
Press, London, 1979.

'Goodbye to all That' by Robin Morgan is reprinted in
Voices from Women's Liberation, ed. Leslie B. Tanner, Mentor,
New York, 1970.

The Dialectic of Sex by Shulamith Firestone was published in
Britain by Jonathan Cape, London, 1971 and reprinted by
The Women's Press, London, 1979.

The Shame is Over has been typeset by
Input Typesetting, Wimbledon
and reproduced, printed and bound by
Hazell Watson & Viney Ltd, Aylesbury

From The Women's Press Ltd
124 Shoreditch High Street, London E1 6JE

For Dayle and Victoria
For Mieke
For the women who occupied the
Bloemenhof Abortion Clinic

Contents

Prologue/Foreplay
No Alibi   3
Time wounds all heals   5
Gordes 1   8
Part One: Dreams at bargain prices
A dark street with high windows   19
Gordes 2   27
Schmalz   31
Gordes 3   45
A second marriage   50
Gordes 4   64
Part Two: The sexual and other revolutions
The moon and sixpence   69
Gordes 5   83
The turn of the screw   85
Gordes 6   97
Not my revolution   98
Gordes 7   117
The prince on a white horse   121
Part Three: Public woman
Hysterical materialism   135
Gordes 8   147
Mother isn't coming   152
Gordes 9   162
Triangle with unequal sides   164
Gordes 10   178
Divide and rule   181
Gordes 11   194
No more smiling   195

Gordes 12   207
All women are lesbian
except those who don't know it yet   209
Gordes 13   224
After the euphoria   226
Gordes 14   242
Cold turkey   246
Epilogue
Gordes 15   265
On the crest of the wave   266
Return to Go   274

Prologue/Foreplay

Just at this moment Alice felt a very curious sensation, which puzzled her a good deal until she made out what it was: she was beginning to grow larger again, and she thought at first she would get up and leave the court; but on second thought she decided to remain where she was as long as there was room for her.

'I wish you wouldn't squeeze so,' said the Dormouse, who was sitting next to her. 'I can hardly breathe.'

'I can't help it,' said Alice very meekly: 'I'm growing.'

'You've no right to grow *here*,' said the Dormouse.

'Don't talk nonsense,' said Alice more boldly: 'you know you're growing too.'

'Yes, but *I* grow at a reasonable pace,' said the Dormouse: 'not in that ridiculous fashion.'

Lewis Carroll, *Alice's Adventures in Wonderland*

No alibi

I am in a hurry. Now that it is clear to me that I have decided to write a book (was that in my sleep, as so many decisions taken in the morning appear to be?) the scraps of my life beseige me and keep me awake.

I want to seize them before they vanish or congeal into anecdotes, dead as holiday slides which, after we've seen them three times, arouse no more emotion.

Language, my problem is language, this is not my language. I could write in colours or in wordless sounds. The scraps I find among shopping lists and notes are remote from me, or so close that I am embarrassed. Emotions that appear too sentimental or too dramatic if they are spelled out on paper. Love. Pain. Words that become shallow, or businesslike, or hard. Cunt. Vagina. Orgasm. Not my langue, but as yet I have no other.

I want to capture my experiences. Those of the past, those of the present. It is more difficult to describe what is closer in time. Meanings have changed. Relationships are no longer the relationships I had in the past. I no longer know what sexuality is. I have no categories any more for the people around me. The labels have become nonsense: my husband, my girlfriend. Distinctions that no longer fit. Work. I work all the time. I'm never not working. Another word for living.

I do not want to make compromises. I do not want to be ashamed. It is difficult. When I wrote in political language or the language of economics, a compromise I made in order to be understood by my allies, too much was left out because it didn't fit into the theories. I write to restore my equilibrium. To balance

3

the marxist language through which I could express most things, but not all. It should be a whole, it must become a whole, but it isn't yet. The personal is political, but for the moment there is the same split in my writing as in my fragmented reality.

A success that is too comfortable, our pain translated in terms of production and reproduction. People come up to me to tell me that now they understand what I am saying. While all these years I have been saying the same thing. 'Your writing is so much better now than it was a few years ago when you still wrote those emotional pieces', says one person.

My pain has fallen out of the theoretical framework. They understand it better without pain. Their understanding is too simple. I need to destroy it. Things are not that easy. Even as I bask in the warmth of compliments, my ego a size bigger, I become suspicious again. If friendship is so easy, then I have said too little.

Again the temptation to leave things alone. To fit in. The old comrades who lie when they say that they always knew how important the women's movement would become. Who fake the solidarity they never felt. How nice it is to believe them. No pain. No split. No hate.

There is a knife in my back. I hear whispers: treachery. Sara is dead. The women next to me on the tram are silent. They hump shopping and children. Varicose veins.

In a lift in the Bijlmer, a new town, Francine was raped. And a week later her woman friend.

In the distance, as if seen through the wrong end of a telescope, I see a woman with empty eyes, a head full of impossible dreams. She is not yet twenty. Mother, housewife. Myself, but no longer who I am. I had almost forgotten her until I met her in the supermarket, shy, she dropped her money, blushed as she bent to pick it up. A mirror image of myself, of what I was, multiplied by so many thousand women driven quietly mad, although no one notices. Crying over a sentimental love story. Not understanding where the pain comes from. I am still that woman, wounded, bitter, suspicious, at the same time as the strong,

4

creative, independent woman I am also. Anger close to the surface. Anger that allows itself to be transformed into political theory, in language that non-women can also read. But I am still angry.

I am not looking for an alibi.

Do not understand me too quickly.

Time wounds all heals

Anna, whom I call Anna because it is a name I should have liked for myself. I mourn for Anna. Almost like myself, I loved her because she was like me, I feel safer with my own kind. Anna, whom I have lost now, it will never be the same, that innocence of sisters playing with their dolls and their dolls' tea service. Warmth of comrades working in the same cause. Belly to snuggle up against. We can never get rid of the mountains of accusations between us, her fear of me paralyses me. I can do nothing more with her. Her husband and children come between us, the flat, rent, children's allowance, in-laws who look suspiciously at me, obstacles I can't overcome. We are not approved, Anna becomes again just the wife of her husband, out of my reach.

And what do I have to offer, I think masochistically. An avalanche of emotions, all my neuroses and traumas that I want to share with her, but no apartment, approval of neighbours, in-laws, or recognised status. I can offer no safety, just the fight for the space we need which no one will give us for nothing. She can't take it, goes crazy from the two lives that can't fit together, and naturally I am the one that must go, no twelve-year-old marriage for me to call on, only that I am breaking up, am dying, but who isn't nowadays.

I mourn for Anna, play the records we heard together and weep. And read: Jill Johnston who travelled to Spain, crying, to fetch her love back again. Hopeless, she could not compete with marriage to a man. And Kate Millett who mourns throughout a whole book for Celia. They are still alive, Kate and Jill. You can come through it. Everything wears out in time but time wounds all heals, Jill says, and with the capacity to love the pain increases.

And then the memories, like a never-ending porn movie in my head: big soft breasts and soft bunny tummy and her back stronger and broader than mine. Her body almost the same as mine, only stronger. Smells, of her hair, her armpits that have a different smell from the other perfumes on the snuffling journey down her body. Her neck, and the smell of new-born kittens. Laughing when she can't get a curly hair out from between her teeth; stop, if I laugh I can't come. Then deep sleep, her breasts first seemed as if they would bump against mine, all four equally soft, we have had children, but everything fits. Sleeping with our arms around each other, her head on my shoulder or my head on her shoulder until we turn in our sleep, my belly against her back or my back against her belly.

When she comes it's a celebration, I have never experienced it so close. I can feel everything with her because I know how it feels, a soft swelling, everything is soft, and then a quicker rhythm. When she calls me and pulls me up to her, she tastes her flavour on my lips. We feel complete, snuggling happily together and forgetting to drink our whisky: the next morning after she has gone I leave the two half-empty glasses so that she seems less absent. At night I sleep alone again in the pillows that still smell like her; I find a curly hair between the sheets, dark, hers.

The porn movie that keeps on coming back. Making love quietly on the bare floors in London without noise at the climax so as not to wake the others in the room. And during the weekend with our women's group we push the beds against each other, covering them without comment with our double bed sheets. (I don't believe anyone thought it strange, but all the same, we didn't dare to make love.) Addicted to her body, sleeping with

6

her so different from when I sleep alone, deeper, dreamless, almost without moving. The next day when I see her coming towards me I believe that she has become more beautiful, but perhaps that is because I see her strong body beneath her clothes. Sleeping together is almost as important as talking together. We grumble about the narrow, chaste beds pushed against each other in the adult educational institute. Rather backache than to have to miss the softness of her body.

Throughout the summer I have been trying to put her away from me, to set myself free. There was still hope when she left, we almost found each other in our sorrow. She said she did not dare go on any more, scared of the emotions that were becoming ever stronger, scared because it would become increasingly difficult to break off, scared that she would in the future cause me to suffer even more than she had already. That is impossible, I say, it's already impossible to experience more pain, we can only go on. Talking about it was already a continuation of the relationship under another name. But she went anyway. I waited for her letter which naturally would say that she could not live without me and that we should go on whatever the consequences, but when her letter came at last it was a chatty holiday letter, distant, about camping, where they were now, that she thought about me still and that she had almost forgotten her bag in a museum out of absent-mindedness and that she hoped I would be over it a bit by now. Pain, pain, I fall in a pit, make wild plans to go to her, sure that she could not be so cold if she saw me, sure that it would not be over if only I could touch her, sure that we would go on even if we told each other it was impossible. And I imagined that I would abduct her and lock her up, or fight with her or murder her. If only she understood something of this pain, I thought, what can I do to make her feel it. But how do you talk about pain to someone who doesn't know what it is, who has never lost someone she loves, married twelve years to the same man, never lost a child under a tram or a woman friend who has killed herself. She knew nothing in spite of having lived longer than me, what did she know about pain.

I wrote atrocious letters saying that I hated her which was true at the time, that I despised her for being a bourgeois frump who opted for her own safe little existence and received a letter back in reply that she was insulted and unhappy. Unhappy. What did that person know about pain. I wrote the final letter, that I never wanted to see her again, that we could never be friends again. And went back to Amsterdam where, when I saw the bed we had slept in together, the plant she had given me, the books we had read together, the lamp with the purple letters on it: anna is a darling anja is a darling, the photo of her on the wall, I fell back into the pit again. I knew she was in the city. Only a little water between us. It is crazy, I thought, so close, both of us paralysed, and was compelled to walk to the telephone, dial her number, listen to endless ringing, put it down, dial again, ringing again until at last, after I don't know how long, finally getting him on the line. I had decided in that case to put down the receiver but the need to hear Anna had become so physical that I managed to say: Anja speaking, may I please speak to Anna as if it was quite normal, as if I was not busy dying on my end of the line. All right, he said, a little put out and ordinary and I heard the noises of their living room, the children, the television and then yes hello, Anna speaking. I didn't know what to say, took a deep breath to try to find words, but the tension was too much and I said Anna and began to cry.

Gordes 1

I want to write a book. Before we left I packed the piles of scribbled pages and notes into a plastic carrier bag with Marx's head on the outside. The book is still only a few sheets of typed paper, about Anna, who was the cause of this renewed fit of writing: an attempt to save myself. And a few sheets about the reasons why I want to write a book: an exorcism of my doubts that continue to return, fear of the nasty side-effects of being published, of being a public woman. Fear of being seen as an exhibitionist. Fear of the people who will now know me better than I know them, and who will condemn me. I can almost call them by name, the people looking over my shoulder as I type. My invisible public. Hans, who will be hurt. Feminists who will say that I am on an ego-trip. Friends of both Anna and mine who will think that I attack her without giving her a chance to defend herself. Men who will say, well, obviously, neurotic man-hater, lesbian, virago. Therapists who will find it all the result of my childhood, too simple a solution. Marxists who will say that what I write is too subjective. Whom do I represent? As a woman with a bourgeois past and a privileged position? What political relevance does it have, this self-pity, rooted in deep individualistic emotions?

I try to argue with them, the critics who look over my shoulder, by writing a defence. But as I am the one who has called up my critics, naturally they do not allow themselves to be so easily dismissed.

Scraps from years ago, in exercise books, among shopping lists, notes taken in class, unfinished articles, angry letters I didn't send because when I wrote them the anger disappeared. They surfaced the last time I moved, I didn't know that I had filled so many pages.

I am surrounded by untidy piles of paper that grow in corners and up against the walls as soon as I take over a new space. I am fascinated by the scraps of writing I find, forget my packing. Love letters, I've forgotten to whom I wrote them. Eli or Michael? I put them in a new pile to take with me when I go on holiday to France.

A borrowed car. Hans, who hasn't driven in years, nervous and silent behind the steering wheel. Armin gabbling next to him, I am lying in the back, on tents and sleeping bags, dull from days and weeks of overwork. The article on domestic labour had to be finished, corrected, then *Our Bodies Ourselves* needed working on, the translations to be revised, bibliography put together, photographs chosen. As well as the article for the family planning journal *Sextant* that I had promised and couldn't put off any longer because we needed the money for the holiday. And a discussion piece for the labour party women, lectures that needed polishing, meetings. When the holiday begins I am empty, with my last gasp of energy I take the copy of *Our Bodies Ourselves* to The Hague, collect my money, three thousand seven hundred and fifty guilders of which five hundred go directly to Annemiek for printing the photographs and one and a half thousand are already spent on loans and unpaid bills.

I am half asleep in the back of the car. See Antwerp glide past, think, but hardly consciously, of Sjef who lives there in one room with a half-painted blue floor and a gas cooker that was even filthier than mine. Of David, with whom I walked through the Maritime Museum, looking hopelessly for a place to fuck because we couldn't wait any longer, a suspicious curator following us. Of Sjors, with whom I spent a weekend in Antwerp at the time of the dock strike. Sleeping in the narrow bed in Sjef's pink spare room, Sjef who brings us tea in the morning, familiar without any outward signs of jealousy, touching me as if he had been married to me for years, to test me, to test Sjors, who asked me nervously if I wouldn't rather sleep with Sjef.

The motorway restaurant just before Paris. The last meal with Ton before we returned from our illegal honeymoon, leaving behind us the adulterous hotel with the bidet and the flowered wallpaper and the squeaky bed. Neon light and sour wine and an internationally poor meal with tough steak and limp chips, where the Paris trance was broken and I suddenly thought with tears in my eyes that this was probably the last time we would have so much time to give each other. I already disbelieved his promises about living apart, divorcing his wife, one week away together.

After Paris we find an hotel. The first confrontation with the respectable French bourgeoisie, an uptight hotel. Hans is suddenly no longer a sociology student, almost graduated with a well-paid position as lecturer, but a tall, untidy young man with too much frizzy blonde hair. I suddenly see that Armin has again managed to have pitch black hands and that he is wearing his heavy gym shoes and has tied their laces round his trouser legs. When, on request, we show our passports, nothing improves, the three of us have three surnames and two nationalities. Obviously

10

not a normal family. I remember that I have left the papers at home which prove that Armin, with his different surname and nationality, really is my child and not kidnapped. But he is nearly thirteen and does not look as if he would allow himself to be taken against his will, also not as if any one would want to, with his black claws. The madam looks disapprovingly at my breasts softly bouncing ten centimeters below decency, but she does not send us away. Giggling nervously we fall on to the beds, blue bedspreads, blue roses on the wall, more blue roses on the ground, still more blue roses on the curtains. I feel as if I am in a flowery aquarium. We make plans. Do you want to eat first in the Dordogne and then weep in Paussan and after that go on to Gordes? asks Hans or the other way round. First weep, I say, then we will have done that and I can eat better. Only a day though, I say. I want to return to the place where Anna and I swam for the last time, a year ago, the trees half way to Mialet under which we sat, cicadas splitting our ears, the hottest part of the day, while I tried to cast a spell over her to make her stay.

The sentimental poem that fortunately was never published, that I wrote the following morning when she was truly gone and I woke up with a sick shock in my stomach and thought of the time ahead, all the misery of breaking the addiction that I still had to go through, jesus how did I live through it.

Together we can accomplish anything:
Change women
Laugh over nothing
Make herstory
Swim naked in Mialet.

She a strong water nymph
Shoulder deep in water
Strokes my shoulders.
Rock firm under our feet
Nothing can touch us.

We walk hand in hand
Unhurt by lewd looks from
Tram conductors, waiters, tomato-sellers

11

Hand in hand we run to the depths.
I jump
And reach again for her hand
But she stands still on the side.

Gasping for air which has gone
I sink slowly
Without her hand
I drown.

To those who meet me
In September
In the Half-moon alley
And ask about the circles under my eyes:
I have only died a little.

We drive on, a better hotel in an out-of-the-way village, romantic creepers against the walls, pleasant kitsch. The owner doesn't look judgemental, but tolerant, and winks at Hans. He doesn't need to see my passport, he knows it all. On the terrace outside we become slowly drunk on pastis while I leaf through the pages and tear out bits I can use. There is so much, too much. It would be a boring book, too many lovers and melancholy love stories with sad endings. I find bits that embarrass me. Did I let myself behave like that, for that boring prick. And which prick was it. Eli or Michael?

Undated scraps that I can no longer place. Annoyed, I put them all back in the plastic carrier. Start completely fresh, don't use those pieces of the past as I saw them while still living them? More pastis. . . I arrange with Hans to stop tomorrow at the first paper shop to stock up with lined paper so I can write. My red typewriter is somewhere under all the luggage, but while we travel I can't use it.

Writing, why do I write exactly? The urge to validate yourself, says someone, the honour. You are someone if people say your name, if you are for sale in a shop. You hear people whisper, look there she is now, god I thought that she would look quite different. I think about my meeting with a woman who wrote three books one after the other and whom I imagined to be a big, strong woman, self-confident. And then this small blonde girl came up to me and whispered, giggling, nice to meet you.

Myth-making, which I contribute to by writing. An authority. The distance that is created when people know more about me than I know about them, their verdict already formed before they meet me in real life. I notice it already when I enter the Women's House and no longer know what to expect. Women who unexpectedly behave coldly towards me, others who just as unexpectedly throw their arms around me. The tendency to keep myself closed and distant until I have learned their verdict, to see first what they think. Or just embarrassed, making excuses when it is completely unnecessary.

The need to assert oneself; naturally I want to be someone who is visible, I want to do more with my life than just endure it as a natural disaster. But to become famous is something else, I don't want it like the politicians have it: professional schizophrenics who only show what they want to be seen, pretty theories that they trot out with aplomb and certainty because otherwise no one believes them. Don't show doubts or emotions because then you will be beaten. The emotions and doubts come at home, for those you have a wife before whom you can show your nakedness. I can't do that any more: preach feminist theories without at the same time showing how little I can fulfil them, how difficult I find it to live them. I do not want to be an authority, to present a model that is always incomplete without the experiences that led to the theory, the difficulties that grow from it.

Kate Millett was destroyed by her book, *Sexual Politics*. Suddenly she was a representative of the women's movement, was invited to give lectures and television interviews, used by the media, used by the movement which needed her but never forgave her because she was made a star by the media which attacked her for her faults, never saw her doubts. Kate knew she had only two ways to go: to disappear, announce her own death, never again allow it to be suspected that she had anything to say about feminism, or to go on, to speak more honestly about how difficult it was for her to live according to the model that was held up to her, that she herself had set up. And yes indeed she

13

will announce publicly that she is a lesbian – because it is necessary, because we can no longer allow ourselves to be ashamed and no longer wish to deny that we love women, although the media screams that feminism is nothing more than a lesbian conspiracy. But at the same time Kate knows that in her personal life she has succeeded in nothing; relationships with women break up too, are no easier than relationships with men. Are the theories therefore untrue, or must we allow ourselves to fail, openly, without shame, proud to fail and to begin again?

I have needed other women who write without shame in order to become what I am. Doris Lessing with her *Golden Notebook* which I lived with long before feminism. Jill Johnston, Ingrid Bengis, Rita Mae Brown, Kate Millett with *Flying* and Verena Stefan with *Shedding*. Women who dared to write about their conflicts. Who made it clear that I am not alone. Rather a public woman than a false stereotype. I want to write for other women, those women who meet me, confident in my feminist convictions, independent, courageous enough to stand up to my full height, fierce if it is necessary (only my women friends see how my hands sweat). We all need strong women with whom to identify, strong enough not to let themselves be intimidated, strong enough to say openly what needs to be said without being frightened by the fact that many people will no longer like us.

But strong doesn't mean having no doubts, no anxieties. Emotions follow years behind our heads.

I can say that those of us in the women's movement should put our energy into each other, should give our warmth to each other instead of always to husbands and children, destroying ourselves in the process.

I can say that we must learn to keep on loving each other, even when we disappoint each other, and even when we don't achieve much.

Has this feminism made you any happier then, asks someone.

Well, no, sometimes, I reply hesitantly. Happy? Certainly it is not easier. We strain ourselves constantly on our own ideals, achieve very little. Sisterhood is powerful: it can kill you. And yet we can only go on, we can't go back any more. Even the deserters who can't live up to their ideals, go on. I go on even after I have withdrawn for a while in order to lick my wounds.

14

Let's have patience with each other and stay honest about what we still can't do. But let's not be ashamed. Sentimental, I say, looking my critics in the eye, sure I am sentimental, I cry in movies. I sometimes hide my vulnerability under a thin layer of cynicism.

Over-sensitive, over-emotional, perhaps even paranoid. I see, as if under strong searchlights, magnified ten times, the daily details of my oppression, the daily details of the pain of other women. I have no defence against it any more, no blinkers. I am right in it, a mollusc without a shell.

Self-pity? Sure. I can swim in sympathy for myself. I can roll in it like a pig in the mud.

Bitter. That too.

But no shame. The shame is over.

Scraps that must become a book. We have ransacked two department stores. New lined paper, an orgy. Red, blue, yellow writing paper and notepads. I caress them, smell them. That sensual moment when you write the first words on the first clean page. With black ink that flows better than a stiff ball-point. Using a fountain pen, my fingers don't become so tired after pages of quick scribbling.

When I am sitting in the car again, more scraps float free, associations that come whirling to the surface because I am tired and empty, have no resistance. Must I leave them like that, connections that even I don't understand? I decide to arrange them later. But they remain scraps. A crumbling life. I don't want to make it look prettier than it is.

Part One
Dreams at bargain prices

I discovered that . . . I should need to do battle with a certain phantom. And the phantom was a woman, and when I came to know her better I called her after the heroine of a famous poem, the Angel in the House. I will describe her as shortly as I can. She was intensely sympathetic. She was immensely charming. She was utterly unselfish. She excelled in the difficult arts of family life. She sacrificed herself daily. If there was chicken, she took the leg; if there was a draught, she sat in it – in short she was so constituted that she never had a mind or wish of her own, but preferred to sympathise always with the minds and wishes of others. Above all – I need not say it – she was pure. . . . And when I came to write I encountered her with the very first words. The shadow of her wings fell on my page; I heard the rustling of her skirts in the room . . . she slipped behind me and whispered: ' . . . Be sympathetic; be tender; flatter, deceive; use all the arts and wiles of our sex. Never let anybody guess that you have a mind of your own. Above all, be pure.' And she made as if to guide my pen. I now record the one act for which I take some credit to myself . . . I turned upon her and caught her by the throat. I did my best to kill her. My excuse, if I were to be had up in a court of law, would be that I acted in self-defence. Had I not killed her, she would have killed me.

Virginia Woolf, 'Professions for Women'

17

A dark street with high windows

Where does my beginning start? I can't deny the confusion in my ancestry. I had an ambiguous beginning which defined me because I needed to rebel against it. My environment had an effect on me precisely because I no longer wish to belong to it. Through my grand-parents I can trace back all the confused lines which still run through my life. My father's father was a factory worker, later unemployed. At one time married to my father's mother who had studied, and wrote and associated with artists. When I came to know them, she among her books and etchings in her little house in Bergen, he living with Aunt Nel in a working-class terrace house, I couldn't understand how these people ever belonged together. They stayed together 'because of the children', and the divorce took place democratically, the sons also voted.

On my mother's side a hollow gentleman's house in Utrecht, on the old canal where all sounds except that of the wall clocks were muffled by thick carpets. My mother's father, a self-made accountant, a bad tempered patriarch who let himself be looked after by his fourth wife and sent my mother out of the house because his third wife had disliked her. Sent to teachers' training college because it was cheap and far away. Only after my birth were my mother and her father reconciled by the fourth wife. My own father finally won favour when he developed into a successful businessman.

Gentleman farmers and vicars and colonials among my ancestors. Proletariat, intelligentsia and nouveau riche. It couldn't be more mixed.

A child of the 'hunger winter', the last winter of the war, with bad teeth and crooked ribs for the rest of my life because I was fed on sugarbeet pulp and potato peelings. Parents who went underground, who married too young and stayed together too long: because of the children. Just like their parents before them and like myself who married too young and thought that I could escape my family home that way.

I must dig deeper to discover memories, happy memories. Perhaps I was one of those children not suited for childhood. An oldish, anxious girl behind glasses.

I had five dolls. The ugliest, which was given to me first, was called Jetje. The others had real hair and eyes that closed and names like Joyce and Claudia and Nicolette. I did not think Jetje was pretty but I felt responsible for her and when I threw all my dolls out of my bed because I had no room to sleep, I allowed her to stay. Guilt, it was there early. And in my behaviour I see something that reminds me of my mother.

A grey street, inward-looking houses, windows too high for children's eyes. We lived between the Weteringschans, the posh street where the real bourgeoisie lived in big gentlemen's houses, and the small streets at the back of them where the petit-bourgeoisie tried to keep up appearances. Only the Stadhouderskade canal between us to distinguish us from the Pijp, the working-class area where I went on Saturdays with Aunt Meg, who lived below us, in a ferry to shop in the Albert Cuyp market.

As my father's business improved we took over the floor below, room by room. While we became more affluent, the street declined in status. Overcrowded boarding houses and a whore who lived further along, screaming arguments across the street. I knew all the places in the street for marbles, but I did not like playing outside. Scared of the gangs of roving boys who pestered girls with chicken claws from the poulterer on the corner and who tried to push girls into doorways forcing them to show their cunts or bribing them with sweets.

I was not pretty, everyone agreed on that. Straight hair that, just as it grew safely over my big ears, was cut short by the barber. The curls of my baby years were gone, to return only much later.

Glasses. A strange nose. Strange teeth. Arms and legs too long and thin.

At least you have got personality, said my father, but that did not sound like a compliment. As if that was my only trump card to save me as a girl, and a dubious trump at that.

And during a game at the international children's camp an Italian boy in the middle of a circle of girls pointed to each one calling bella, bella until he came to me and after a short hesitation said intelligenze.

I see two children. A girl who plays quietly in her room with her dolls, reading, dreaming, an internal world shared with no one.

And I see another child, rebellious and disobedient. Chief of an Indian gang. Fighting with her brother. Hot-headed, mischief-maker, surely, those were the words used. Scenes when I refused to do what my parents demanded, refused to empty my plate. Until I was boxed on my ears or banished to the dark toilet. No tears until I locked myself in my room and they pleaded from the other side for me to please come out again. The apologies I had to make, even if I thought I had done nothing wrong, I delivered with my chin in the air and as much contempt as I could put into my voice to make it clear that I was not sorry, but spoke only under duress.

Obstinate devil, the teacher called me, who hated me and, in a failed attempt to put me down, struck me so that I fell against a table. You probably asked for it, said my father.

I knew I never wanted to share my mother's fate. I saw her disappear more and more into the housework, even though we had help. Tuesdays the staircase and the bathroom. Wednesdays the upstairs room. Thursdays the kitchen. I saw that my father and my brother never lifted a finger to help her and so I didn't either. I heard my father complain about the food and so I complained too.

A fight over my room that, according to my mother, belonged to her. According to me it was mine. Screaming arguments when she threw away something I thought valuable which I hadn't tidied away. And I refused to make my bed. When I took off my clothes I let them lie where they fell. Not a daughter with much solidarity, but insofar as I saw she was unhappy, I thought it was, after all, her own fault.

I planned to marry on my twenty-fifth birthday and anyway my life would be quite different from that of my mother.

How I would achieve that, I did not consider.

Granny Jet, who lived in the witch's house in Bergen, never called me a mischief-maker. She did call me witch, but that was with a look of understanding, a shared name: she was one herself. Granny Jet, with whom I could share my interior world, with whom I arranged exhibitions of my drawings and who asked me for medicines when I was a herbalist under one of the trees in her big garden. She supplied lemonade when my cousin and I dressed up in clothes from one of the mysterious trunks in the studio and furnished a temple under the big fir tree. Granny Jet who was big and unconventional. Who had written six books, on the depression, on women's lives, on the way her marriage had slowly paralysed her, had caused her to give up her studies, had hindered her writing. She lived with a communist artist whom she did not want to marry and when she'd had enough of that too she went to live in a converted barn in the garden next to the big studio, on which was painted: melt the swords into ploughshares.

I was there when she died. I had not seen her often during that time, caught up in the middle school world. I was no longer fascinated by the boxes of cut-out pictures from stewed apple tins and chocolate boxes, the old goose-board games and the books that lay a little dustily on her always untidy cupboard, between packets of old letters and still more little boxes. I considered myself too old still to be playing with them.

My uncle, a doctor, rang us up when it was time, to ask us to come immediately. She had postponed her death until we were there. Exhausted, she did not fight it, no longer interested in city life, modern life. Only enjoying concerts on the radio, walks through the garden and the dunes, feeding the tits. She said goodbye to me, almost inaudibly, and while I held her hand, sitting on her bed in the tiny upstairs room in her witch's house, she shut her eyes and slowly stopped breathing, slowly became colder. When it was over no one cried. Aunt Willie had made vegetable soup for us. We buried Granny Jet a few days later without fuss in a small cemetery in the dunes. She looked beautiful, peaceful.

Years, years later I cried for her. A delayed mourning, when I read her books and understood her for the first time. And suddenly missed her so much. I know so little about her, we would have had so much to tell each other.

Nightmares. Always the same. Darkness, a high tower, the ground around it invisible. There are thin old women dressed in black sitting in a circle on the tower. I try to talk to them, but they mumble to themselves or pray and don't listen to me, look fixedly in front of them. There is a hole in the wall. To the beat of my heart they fall one after the other with a scream downwards through the gap. The others shift one place up, wait dumbly for their turn. I twist, sweat, try to scream, to warn them, but no sound comes from my mouth. Then when it is my turn and I am pushed by the women behind me up to the gap, I wake up.

Suddenly I was no longer the second smallest in the class, but the second biggest. Small, new breasts, my hair in a pony tail. Because my maths was poor I was sent to a school for girls, which taught domestic science, typing and languages. I stood it for three weeks. Demanded to leave. The girls divided into two groups, the dolly girls with wobbly high heels and ice-cream-cone bras whispering about boys. The girls in the other group wore twinsets and sensible shoes, grey mice who had no interest in boys, but in nothing else either. I did not want to choose, I did not want to belong with them.

So, therefore, to the Technical School, although I was panic-stricken by maths from which I rescued myself only by a sophisticated crib system and my most innocent face. There were two girls in the class then, the pretty girl and me. Her hair was fairer than mine and she had no glasses.

Dilemma. I could not conceivably compete with her. I did not even get angry when the most popular boy in the class phoned to invite me to a party and then unthinkingly added that he wanted me to go with him because the pretty girl couldn't go. I went. Thankfully. I quickly understood that I must choose. If I was not pretty there was still the role of comrade. The pretty girl was invited out, but she was also disliked and gossiped about. I developed the role of comrade, in which I was neither disliked nor talked about. But I was also not invited out all the time. In any event I was allowed to join in with the boys, and they took me seriously.

After school my gang smoked roll-ups and secretly drank cheap sour wine that no one really wanted. I was allowed to go skating with them and went, although I hated skating and fell and got cold toes. I was called Adriaan – one of them. Jonas also belonged. Jonas, tall, silent, thin, shy, hiding behind his glasses. Jonas brought me sweets and lent me his Dave Brubeck records and took me to parties on the back of his bike although he knew he couldn't start anything with me and that he, no more than the other boys, could not get past the elastic obstacles of bra and suspender belt during the secret evenings when parents were away. Candles in Chianti bottles and drunk gasping boys round my neck, I let myself be protected by Jonas, who demanded that he should be the only one to put his drunk head on my shoulder. Jonas, who knew nothing of my double life, my secret.

Austria. Holiday with my parents, romantic lakes and ruins, schnitzels and subservient service. In Austria I understand that we are well off. I hear it in the 'Frau Director' with which my mother is addressed. I notice it in the envy with which the daughter of the hotel owner looks at my clothes. My first bikini. Through the eyes of the local boys I feel pretty for the first time. They look at my legs although I am just fifteen. My dresses are prettier, more fashionable than those worn here. I cherish the attention I am experiencing for the first time. On one of the lakes where we often go, I meet Toni, tanned, athletic. I hardly understand him, but that scarcely matters, the game is the exciting part, make as if I don't see him, wait until he makes the advances. The boys in my class would never put up with that. Adriaan, they would say, cut it out. But not Toni, he continued to follow me and ride his motor bike nightly back and forth under my window. An inevitable first kiss, that tasted strangely of garlic. Not enjoyable, but certainly exciting. We only see each other occasionally, on the air mattresses floating between the reeds so that my parents can't see me. But my mother notices anyway and before we return Toni is allowed to introduce himself. He does it with a handshake and nod of his head and a mumbled Gnädige Frau, the respectful form of address which my mother takes eagerly as her due. My father looks critical.

Exchanged addresses. On the journey back I suffer from love-sickness. We write letters, I in awkward German, he too, but I can't judge that yet. I begin to know more about him. Son of the railway official in the town that has two lives, a summer life with tourists, an inward-looking, conservative winter life. Toni goes to Germany to get a technical education, dreams of becoming a qualified engineer. I think that sounds beautiful.

You can ask him to come here to visit, says my mother. The week before he arrives I become terribly nervous, hope he won't come but don't know why. When he arrives I am disappointed. He looks smaller in his badly fitting suit, his trouser legs a little too short. Without the romantic trappings of the Austrian lakes and the pink cloud on which I floated because, out of vanity, I was not wearing my glasses, he did not look like the film star I had gradually begun to imagine him to be. But I put that feeling aside. We communicate awkwardly. Talking is quite different from writing love letters. And he doesn't want to talk, but to fuck. Without letting up he conquers the ground centimeter by centimeter. What was ceded yesterday I can no longer refuse today. I feel little except the excitement and the sensation – if the boys in the class could see me like this.

My mother sends Toni to wake me with the news that we are to have breakfast in an hour. In the short nightdress that she bought for me, there is little to defend. I remember vaguely that before Toni came she said something about safe and unsafe days but I hardly listened because I was planning to marry on my twenty-fifth birthday and did not expect to go to bed with anyone before then. Toni is unstoppable. Against so much pressure and force I have no defence. Obviously my skinny body has aroused his need. I am responsible for it. And on top of that, what else can one do with someone who continually has his hands on my breasts, hands under my dress, his knee between my legs. It is painful, the sweaty toil on top of me does not resemble the sweet cloud that people on films appear to sink into while in the background violins begin to play. But I at least have the satisfaction that I am the first in the class, although I will never say so.

My mother has tears in her eyes when I come embarrassed to fetch a clean sheet. She calls Toni to her. You do love her, she asks. The next day it still hurts, but Toni wants to do it again and again. It is an important business, I see that clearly. He suffers if I won't go to bed with him, and that is my fault. I learn that if you have said yes once, you are never again allowed to say no. Against his passionate perseverance I have no defence, even if I am disappointed each time when he becomes much colder and more distant once I have given in. In my books men are always more loving afterwards, but with Toni it is the other way round.

He goes away. Then I am less confused and the romantic feeling returns. We write letters again. A year later when we return to Austria we see each other every day. Fucking on the divan in his parents' front room when they are not there, with a towel for the stains. Or outside among the reeds, where the flies bite us and my bum is scratched by the stubble. Or he climbs into my hotel window at night. After a few weeks, when we're leaving, Toni buys me a gold ring with a little stone. Are we engaged now? I ask. At school I still don't tell. The ring is in a little box.

Then I become bilious in the morning, vomit in the toilet and later during break at school. I get peculiar urges for food, all at once want to eat only hotdogs with ketchup which I throw up immediately I've eaten them. I think I have flu or somesuch, or that I've eaten something to upset me. My mother notices, says nothing, but looks as if she knows something. The biliousness continues. My mother takes me to our doctor. I am sixteen.

Gordes 2

In Aubenas, where we are stuck because the car has broken down and it is Saturday and it can only be repaired on Monday after the fourteenth of July holiday, we have our first big fight.

I begin to feel something of a post-natal depression, the kind I always have after I have worked too hard, after I have delivered something. I want to rest, have nothing I must do, nothing to be responsible for. I don't need much, my papers, a book, a place to sit or to lie, something to drink. Armin is bored without water to swim in. He has read his books, he doesn't want to sit on a chair on the terrace. The shops are closed. He walks three times past a shop window with silver coloured jeu de boules balls, works out how much pocket money they will cost him, comes to complain to me. But even the promise that I will put something towards them only comforts him a little. Hans is almost the same, a sullen face. One can only eat in a restaurant twice a day. I feel I am out with two spoiled children. I say to Armin, come for a walk with me, just to get away from Hans's dissatisfied face. But Hans follows us. After we have sat down glumly on the wall in the sun and I have tried again, without success, to concentrate on my book, I have had enough of his demanding presence and say that I'm going to have an hour's walk, alone, and that we can make a date to meet somewhere at five o'clock. Hans looks hurt. I try not to care, to go anyway. Disappear to another terrace where I sit down with a sigh of relief, order a pastis and let myself sink into my book. I shut out the men around me, who try in a routine way to attract my attention, by looking over and through them. Three-quarters of an hour later

27

Hans is sitting with me again. I have come to my senses, he says, it is over now.

That night we have a real row. I ask why he sat in his chair looking so dissatisfied that morning. Jealousy, he says. Yesterday evening when I fell asleep you were still writing in that exercise book, this morning when I woke up you were writing again. As if you had written all night through. I am jealous. I would like to write like you, to be so self-sufficient. What do you expect from me, I ask, guilty: that I constantly look into your eyes? Must I amuse you, can you do nothing for yourself? Leave me in peace, I say, I sleep with you, I eat with you, I talk to you. I also need a few hours to myself, I don't want to have to give you my attention all the time. Now Hans is furious. Goes outside. I can see the holiday fireworks from the hotel window. Go on alone, I say, I am staying here. The need to be alone is overwhelming.

When two Dutch women offer to take us with them to a camping site until the car is repaired, things improve. There is a swimming pool. We put up the tents, ours and the pup tent for Armin. In a final burst of energy I make a list of what I still need to do in the holidays: some letters to be written, to Armin's camp that he isn't coming, to Barbara, the last bit of bibliography for the Dutch edition of *Our Bodies Ourselves* to the publishers, a review of *Fear of Flying* for *de Groene*, a weekly paper, that I have already promised and which I can no longer get out of, a review of the diaries of Anaïs Nin for *Lover*, a feminist magazine. When the list is complete I am exhausted. It is too hot to do anything with it. Scraps of my own book pester me. I am kicking the habit of working, as if I have worked on speed. Exhaustion in my body while my brain continues to work at full speed and I don't know where the switch is to turn it off. The result is irritation, restless as a dog that can't find a satisfactory place to lie down. Compromises with myself – when I write a letter I get the feeling that I am working and become more restful. I read five books in four days and tan only my back.

Armin swims, an otter with smooth brown skin, brown, almost edible shoulders. Seagreen eyes, a little aslant under his bleached hair, one of his ancestors of Asiatic descent, Mongolia. The same long fingers as mine, the same skew thumb. The same curve in his back. Flesh of my flesh. So much easier to love him, now that he can look after himself and I am older and at last have a genuine liking for him. Guilt that is never quite gone. Did I love him enough when he was little, myself a child of sixteen, seventeen, not even able to love myself? I am more forgiving towards my parents – who also did not want me, nor am I ever sure they loved me. (Why do I keep such a taste of sorrow when I think of the past?) And Armin, is he making up for what he lacked? He dives right in front of me, splashes, grins at me. My little friend, even if you are no longer so little. Vulnerable behind your boy-facade. And thank God, still a child when he needs to be.

Come sit close to me and watch television, he says. I like that. Understanding looks, jokes no one else can understand, a thin line of communication between my world and his boy's world. We fight for a while in the water over a ball, until I get a mouthful of rancid chlorinated water and have enough of it. Old lady, says Armin, friendly.

Two days camping and it becomes increasingly hot. Heat as heavy as lead on my head, I breathe pudding, become a cauliflower, vegetate only, stupid and dazed from the heat and too much eating and drinking. Good, says Hans, stop working a while, and he pours me a glass of wine. Then I wake in the middle of the night when it is cool and the wine has worked itself out. Sentences like waterfalls around me. I long for my red typewriter, but that is in the broken-down car. And I can hardly, in the middle of a camp site at four in the morning, begin to rattle.

At night in the tent. A cotton triangle of intimacy next to other triangles. I constantly forget that there is no more than a piece of cloth between me and other people. Jump when I hear someone cough nearby. We talk. Do you remember the time I went out to dinner with Ellie and you asked if we had made love and I said no? asks Hans. We did make love, I mean, more or less, in the car . . .

I observe my emotions, suspicious that I am not busy supressing my jealousy. But I feel no jealousy. Certainly surprise. Why didn't you say so, I ask, all the other times it didn't matter? I think it was because I didn't know myself why I did it, says Hans. Just because you wanted to, isn't that enough? I ask. But Hans wants complete stories, rounded off with interpretations and future expectations: I did tell Annemarie. Then I become angry, because I find it disloyal. But I understand completely. Annemarie and her confused relationships, for her he doesn't need to make it into a good story. You are turning me into your bad conscience, I say, as if I am purity incarnate. I don't want to be your conscience.

I am not pure. Only much more careful than before. I have settled with my past lovers, there is no one I want to return to, unlike Hans who occasionally returns for a while to an old girlfriend. Scared of new relationships which disturb my peace. Scared of too intense relationships with women with whom I want to continue to work, to make love and to dance with, without the dramas that blow up, that almost split the women's movement, as happened with Anna. Suspicious of men, there are few men with whom I would still want to have a relationship. I don't know how to do it any more, have forgotten how to flirt, how to get stomach cramps from suppressed excitement, the double meanings, the rituals. If I do sometimes feel an attraction, butterflies in my belly, it is not difficult to turn it down. I have never flirted with Hans. A peaceful, friendly work relationship that only changed when we both came back from holiday with broken triangular relationships and could comfort each other. I had to chase him a bit, he could not understand it, a woman pursuing him. I invited him to the commune party. Now he will have to, I thought, and sat pointedly next to him, close to him. He still noticed nothing, but looked nervously at his shoes of which he was ashamed, upset his glass. Don't overdo it, I thought, and danced a bit with my women friends. When I turned round he was gone. Damn, failed, but I found him again downstairs, pushed up against the kitchen cupboard. If it doesn't work this time, I give up, I thought, sitting next to him again, under the eyes of the high priestess of the lesbian front, who sat spying on me from the other end of the kitchen; in the end I got him. All the beds were occupied by party-goers, not one for us to creep into and I had to catch the plane for London early the next morning. We'll save it for my return, we said, and kissed goodbye at the Amstel river and afterwards Hans took the night bus home. All through the conference in London I thought about him and about fucking and if I had made a mistake and if it was the drink or if he really wanted to. And what stories the lesbian front would be telling about me.

In Aubenas I see a wall poster of the French Communist Party. First I liked it. Women's faces, the text: so many thousand women demonstrate with the communists. A beautiful poster, at last attention paid to women. Until I begin to reconsider. Would they have written so many *men demonstrate with* the communists? Obviously communists are men and women may participate. There is no question of a grammatical error.

We aren't going to Paussan, I no longer need to go on a pilgrimage. If we don't go to Gordes now, An and Eric and Hanneke will be gone and we want to see them.

Schmalz

Pregnant, the doctor said to my mother after I was sent to the waiting room. I do strenuous exercise and jump off chairs. It doesn't help. My mother says that she will find out from a woman friend who is a nurse if there is anything we can do. Comes back and says no, apparently there was a doctor who used to do abortions, but he doesn't do them any more. I don't ask if there are any other possibilities. It doesn't occur to me to go to a doctor myself. I decide, after a few crying fits, to leave things as they are. After all, I liked dolls, which with difficulty I had stored in the cellar because I thought I was too old for them. On top of that, to be able to get out of the house, to have my own home, not to have to fight any more for possession of my room. Never again to be hauled out of bed by an angry father because I had forgotten my bicycle outside. Never again to have to ask for pocket money. Never again to have to do homework. To be able to make my own decisions.

I walk with open eyes into the trap which had caught my mother long ago, without even considering the consequences.

My mother told my father who walked past grumbling and didn't dare look at me. She went to talk with the head of the school, who called me to him and asks if I have done it with all the boys in the gang. I blush and stammer and get angry only when I am home. I am expelled from school. A bad example for the other girls. The head of this progressive Montessori Lyceum is naturally not personally against my writing the finals, but the parents' association, the school committee. . . .

My mother writes to Toni that there must be a wedding. He hesitates and then says yes: to be son-in-law of a well-off family is more attractive than the future in his village. My mother arranges the wedding papers. I do not return to my class after the Christmas holidays. I don't tell any of my old friends why, not even Jonas, who hears it from someone else and drinks and misbehaves at parties and later makes a clumsy suicide attempt in a place where he will easily be found in time.

A lime-green two-piece with an orange silk blouse. The dressmaker asks discreetly if she should leave a little room in the waist. A good suggestion because Toni is still somewhere between Santa Cruz and Houston as mechanic on a ship and by the time of the wedding I am five months pregnant. A quiet wedding, one uncle, one grandmother. A solicitor who is a friend of my parents, his wife. No celebration, no friends of mine or of Toni. My father relents a little, has talked with Toni who promises to study further for engineering qualifications. The solicitor hints that I should make something out of the marriage to compensate for the trouble I have caused my parents.

In their house, now on a chic canal, we have the right to the official guest room. It is strange to be allowed, to be expected, after that sneaking across the corridor. It does not improve our love-making. It is no favour that I yield to Toni in exchange for the ritual of loving words and tenderness. It is now a right. Being in love is childish and I have to make up for the fact that Toni has exchanged his freedom for a marriage by patiently enduring new sexual experiments.

I become fatter and don't vomit in the mornings any more. Tender looks from people on the street, a young little mother. It makes up for a lot. My mother takes me with her to an expensive shop for the baby layette. Progressive, yellow and blue diapers, no pink. I have no idea what babies need. I let my mother put powder boxes, cotton wool swabs and bath thermometers and navel bandages on a pile. Aren't you excited, she asks, as I look a bit dazed. Oh yes, I say. The baby moves in my womb as if butterflies were bouncing against my insides. I can't imagine it. It could just as well be a parakeet or a teddy bear. Toni says he is delighted with his heir, who must be a fine boy, well set up, but it sounds no more real than my baby doll.

Why did no one tell me it would be so painful? I had prepared myself, done exercises, breathing. The first labour pains come at six in the morning. I say bravely that it seems perfectly bearable, have promised myself to be brave, not to cry. But as contraction follows contraction I forget my breathing exercises. I drown in pain, I am pain. Hear myself screaming, cursing the doctor who is late, threatening to jump out of the window if it doesn't stop at once. Hear the nurses whispering that there is something wrong. When the doctor comes I ask what is wrong. You are having a baby little lady, he says. Then I hear the nurse saying the child is in the wrong position. I have no idea how bad that is. I couldn't even care. I want to be rid of the pain, me dead, baby dead, it doesn't matter as long as it just stops.

Then something fantastic happens. The pain stops and I feel my whole body working to press down to let the child come out. My body does what is necessary completely outside my will. Gently, gently, says the doctor, but I can't hold back any more and after a few contractions I feel it slide out and I see the doctor hold a little blue body up high. Dead, I think, when I see the blood, but then I hear a thin baby wail. A boy.

A little later when he is cleaned up and wrapped up and put in my arms I don't recognise him. My child? This wrinkled monkey with hair growing deep into his forehead, with hands that clutch my finger like birds' claws, a real baby?

On the way to Denmark, to the women's camp at Femø, we need to stop somewhere in Germany, four women in a Volkswagen. We look on the map to see where we have the best chance of finding a youth hostel, although we ask ourselves when do you stop qualifying as youth. I am twenty-eight. Lübeck we decide, right near Travemünde where we will catch the boat to Denmark.

Just before Hamburg I realise what Lübeck means: for the first time in almost ten years I will return to the city where I lived for a year as new housewife/mother/wife. I try to remember the address, but I can't think of it. That whole year has seeped away like a grey stain. Nappies, I remember vaguely, and that it was always cold. When we get to Lübeck, I see streets I recognise. A nightmareish strangeness comes up out of my belly. I recognise shops, almost the same except now there are wanted notices everywhere for the Baader-Meinhoff 'terrorists'. I say that I want to try to find my house, say then for the first time that I have lived here, ask if someone will go with me because I don't dare go alone. Almost blindly I look for the house. It must be near the harbour where Toni worked as a mechanic. Here is a church which looks familiar to me. When we turn the corner isn't that the food take-away? Then I find the street, Engelswisch, see for the first time that they are almost mediaeval houses, pretty and romantic if I didn't have those memories of cold, dark passageways. I hesitate, don't know for sure which house it is. Walk stooping through an alley between the houses that is only one and a half meters high. Recognise the old street lights, the alley. Turn around and feel the blood drain from my face. The kitchen curtains are still exactly the same.

Overslept again. I just wanted to sleep another half hour after he left. The dirty breakfast things are still on the table next to the bed. Grey light outside. It is surely almost eleven o'clock.

34

Now I hear why I have woken up. The sound of Armin's crying, thin but penetrating through the floorboards. Must go downstairs. What must I do today. I am out of nappies, need to do the washing. Nothing exciting today, went to a film yesterday, can't go again today. Fire is out. If the fire is also out downstairs, Armin will have icy feet again. Same clothes as yesterday. No point in putting on something else, no one sees them. Rubber band around my hair to keep it tidy, if I go out I'll wear a cap anyway. Armin's crying is getting shriller. I listen to hear if the landlady is in the passage so I can go downstairs without her walking behind me to tell me I can't leave the washing hanging on the line at night. Armin's little feet are grey-blue, must take him to the doctor, something wrong with his circulation. Wet nappy, cold body. Smell of piss in the kitchen, yesterday's plates still on the table, congealed fat. Bucket with dirty nappies. Armin happily eats his banana sandwich. Wants to play, make jokes. I try to be a cheerful mother. Succeed for ten minutes. Then the kitchen overwhelms me, the nappies, the washing up. Fires to make up, lug coal from the coal hole, where the darkness frightens me. It begins to rain. Jesus, yesterday's nappies are wet again. I must still vacuum upstairs, coal dust is like a black film over everything, it clings to my bare feet, I take it to bed with me. Sour smell from beds, from sleeping too long. I want to creep under the blankets again, to sleep. But Armin gets cross if I put him in his cot. He wants to play. I carry him with me upstairs where I am making up the fire and vacuuming. When I have made up the beds, Armin turns over a box of rubbish. The dust from under the beds mingles with it. I turn on the vacuum cleaner again. The chimney won't draw because of the weather. Smoke in the room. Take Armin downstairs again, put him in his cot so I can fetch the vacuum cleaner. He begins to scream from anger, thinks I am leaving him alone when I go upstairs and don't want to risk him burning himself at the fire or pulling the breakfast things off the table. Vacuum cleaner and dirty sheets downstairs. Manage, with beating heart, to avoid the landlady. Armin's screaming dulls me. I almost hit him. Unreasonable screaming, if he didn't scream like that for god's sake, it echoes in my head, cuts out all pleasant deadening thoughts. I give him another banana, although it isn't allowed. He is already too fat. Next week explain again why he hasn't got thinner, at the baby clinic where I sit between grey anonymous mothers who peer jealously at each other's children. Not at me, I don't count, Armin doesn't even have a wool suit to show off in. Struggle with the sheets in the plastic tub. How do other people wash sheets, great clumsy rags, water on the floor that mixes with the dirt. Must mop the floor soon. I almost vomit on the nappies that I have left standing too long, breathe through my mouth. What should we eat today. Bought a book yesterday, money almost gone and it must still hold out for two days. Don't dare to ask for more. I can cook tripe again but in that case I must go shopping now otherwise there isn't enough time to cook it.

With my arms in the suds I re-run yesterday's film, scene by scene. Crime and passion. Beautiful girl, more beautiful than me, small pointed breasts. No glasses. Dark mysterious man who falls in love with her at once, waits for her outside, follows her. No one ever falls in love with me, I was beautiful for only one year. Don't think about the future. Leave it vague. Replay the film, picture by picture. The moment when he bends over her sleeping face, lips touching her hair. Suppressed passion. Not the same as Toni who doesn't even take the trouble to caress me, grabs my cunt straight away, body heavy on mine, ridiculous pumping, if I move with him it is only to get it over as quickly as possible. Then I can sleep, dream, perhaps of the film, of myself with small pointed breasts, without glasses. Hang the nappies up outside. My hands are stiff and cold and blue as Armin's little feet. I struggle to get him into his coat, shoes, he can't sit still for a minute. Push-chair, cap over my hair I have forgotten to brush. I make up my eyes in the small cracked mirror. I look as little as possible at my face which stares back at me.

Outside. Grey. First the butcher, that is the worst, people push in front of me and I can't get angry because I'm only buying tripe. Other people buy that for dog food. My mouth waters, pork sausages. Shall I get an ounce of left-over pieces, but then I won't have any money left for bananas for Armin and a piece of chocolate for myself. If they weren't so patronising towards me, if they talked more clearly to me and I didn't have to ask over and over, how much please. I see my green coat through their eyes, it was quite good last year, with its new imitation fur collar, but it isn't any more. Outside I am overcome by hunger. Something sweet. Cake too expensive. I want white bread, not sour German bread: but I can only get white bread on the other side of the shopping precinct. my mouth waters. Think now only of white bread with chocolate spread. I can get it in the department store. They also have a department there with slightly damaged paperbacks that I always look at. Aldous Huxley in German and Han Suyin. I was there the day before yesterday, but perhaps they have something new now. Awkward with the push-chair on the escalator. Armin thinks everything is wonderful, I must watch constantly that he doesn't put his dirty hands on the counters and pick things up, scarves, soft handkerchiefs, that I have to put back with a face red with embarrassment before anyone else sees. I stand engrossed by the books, no new ones, but there are some I haven't looked at properly. Armin grumbles, tries to climb out of his pushchair. I pull myself away, no money. Buy chocolate spread, margarine, schmalz for the bread. German bread for Toni. Swedes. Hesitate at the chocolate. No money. Apples and bananas for Armin. Milk. A packet of soup to make the tripe edible. Drink department. Cheap vermouth, I give in. Guilt feeling towards Toni. In the end I buy white bread, which isn't at all necessary. And I want vermouth to get a bit drunk, not to think, but Toni always wants to fuck if he is drunk. If he isn't drunk also. It makes no difference.

On the way to the baker, shop windows. The black fur coat is still there. If I had that and no glasses and no stretch marks and those small pointed breasts and wasn't married and had no child . . .rubbish. Window with sheets all in different colours. Quite different from the grimy rags that I can no longer wash white. A clock chimes. Jesus, only three-quarters of an hour before Toni comes home. The washing up is still to be done and the dinner isn't ready. Armin laughs at the bumpiness, my awkward attempts to get home quickly over the old pavements, thinks it is a game. Dark street, dark house, dark stairs. Put on the meat, cut the swede into pieces in the pot. Push the washing up into the cupboard, sandwich with margarine and chocolate spread. Cram it inside and another one. Feed Armin. He doesn't hurry, sits happily gabbling meaningless sounds.

Toni will be coming home soon then Armin must be in bed, otherwise there will be an argument. Toni will not eat if Armin is still sitting at the table, can't bear his whining, his gabbling. I look out of the window, still no one in the alley. Kitchen full of the smell of swede. Condensation on the windows. Forgot again to buy something for the mice. I have no appetite any more, certainly not for tripe, dirty stuff that I cut into strips. Make pudding from yesterday's old bread. If only Armin doesn't cry when Toni comes home, if only Armin just doesn't cry.

Toni travelled ahead to Germany, found work in Lübeck harbour as a mechanic. A house close to the quay, or rather two rooms, one above the other. The bottom one is both the kitchen and the place where Armin's cot stands. A rough area, at night drunk sailors vomit and piss under the bedroom window. Greasy flowered wallpaper. A mouldy smell that you can't get rid of. I don't complain, try to make what I can of it. Hang prints that I have brought with me, make orange and yellow cushions for the camp beds where we sleep.

Suddenly I am a housewife. Now revenge for never helping my mother. I can't do anything. Don't know what to buy to eat, don't dare buy spinach because I don't know whether you buy an ounce or a pound let alone whether I can say it in German. And I get so little money from Toni. The chops I bought for the first meal because they looked easy to cook, we couldn't afford. But Toni expects his meal to be ready at five o'clock when he comes home and if he doesn't like it he pushes it silently away from him.

I wage a battle against the washing up, the dirty nappies, the mildew in the cupboards, the mice which turn out to be rats. I didn't know that one child makes so much mess, treads half-eaten banana into his blanket, smears shit on the walls and pulls off the wallpaper. I didn't know that a child needs to put on clean clothes so often, needs to eat so often, can cry such a lot.

Arguments. Toni doesn't want to be bothered with a child. When he comes home Armin should be in bed and not make another sound. If Armin cries, he says he needs a good hiding and that I spoil him and am turning him into a weakling. I see the fear in Armin's eyes when Toni comes near him. I try to keep them apart, don't touch Armin when Toni is there because then he starts a jealous scene. And once when I came back from shopping Armin's buttocks were marked with blue bruises, beaten with a curtain rod because he would not stay sitting on his potty. I no longer dare to leave him behind with Toni.

I write a diary. About depressions that keep coming back, although I don't understand why. I have, after all, no reason for them. I have a husband who loves me, a baby, my own home. I am ashamed that I am unhappy. I write cheerful letters to my mother.

I escape in reading. First the books I brought with me, then romances. We have no television. What is happening in the world goes completely past me. I read the daily paper once in a while, but mostly I don't know what it is all about. I put on the radio only to listen to music which keeps me tranquilised, to which I can dream. On the street I hear that Kennedy is murdered. I don't feel it has anything to do with me.

In my diary I write about the suicidal moods when I feel my life is over and there is no way I can change it any more. I show Toni my diary in an attempt to talk to him about it. He says what I write is worthless rubbish. Says I am a lewd bitch when he reads an erotic poem by Rilke which I have copied out. I offer him the key in the hope that he will understand more about me if he reads my diary more often. He says that he doesn't need it and lets me see that he can easily bend open the cover anyway. I must try to become a worthy life's companion, I write. It does not sound convincing.

I write:

'If only I had never married. How banal. Just now he said something lovable again. We talked about Mrs B, that she is a good wife. She has no children, says Toni. It is a crime that I have a child. I often wish that I had had the chance after all to have an abortion as Toni wanted. Perhaps then

I would not be married now, or perhaps yes, but then I would have known what he was like. Perhaps he would have known me and appreciated who I am. In any case there would then have been a way out. Wait until Armin is big enough to stand on his own feet and then go away. Leave when I am still young enough and not too disillusioned, or otherwise kill myself. It isn't nearly so dramatic as it sounds. Toni would easily recover. At most he would feel misunderstood.

'Now what is women's emancipation really worth? It only shows on the outside. If you aren't the sweet subservient wife and also make demands you still get disapproving looks. Making demands is still the privilege of the husband. "You would like to sit comfortably reading while I do the housework", says Toni. Nothing else occurs to him if I ask him to pay more attention to me. How scared they are to be ruled by us. I wish that I could talk with someone. With whom? Whom do I have? No one. Banal. But I shall have to endure it for a while yet.'

And then in a big scrawl:

'Beautiful promises. He says he will no longer interfere with Armin's education, but he will take steps if it goes wrong. Just now he hit him because he dared cry a bit.'

Then thick lines through the words. The pages half torn out:

'You will be ashamed later on at what you have written.'

I write to myself. 'It is just a bad mood.'

I write less and less. My writing becomes smaller and smaller. On the last page are only the titles of the books I am reading. Toni says my dissatisfaction comes from all my reading. My books stand on a shelf I have put up next to his one book that he never opens: Nietzsche's *Also Sprach Zarathustra*.

I have no one to talk with in Lübeck. Once or twice Toni brings colleagues home with him. Unmarried. One has a red sports car. Toni obviously envies him, makes insinuations about his lost freedom. They talk about women, about how one of them has an over-demanding girlfriend who began to nag about marriage in the middle of the night and whom he threw out without her clothes and how she had stood banging on the door crying until he threw her clothes out of the window. They laugh. I say nothing, look at my toes, fetch more beer, cut sausage in pieces. The conversation dries up. I see myself through their eyes, my severely pulled-back hair, my glasses. A frump. A dull bookworm. Not their sort. The visit is not repeated.

My mother comes to stay. I am ashamed of the kitchen, try to tidy up before she comes, but she silently picks up a cloth and begins to scrub the greasy chairs that I had overlooked. Once we go out to eat, my mother pays; the luxury of sitting in a restaurant, a glass of wine, no plates to wash up. I had forgotten it was possible. When I was a child I had been bored by the endless wait for my steak with chips and apple sauce on Sunday outings with my parents. But I can't talk to her. Toni acts the model husband when she is there. Is charming. Fills up her glass. Helps her put on her coat. Says that she has a wonderful daughter who has learned to cook very well.

In the little park where I sometimes sit with Armin a Danish woman comes to sit on the bench next to me. We exchange a few sentences. She lives here because her husband works here, just like me. She knows no one, has no friends here. Perhaps we'll meet again, she says as I leave. But I avoid the little park for weeks. I have become frightened of people.

Toni begins to bet on the horses. After tea he goes out again to a betting shop on the docks. I go with him (only once), but become bored and am afraid of the kind of men who hang around there. Toni becomes a fanatic. Buys racing papers, makes calculations on pieces of paper. He says that it must be possible to find the ideal system of winning. After a few months betting he stops work and devotes his whole day to the horses. He has saved money, has given me very little for housekeeping. With this money he now wants to go to France to see the horse races at

41

first hand. He buys a Volkswagen bus that he converts so we can sleep in it. We give up the house in Lübeck, I pack my books in a box.

In France the season is over. Museums are closed. It is cold and windy on the Riviera and there are almost no people. We eat what I cook on the small gas stove. I daren't go to restaurants and anyway Toni wants to save money for his system; he needs a lot of money in reserve. Now and then I try to talk, about how we should plan the future or if we are going to go on drifting, but my attempts at beginning a discussion set off such scenes that I learn to keep my mouth shut. I refuse to talk German any more. I refuse to do anything for him except silently cook his meals and silently endure, every other day, his sexual appetite. I become sick, diarrhoea and kidney infection. A French doctor whom I don't understand gives me pills that don't help. I have a temperature, am always cold. Toni decides finally that we must go back to Amsterdam where we can stay with my parents. On the way back I daydream feverishly about suicide. It seems to me to be such a solution, not to have to struggle any more. But to leave Armin behind with Toni, that I can't do. There is nothing else for it but to go on.

My parents throw us out after a week or so when it is clear that Toni doesn't want to work. They give him one week either to find work or find a room. I feel marginally more solidarity with him than with my parents. I go with him. Toni doesn't look for work but does find a room. In the Jordaan, a neighbourhood that I don't know – as a respectable well brought-up bourgeois daughter I never went there. One room divided from a furniture shop by a thin hardboard wall. There is only one window in the room, the door opens directly onto the street. There are draughts everywhere. It is possible to keep the room warm only by turning up the paraffin heater as high as possible. A curtain divides the kitchen area, with Armin's cot, from the living area. The toilet, which has no door, is broken and must be flushed with a bucket of water. I try to make something of it. Stick pictures from women's magazines onto the kitchen wall, paint the chimney breast bright blue with a pot of paint given by the landlord. I put three coffee cups on the mantlepiece that are the same shade of blue. I bake doughnuts on old year's eve for Toni and Armin and me.

Toni is away during the day. To a café on the Dam where you can bet on horses. One day I buy a bottle of lemon gin and drink it up all at once. Then cry myself empty over a record of Charles Aznavour that I play over and over again. ('Yesterday I was still twenty, but I have wasted my life, my friends are gone, love is dead before it is begun') Vomit in the toilet, am ashamed in front of Armin.

I become more and more frightened, but I don't know what of. Of people. I go less and less into the street, only if I have to shop. I don't dare go to the launderette because there I need to ask how to work the machines. I wash by hand, hang the washing up in the room. I only go to supermarkets where I don't have to say anything. If I go to a shop where I need to ask anything I rehearse it beforehand for fear that I will forget what I came for when I am there. If I can see who is at the door, Jehovah's Witnesses, I don't open it, stand with beating heart behind it. Then I no longer dare to cross the busy street nearby. I finally stay only on the street where we live.

The money is almost gone. Toni's system will not succeed. He becomes more and more bad tempered. I barely talk any more. I say once, in an attack of courage and despair, that I want a divorce. Toni laughs at me. Why? he asks, where do you want to go? I don't know. I don't know what I want. The future is an enormous hole full of washing and shopping. There is nothing that I am proud of, there is nothing that I want for myself, I feel like the empty packet of crackers that stands on the table. A container with nothing inside. Why should I want anything?

But when I come back one day from shopping and find Armin beaten black and blue, something snaps in me. I hear myself scream with a voice I do not recognise. For myself I can't fight, I hardly exist, but for Armin . . .

I realise that I must leave, it doesn't matter where I go. I want a divorce. Toni says rubbish, can't happen and that he can keep Armin if I run away, or come to fetch him if I take him with me. After all he is an Austrian child, in Austria the father always has custody.

I go on strike, don't cook for him, am silent for days on end, refuse to be fucked. Tip over a pot of tea that I have made for myself when Toni puts out his hand to help himself. Shut my eyes waiting for the blow that must follow, but nothing happens, too much rebellion against his authority bewilders him, he doesn't know what to do any more.

When Toni tries to force my unwilling body I dig my nails in his back, feel the skin tear, blood under my nails. Toni curses. Gives in, wants to do a deal. If I fulfil my wifely duties, as I should, three times a week, for two months, he will let me go. I take him up on it. The only arguments we then have are if he thinks a new week has started and wants to fuck and I say that it is still the old week and he has already had his quota.

After two months I silently pack my things. My few clothes, books, Armin's toys. I have been to my parents to ask if I can stay there temporarily with Armin until I have my own flat, or if they will lend me money. When I shut the door behind me, Toni sits with his back to me and says nothing. I leave the blanket, which is actually mine, with him.

Years later when I return to that part of Amsterdam – which I have always avoided – I no longer recognise it. The house is demolished. The neighbourhood looks cheerful, window boxes, trendy shops. I can show a friend up to which doorway I dared to walk. It looks distant, unreal, as if it didn't happen to me. I can only talk about it in an ironic voice. It seems so banal, such a cheap, old-fashioned Victorian melodrama. I feel for the first time something of the old fear when I see right on the corner the old snack bar that hasn't changed. As if they are the same cold chickens in congealed fat under the blue neon lights as ten years ago.

I was allowed to remain an 'adult' in the few months before I turned twenty-one when I got divorced.

The last memory I feel boiling up from the depths. A queasy sick-making feeling in my belly. An old fear.

Armin three days old. I am still in the hospital. Toni comes to visit, waits until no one is near and then whispers, I have thought it over, if we give him enough sleeping pills we will be rid of him. And he needn't feel a thing.

I cry at night. Look at Armin's little fists, feel my breasts filling up with milk when I hear him cry. For me he now becomes a living child, now that I realise that I will have to protect him. I choose for him. No longer an unwanted child.

The doctor says it is normal that I cry. All mothers do that.

Gordes 3

Gordes is beautiful as we approach it, a fortified city, built up against rocks, almost a stage set. The mistral blows. My teeth are gritty with dust. Terraces round a square, stalls with vivid fruit among the dusty sandy colours of the castle and houses built from natural stone. We look into a yellow Renault, anxious to see whether it belongs to An and Eric and Hanneke, when I hear a joyful yell and see An come running with her arms wide open. When we sit at the sidewalk cafés I realise how happy I am to see them. We chatter, gossiping chaotically, telling each other about our fights which suddenly don't seem so tragic any more now that we can share them, when you can laugh about them. Carafes of cold white wine. We become slowly drunk. I think it is wonderful to laugh again, to repeat three times how happy I am to see them, to hear An say how happy she is to see us, to pour more cold white wine.

Proudly they show us their house, one room in a sort of palace in a narrow street reached by stone steps. A monumental front door, an enormous hall with wide marble staircase, behind that their room with comfortable shapeless chairs, cool behind the thick walls and shutters. Then their greatest pride, the garden which lies on the other side of the village, past the churchyard, on the edge of the steep rocks. A squeaky metal gate in a high stone wall, behind that the garden, dry and hot, a garden house of heavy stone, cold inside, derelict. Old reed garden chairs, empty bottles, old kitsch on the walls. The balcony sticks out over the edge of the rocks, meters below still more rocks, woods, a wide meadow, the pink stripe of Rossignol in the distance. I am enchanted, want to live there, sit on the balcony where no one can see you, no one can hear you, where you see no life except cicadas and in the distance, toy motorcars on the road. An says I can sit there the next day when she is away and gives me the heavy key to the gate. I am happy.

We eat, talk about food and about relationships, favourite subjects. When I talk about my irritation when Hans wants to do everything together while I have such a terrible need to be alone, An radiates recognition. When Hans explains how difficult it is to be on holiday with someone who never wants to go anywhere because she is just as happy to remain reading, Eric sits nodding. Eric drives us along the winding road to the top where our tents are on the camping site. Armin is almost asleep in the car.

When I want to snuggle happily and a bit tipsy down between the sheets, I notice that something is wrong. Hans is sitting in the corner of the tent. I get a flash of fear that he will attack me, that he will grab my throat. But he makes no movement. What are you doing tomorrow, I ask neutrally, to break the silence. Then he bursts out. What do you care what I do, why don't you just say you want to be alone, that you aren't the slightest bit interested in what I do? Then the rest, a stream, that he is jealous if I dream of someone else, he is jealous if I write, when I can so clearly do without him. Jealous of my contacts with women, the ease with which I can talk to my women friends. Jealous that I am going to the garden tomorrow, that I didn't suggest that we go together, that I know what I want. He says mean things also, things he knows are untrue, but now he is on the other side of a wall and says anything he can think of to hurt me. I feel crushed, had not expected this, so much aggression at a moment when I was completely satisfied, after a good evening with friends who are, after all, his friends too. He falls asleep, exhausted from anger.

I lie awake, turn; I have a headache, am bilious. I worry. How can we ever solve this, what can I do if he is jealous of everything I do on my own? We are trapped in a circle, the more he tries to do things together, the more I need to separate myself from him. And then he has even more cause to be jealous.

The next day I feel sick. I don't want to see Hans's guilt-stricken face. I don't want to answer the question, do I still love him. He wants to know if I think of him when we make love, if I need him. I don't know, I want to go away alone, not be involved with him. He is sorry about what he said, it is my own problem, he says, I must find a solution myself, you must have patience with me. But I want nothing to do with him, not with his aggression, nor with his guilt-stricken face. Leave me in peace, I say, it is enough for the present. I go to the garden.

On the way there I buy bread and ham. A bottle of water, a bottle of wine. The gate screeches open, I lock it, take off all my clothes, pour a glass of water, then a glass of wine. The balcony. Silence, only the cicadas. I don't write, as I had planned, I am busy recovering, drawing deep breaths, emptying. Sun on my body which I wet with water when it gets too hot. Rivulets of sweat under my arms, between my breasts. My headache ebbs away. At the end of the day I am peaceful, my sickness over. I go to the village, the terrace, where I hope to find someone. Just enough money for a lemon drink, but no one comes. I decide to walk on the road to the swimming pool and the camping ground. Half an hour through the dry heat, mistral at half strength. Strange derelict buildings of loose stones on the way. On the terrace next to the swimming pool sit An and Eric, Armin floats in the water. How is your fight going, asks Eric. I don't know, everything is fine with me, now. Armin has told them everything, he was kept awake by the screaming. Everyone must have been listening intently, cursing us. Armin waves from the water. I drink ice-cold beer. In the middle of a crisis, I fall back on the primitive needs of my body. Sun, silence, a cold drink. My body restores herself if I let her go her own way.

Then Hans comes back with the car. I don't really want to see him yet, his nervous face, full of question marks. I don't want to talk, I say. OK, he says, let's go and eat.

At night in his sleep he jams me tight between his sweating

body and the suitcase. I try to push him away, but as he always rolls back, I move over to the other side, closer to the exit.

When he wakes he asks first, are you planning to leave. No, I say, I am not. Then we talk more peacefully. About his difficulty in being self-determined, not making himself dependent. It is fine when I am alone, he says, when you aren't here. Why don't you do more things alone? I ask, but that is something he isn't used to, he must force himself. I feel old, having been alone so much that it has become a luxury which I don't readily allow to be taken from me. Hans tells me about his dream holiday, two weeks completely together, walking hand in hand, in love, making love. I tell him about my dream holiday, a whole lot of space for myself, peace, nothing I need to do, meeting each other now and then as friends, eating together, sitting next to each other in cafés and talking or being silent or reading. Perhaps, now and then, if we are very close, making love.

Hans actually wants to be my muse, hopes that he inspires me, supports me, but writing is something I do under my own power. He feels superfluous when I don't need him. I feel guilty about that. He looked after me in the days before we left, and I was working at full speed, he cooked for me, made coffee, said little. He expects his reward now. I feel guilty.

I realise we are caught in the traditional man-woman relationship, but now completely reversed. I find it no happy discovery. You must have patience with me, says Hans, when I say that I recognise everything he does from before, from my own behaviour. Wait at the telephone, take no initiative, erase yourself and then expect a reward for that, think that you are the only one who gives and because of that nag someone to death. And not understand how anyone can be so heartless as to walk away and still bang the door shut behind them. I understand now what pressure someone can put on you just by saying I need nothing, I only want to sit here and look at you. I ask nothing from you, only that you are here. I only want to lie against you.

You are a few years ahead, says Hans, you must give me time. And what about me then, in the meantime, I say, must I stop growing until you are finished? Then I am your therapist. I don't want to be your therapist, go and find a real one, one you pay.

But we can touch each other again, swim together.

48

Laughing with Armin who had stayed out of the way until he sensed that it was over and that he could come to fetch a new bottle of fizzy orange to which he is addicted.

I write short pieces about Toni. Hardly believe it myself, that it was me, the woman who let herself be battered. I remembered my black eye for the first time when I interviewed two women from *Blijf van m'n Lijf* (Women's Aid). The rape only when I talked with my consciousness raising group. Experiences that had no name, which I had experienced in such isolation that they remained buried in my subconscious. Only afterwards did I realise that I had been crazy and that no one noticed it as long as I continued to behave normally to the outside world. And even if people had seen my black eye, Armin's fear? Private, not the responsibility of other people, something to be ashamed of.

Existential anxiety, that I have never completely lost. Not because I am afraid it will happen to me again but because I live in a society where it is possible. Where women have no protection from what can be done to them in their 'private' lives. If a black man is beaten up in the street, that is politics. If a woman is battered in her home that is a private problem, a disturbed relationship. When workers have no say over the production in their factory, that is politics. When women have no say over their own lives, don't dare walk away because they have nowhere to go, because they are afraid of revenge or that their children will be taken from them, then that is private. They must solve that themselves, each one alone. And if we get angry our left-wing comrades tell us that we are neurotic and hysterical. That we forget the main dialectic. That we are being apolitical. That we are opposing men when we should work together.

A second marriage

In the months before I finally leave Toni, I dream occasionally about Jonas. Without being able to give myself a reasonable explanation. Perhaps because he was the only person I remember as just being nice to me. He brought along sweets for me without wanting anything in return.

Perhaps because he is so unthreatening, just as shy as me.

I live with Armin in one of the spare rooms in my parents' house. While I have been away my brother has taken over the attic floor. I should begin to think about the future, but for the moment I am resting. My parents are on holiday. I stay with Armin in Amsterdam. A luxury. There is a bath, a television, a toilet that flushes in the ordinary way. Every morning I make a pot of tea for myself, toast, real butter. Open the window and sit in the sun. Only that. Toast with butter, tea, sun.

The nightmare is not quite over. At the divorce I am awarded custody of Armin, but Toni is given access. Toni has no desire to see his child, but is sorry that he agreed to the divorce. He tries to get me back, uses Armin to put pressure on me. He has so often threatened to take Armin that I have become really frightened that he will. It would not be difficult for him. The border between the Netherlands and Belgium is open, once over the border and I will never get Armin back. There is no extradition treaty between Austria and the Netherlands. I dare not let Armin go out alone with Toni, must therefore accompany them. Saturdays I sit with Toni in the Vondelpark, where he threatens and pleads in turn. Offers to throw himself off a cliff if I will go to bed with him one more time. If I knew for sure that he would keep his word, I would have done so.

The neighbours tell my parents that Toni stands every night across the street in a doorway.

I hear from my brother, who was in the same class, that things are not going well with Jonas. He is drinking, has failed his finals twice. Is now doing national service. He comes to visit, Jonas. The television as excuse. We don't need to talk then. Comes again, with a friend whom I also knew at school. They stay late, I make fresh cups of instant coffee continuously, don't want to lose them. Because I want to see Jonas, scared that he won't come back. Because I am afraid at night when I sleep alone in the house.

Suddenly I see the light burning on the house telephone. There is someone in the house. I panic, get gooseflesh from fear. Jonas and the friend search through the other floors, while I run to Armin's cot to see if he is still there. Jonas glimpses Toni as he runs out the door. He had climbed on the gable to the roof, jealous of my visitors. Jonas and the friend stay the night, sleeping on the couch, while I lie in bed and jump up at every sound. Saturday Toni tries to find out if I fucked with them. I say nothing. He makes allusions to the pistol he owns, the steps he can take.

At night I am really scared now, I hear footsteps, don't know whether they are real or not. I fetch Armin into my bedroom and lock and barricade the door with a wardrobe. And I still lie awake until it is light. I phone the police, aliens division, to ask if they can do anything, but they answer, lady, we can only interfere if he has done something, broken in or shot at you.

I talk to no one about the past year. Have no words for it, no names for what happened to me. No one has noticed anything. I cooked on time. Armin wore clean clothes. I read. I had no friends but that is normal if you are just back from a foreign country. I do not realise myself that it was unusual, the way I lived, how I felt. I understand only that I am doing my best to start a new life.

I have no idea what I should do. Never finished middle school. A girl who was at school with me is invited round by my mother.

She is at the Social Academy. I can't picture at all what it is like. Something to do with people. She says that you can be accepted after an entrance exam without school leaving certificates.

I present myself, have a talk with a social worker, to my dumb amazement I am found to be suitable. I do more things that scare me. I go with that girlfriend to a meeting of the Society for Sexual Reform where I hear myself discussing sex with the others. Theories about free love, information on contraceptives. As if I know anything about sex, except for the sessions with Toni which I endured three times a week with clenched teeth.

Then the money. My first experiences with officials and forms to fill in and hours waiting on benches, experiences like many that would follow. I appear to have fallen into a hole in the social welfare laws. No payment as unmarried mother because I am married. No alimony for myself because I am the 'guilty' party. The fifty guilders I should get for Armin don't arrive and Toni has disappeared. In the years that follow I receive regular letters from the Council for the Protection of Children, that the amount of money that I do *not* get has been raised. I also don't get unemployment benefit because I have never worked. I don't get welfare because I am a student, not even for the creche for Armin. I don't get a student grant because my parents are too rich and I am not yet twenty-seven. I don't even get child allowance.

To appeal to a higher authority doesn't help. Get a job, madam, says the welfare officer. When I work out for him that I will cost a lot more money if I take an unqualified job now and will need years of additional allowances for Armin, while they will be rid of me after the four years which my training will take if they pay for Armin's creche, he snaps at me. It is not the money, he says, it is the principle that counts.

More bureaucrats. By marrying an Austrian man I become an Austrian woman. I need a solicitor for the divorce. I can get one for nothing if as a Netherlands citizen I can show I haven't enough money. But in order to become a citizen of the Netherlands I must first get a divorce. And for the divorce I need a solicitor.

Papers, papers. Sometimes I almost forget why I am waiting.

52

Was it for social security or was it for the certificate of inadequacy I ask for by mistake at the cubicle when I need to ask for a certificate of inadequate means.

In the end my father finds out how much I would have got on a grant and pays me that.

Then a house. I take the first I can get. A derelict flat in a working-class area. The surgery of a senile doctor who had died. The man who shows it to me says you aren't really going to live here?

Two rooms, an alcove, a small kitchen, an enclosed balcony. The floor is so uneven that I trip. No shower. It is filthy. Pieces of cotton wool on the floor. Thick layers of grease on rancid vomit-green paint. A greasy line on the wallpaper where people in the waiting room had sat with their heads against the wall. Urine splashes on the wall in the kitchen where specimens were taken. A timber merchant below. At eight in the morning the circular saw starts, and stops again only at six in the evening. The balcony looks out on corrugated iron roofs. In the morning between ten and eleven a slanting sliver of sun shines in. I shall have to let out the front room to pay for the rent of the room plus alcove. I take it.

Jonas continues to visit. I feel comfortable with him. Two scared failures. I don't have to pretend to be anything that I am not. He doesn't either. When he has weekend leave he comes to help me. I have been scraping dirt off the walls for weeks, filling in holes, pulling off generations of wallpaper. A lot of white paint on the walls, the ceilings. A little room for Armin in the alcove. A dark blue bookcase in my room, a writing table. Chinese straw mats on the floor. An orgy of colours. The kitchen all shades of yellow. A midnight blue toilet including the chain and the lid. A red hall with red collages.

I am happy. Cook what I want, or don't cook. I eat fried herring, which Toni didn't like, for days on end. Cats. One red, one black.

Toni disappears without a word. Not even a card on Armin's birthday. Until, a few years later, he stands unannounced with his parents at my door, to view the child. I don't let them in.

Jonas and I are in love, that can't be denied any more. He is teased about it by his fellow servicemen. Carefully we begin to make love. Jonas for the first time. His shyness makes it suddenly not terrifying for me any more. Now I am the one with experience. I show him carefully. On a mattress among the tins of paint on the bare wood floor, self-conscious under a blanket. Jonas grateful, moved. For the first time someone who doesn't just appropriate my body, but finds it beautiful, appreciates me. But at night he still goes home to his parents who look reproachfully at him because he is with a divorced woman with a child. Until one time I hold him back and he stays sleeping on the mattress in the now tidy, empty room. Checked sheets I have made myself. An oil lamp because the electricity isn't yet switched on. In the warm light we see each other properly for the first time. His thin body with freckles on the shoulders. The shoulder blades stick out like abortive wings. Eyes blind without glasses, like a mole. Trembling hands. And I see myself in his eyes. The breasts with which I have fed Armin and which Toni said I had sacrificed to that spoiled boy without thinking of him, look suddenly beautiful when Jonas shyly and ecstatically touches them. In the soft light of the oil lamp I don't have stretch marks either.

The next day his mother and mine are sitting next to each other on the still rolled-up carpet, both of them with tears in their eyes. What must become of it, says his mother, you are still in the army, you haven't even finished school, you don't even know what you want to be. Do you love each other? she asks. Jonas and I look at each other, while at the same time continuing to put my books in the bookcase. We have not talked about love. Well, mumbles Jonas, half denying half confirming. But I am stronger, now. That is our business, I say. My father tries once more. Says that he gives me an allowance to study. That my flat is for studying and for nothing else. But I don't give an inch.

Jonas and I laugh at our parents' fears. At his, who see his association with me only as the continuation of the line of failures, his drinking, his inability to pass his finals. At mine, who still

54

have hopes of a smart solicitor or businessman who will save me. As if it is possible for us to fail more than we have already failed.

When we are on holiday in Spain, Jonas buys me a gold ring as a surprise. I buy one for him. We send a postcard to our parents announcing that we are engaged. Then they are less worried, leave us alone.

When he has finished his national service he stops sleeping at his parents' house. The few things he owns are already with me, a few books, a shelf of clothes, his jazz records.

We become settled. We live on six hundred guilders a month, a hundred of which he has after much wheedling squeezed out of his parents who say to him you don't need money, you can sleep and eat here. Until the time I go to talk to them, braver than Jonas, and point out that their son is maintained now by my father. His father can't bear that idea and they give him the hundred guilders. We manage. Jonas doesn't drink any more, we are rarely in bars. In Germany I have already learned how to live cheaply. Occasionally Armin is given clothes by my parents who want him to look smart when he is with them. Once in a while a film to look forward to. Once every six months a jazz or Stones or Beatles record as a treat.

To everyone's astonishment Jonas registers at the Social Academy. A year after me, in social work instead of cultural work, like me. While everyone sees him as the most asocial person possible. How can he help other people? But he says nothing, perseveres in spite of negative advice after a psychological examination, goes to work.

We study. Eat twice a week at his parents, Tuesdays and Sundays. Sunday morning we eat eggs and bacon. Once a week Jonas cooks kidney stew, the only thing he can cook besides eggs.

He begins to talk about the future, that I will finish studying first and look for a job. Then, a year later, he will be qualified and then we will make a baby, which I will look after while he works. A girl, he knows it already, with thin legs and brown eyes. And then perhaps another child.

I learn to speak. Slowly. As if for the first time like a child learning to walk. I hear with surprise my own words in the discussion club, notice that I have an opinion, that it is listened to. I learn to think. I sit in the front row in the Social Academy, listen, ask questions, write notes in handwriting that is at first still cramped. I read again, for the first time books with something in them, not only romances in which to lose myself. I can't yet make any distinction between the ideas that the different lecturers put forward, still don't know why it is that I dislike the right-wing economist and not the left-wing sociologist. I am a sponge that has lain for years without water, I absorb, I feel that I am becoming bigger. I pass all my exams, get good grades for all my essays. I can hardly believe it.

In the second year I need to do a short practical course. I have never yet worked except for housework. I have no idea how other people live, know only my own protected environment and my marriage with Toni. But I still think that is an exception, my fault for choosing the wrong man. I am sent to a watch factory for three weeks, as a packer. I begin at eight, finish at six. A half-hour break in the middle, ten minutes tea, ten minutes coffee. I stand at a table where I fold labels round watch straps, two guilders fifty at the supermarket, four guilders for the same strap at the fashionable shops. Pain in my back, minutes that last a quarter of an hour. I try to make contact with the other women, but it is difficult. I am afraid of them. They look mistrustfully at me, I am only a holiday worker, not a real one. And we can only talk in the break, in between we stand too far from each other and the machines drone all through the day. Only the women who have worked there longer may talk to each other. There is only *one* key to the toilet so that women can't even smoke a cigarette together. And in the coffee break we have only ten minutes, quickly take the lift upstairs. Petra teaches me a trick: how to drink the boiling hot coffee without burning your tongue in the five minutes you have left. Petra first stuffs her mouth full of cake and then gulps down the hot coffee at the same time.

Petra is fifteen. She is the youngest of a gang of girls who have left school early. When they get a chance to talk with each other it is about the boyfriends they are going to see at the weekend.

They talk about new shoes. Petra wants to marry, she wants to leave the factory where she earns practically nothing. She is trying to become pregnant. She tells her boyfriend she is on the pill. When she is successful and her boyfriend wants to clear off, she sends her father after him. She tells us triumphantly that she is having the banns read. She is only staying on a few months at the factory to earn money for the baby clothes. The other girls are jealous of her. They all want to leave. I sit with them, say nothing. Don't say, be careful what you do. I don't yet see the connections between her life and mine. My life was an accident and I have escaped. I live with Jonas now who is a darling. I also see no connection between my life and that of the older women, the cynics who have positions in the next department and don't talk about shoes and engagements because they are all married. I also don't let it penetrate my consciousness what it means when one of the women tells me that before her marriage, she worked in the factory and that she was glad when she was able to leave. But now the children are at school she has come back because it is worse at home than here. They don't listen to each other, the younger and the older women. The older ones say just you wait until you've got two kids, you'll sing another tune then. The girls don't want their illusions taken from them and think that for them it will be different, quite different, because they will get a good man with a good job, a house of their own, two well brought up children. I don't want to listen either, I don't want to belong with them, I don't want to think about Toni any more. I think, secretly, it is their own fault if they stay housewives. I have escaped. I am a student.

A second confrontation. A year's work in adult education with apprentices. Groups of young men. I am even more scared of them than of the girls in the factory. I am given two groups all at once, without preparation, without help. One group of apprentice telephone cable layers and a group of apprentice postmen. Among them are youths of eighteen. One says that he would like to take me out, but that I mustn't think I can teach him anything. They haven't left school to be ordered around by a teacher in a musty classroom. I don't yet understand that this is class bitterness, that they take it out on me because I am a woman. I explain I am there to work out a programme together with them. Then they say, all right, football. I explain they must learn something, but they can choose what they want to learn. They don't want to learn, they have to do that already at their jobs, they haven't left school for nothing. I try with enticing tit-bits, with films, with sexual information, with information about how they can avoid national service if they want. I give them projects with street interviews, taking photographs. Occasionally they are interested. But if I try to bring the discussion round to their work situation, as I have learned at the Academy, they rebel against it, fight, start throwing the chairs around. I learn that there is no point in appealing to their sense of responsibility. The only thing that helps is screaming that they must stop goddammit and that if they don't tidy up their stinking mess immediately and shut their mouths they can stay sitting in the building until they weigh one ounce. Even the heavy bully at the back listens to me with some respect. Child, how your language has changed, says my mother, when I go to eat with her after such a Wednesday afternoon.

One of the groups gets the taste. The postmen make up their own programme. They study the budget of the adult education centre to see where they can get money, call the director to see them who tells them kindly that there is no money left over, until they show him that there is a slot for unexpected costs with which they can do something. The director gives in and later calls me to see him. It is fine that I have been able to make the boys so enthusiastic, he's not complaining about that, but will I please not interfere in areas that are not my concern and keep more strictly to the programme.

They are quickly discouraged, fight with each other over the programme and then look helplessly at me to ask if I will take the decisions. I refuse, fetch the tape recorder so they can hear for themselves how badly they listen to each other. Teach them the technique of meetings. They appoint their own chairman, write up the decisions. They become more daring, invite a police inspector. They wipe the floor with him. They become overconfident, all walk into the company lift reserved for senior officials only. The week after that I hear that the group is split up and a number of boys have been transferred to another department.

When I walk furiously into the director's office to ask him why he has taken that decision without my approval, I see him sitting with a red face behind his desk. Don't you forget that you are here to learn, he says, and that I take the decisions here.

I hear from my supervisor that a request has come in to withdraw me from my course. A euphemism for expulsion. My year is almost finished. It would cost me a whole year of study. Perhaps you aren't pleasing enough, says my supervisor. I look at him amazed. Pleasing? Surely that wasn't the instruction. At home I puzzle it through. What lies behind the director's wrath? Not that I work differently from him, who still believes in a rigid programme of two hours sport, two hours craft work and two hours social study. I have not considered that I am younger than him and a woman. I see how Eileen behaves, the other woman who works there. How she runs crying out of the group if she is teased and then calls the director to bring the boys to order.

I decide to finish my course, to keep my studies going. I wear a dress more often. I let the director carry my typewriter. I ask no more critical questions at the staff meetings. When the year is over he gives me a little compliment: I am so much more approachable than I was at the beginning. While I say nothing any more. With a wink he says that he will certainly miss me.

Why is it that Jonas looks almost happy when I come home crying from work and he can comfort me? Why is it that he seems to become steadily thinner and paler if I am successful? What is happening to us?

We don't talk much. Jonas is no talker. He seems satisfied with the secure routine, the secure ritual of Sunday breakfast, the secure ritual of our love-making, still the same narrow bed that I bought with my father's money, who was not to know that I wasn't planning to lie in it alone. Jonas's white face, his eyes shut, at night he dives into me as if he is drowning, falls asleep with his arms still around me. Safe gestures, each other's bodies that we know inside out, a hand on a hip that does not lie still but begins to move the silent code for a series of movements that always ends the same way. My body reacts according to the pattern we have built up together, it functions. Jonas knows precisely my secret places, my rhythm. He knows my signals which denote if and how I want to come. He doesn't need to ask any more if it was good like that. He doesn't need to ask if I have come, he can see that, hear, feel. He can also feel if I don't need to myself, but make the movements with him because he wants to. Why do I dream at night of the intensity of the first times, when we did not yet make love so efficiently but our skin seemed to give off electricity? Why don't I tell him what I dream about?

Jonas counts what average I get for my exams. An 8½. He works hard. His average becomes 9¼. He is satisfied. If I go out at night, he says nothing, but becomes paler. If I go away for the weekend to a conference he sits silent in a chair. If I ask if he minds my going away he says that I should know what I am doing. If I come back enthusiastic he is barely approachable. What is it then, I say. Nothing, he says, without changing, what should be the matter? I insist, persevere, I feel there is something, want us to talk. Can't bear his silent suffering face that becomes paler and paler.

Then come explosions where eventually he screams, cries and then can tell me that he is afraid of losing me, that he sees how I am steadily finding more contact with other people, steadily becoming involved in more things from which he is excluded. And I say, Jonas, as long as we can talk like this with each other you haven't lost me. If we only talk. And we make love with an intensity that seems like the old passion. I fall asleep satisfied. I love him.

The following day he has forgotten that we have talked. When I tell him during the next explosion that it is exactly like last time, he denies it. After a while I don't try any more. Notice that when I don't begin to talk absolutely nothing happens. I try not to see his white face, no longer ask him any more if it is all right if I go away. Now and then I ask him to go with me, but then I sit the whole time watching him, to see if he is enjoying himself. He doesn't love meetings like I do. Feels an outsider at the meetings of the Society for Sexual Reform where I am elected to represent the sexual life of around four thousand eight hundred Amsterdammers. He is at a loose end at the youth club which we have opened and where I, unhindered by any knowledge of the subject and full of enthusiasm, make programmes about homosexuality, pornography, abortion, contraception. He paints chairs. Jonas, Anja's friend.

I make new friends. People I can talk with, work with. Three evenings a week I work in the youth club. It is a stormy time, the late sixties, there is something new in the air. Into the space which is later to become Café de Pieter, a political café, which we have carpentered, fixed up, painted with our own hands, come thirty to forty young people a night. Highly inflammable discussions about relationships, about sex. I argue strongly for the possibility of more than one relationship at the same time, of open relationships. And then look nervously behind me to see if Jonas is there, if I have hurt him. Then the incident when the gang of young people who usually gather at the Central Station are beaten up by sailors from Den Helder. The next day, hoarse with indignation, I walk on the Dam with pamphlets to invite them to our club. They come, about twenty to thirty, suspicious at first, but later more relaxed. They help us with carpentry, only one dares to participate in the discussion. For about three weeks it goes well, until there is again, for one or other reason, unrest in the city. The boys who come inside are excited, aggressive. On the first floor someone is singing French songs. Can't they sing something you can understand, says one of the boys. It seems to be the signal for the rest to go wild. One of the regulars, who has just come from a wedding, has his best suit on still; he must be the first to suffer. One by one the buttons are pulled off his shirt. Fights break out, one of the boys who is locked in the toilet pulls the washbasin away from the wall. Another is busy throwing plates one by one through the window down to the street. I see two others disappear with a keg of beer. I walk round screaming, idiots, if you carry on we'll have to close, is that what you want? One of the boys nods that I am right when I get him in a corner, but in the meantime the others have smashed a pile of beer glasses to pieces.

The club has to close, we are given notice and before we can find other premises the fire is out. The sixties ebb away. The Society for Sexual Reform becomes more strait-laced. The youth club changes into a nightclub for hip people where naked girls with red and white and blue painted tits dance round on a stage. It isn't difficult to walk out at the first argument. Jonas follows.

61

That summer we have no money to go on holiday. Jonas has just a few weeks before he must begin his placement. I find a brochure from an adult education institute near the coast, three weeks creative work, subsidised. I write that we want to come if Jonas and I can share a room and if we can bring Armin with us. It is allowed. We leave with few expectations, a pile of books in case it becomes boring. I choose a theatre course. It means little to me, but I think it will be good for me, will help me with my fear of audiences.

A chaos of creativity. I open out like a flower. Conversations into the night. Improvisations with our bodies. Not the theatre where you interpret a specific role, but living theatre. The education institute as micro-society is our practice material. Arguments when we irritate the group that is busy with wood and clay by putting on a play under their noses criticising them for being unpolitical. Arguments with an architect, who wants us to play games with models, when we build our city with big white blocks with Philips and Shell written on them round a toilet bowl out of which comes church music.

Naturally I fall in love. Paul, an actor with a supple body. I meet Bahasj, a woman who will come to live with me in the future. I have no time to sleep. An intoxication of work, I don't know what is more important, to be near Paul because I can work with him, or working with him because I am in love with him. At night we walk through the woods at Bergen. On a square in the village we put on a parody of *West Side Story*. Make plans about what we will do the next day. I have never felt so free. I begin to see something of the potentiality that is in my body, creativity that never emerged while I was a housewife.

I can't bear the tension any more, the conflict between the intoxication of working and being in love on the one hand and the oppressive, silent presence of Jonas on the other. Jonas must have noticed it, but he says nothing. He doesn't even ask anything when I lie in bed dejected at night. Caresses me clumsily. Says nothing. I must speak with you, I say the next night. I can't go on. I tell him that I am in love, that I have no idea what I will do with it, but that I can't bear his presence any more. He cries, he doesn't want to believe it. Shall I go away then, he asks, hoping that I will hold him back. Yes, I say. And when I see his white face, I say, let's not see each other for a week or two, and then talk again.

He goes, takes the car. Stays with friends who phone me up the next day. Tine travels to Bergen to talk to me. You can't leave him in the lurch like this, she says, he is completely at sea. He could easily do crazy things. I can't go on, I say, I can't go on. No, it isn't just the being in love. But I can't explain what it is. You don't love him any more, says Tine. I don't know. Love, it doesn't seem relevant in comparison with the wave in which I have been swept up, my own growth. And when Tine leaves, I forget Jonas, we work, write scripts, think together, rehearse. I feel guilty that I don't feel guilty.

When Jonas travels to Bergen two weeks later, I know I don't want to be with him any more. He can see it on me when I wait for him on a bench outside. I have been thinking, he says, if you want a relationship with Paul, I don't mind. I can't do that, I say, I can't keep up two relationships at the same time. But I know that it isn't about two relationships, but about two lives. I can't tell Jonas how I come to life when he isn't there, how free I feel if I don't have to take responsibility for him, how he stunts me, not by forbidding anything, but through the guilt feelings he arouses in me. Are you sure, he asks, and when I reply yes, he says, then I will kill myself. You blackmail me, I say furious, I will not let myself be blackmailed. No, says Jonas, I only tell you the truth. But I stay talking with him until he promises that he won't do it.

When I return to Amsterdam with Armin I find the photos of Jonas and me torn up on the floor. But I have no regrets. Not even when Paul confesses that he has tried but he can't start a real relationship with me because he is a homosexual. Not even when Jonas's mother stands crying on the doorstep to ask if I won't take him back because without me things go so badly for him. Not even when I notice how difficult it is to be alone with Armin again, when no one else puts him to bed, fetches him from school, does the shopping.

It is painful when it can't happen with Paul. I feel lonely. I have little to hold on to, no certainties. Not yet finished at the Social Academy, almost no money, Armin to look after. I have no idea how I will have to live. But I am obsessed with theatre, I live vividly and intensely. I can't imagine I will ever want to return to a marriage, to looking after anyone else, except Armin, whom I can't desert because he is my child.

It's my turn now.

Gordes 4

At night we eat in the little palace with An and Eric and Hanneke. I am delighted that they are just such greedy guts as we are. With the same well-fed, rounded bodies with a tendency to drink too much and get fat. We take cointreau with us for later, when we can't get any calvados. Eat artichokes and huge salads and peppers filled with lamb. And talk about relationships. Eric tells us about his fear that Hanneke and An will want to live together, without him. Hans tells us about his jealousy of my women's group. I need them, my women's group, that is true. I would not want to give them up for any relationship whatsoever. But there is nothing at all mystical about it. And if you meet a woman again with whom you want to make love *and* work? There are really not many women with whom I could do so much, just as there aren't many men. And I have breakfast with you, I say to Hans, more often than with my women's group.

Then someone asks after my book, as if it is a well-developed pregnancy. It's growing, it's growing, I say, and tell them about my difficulties. How I can only write about myself if I also write about the people who are important to me. I can't leave them out, like Anaïs Nin, who had to leave out her husband and with that created a completely false picture of herself : the independent, unattached woman, while all the time there was this man, in the shadow. I only noticed it at the end of Part One when in a mysterious manner she had a baby. I don't want that. But how honestly can I write about other people, how bitter will it sound? You are thinking of Anna, says An. And of Ton, I say, who is already politically bankrupt. It will look like kicking someone who is already down.

Can't you write under a pseudonym? asks An. But I have thought about that for a long time and rejected it. I should have started earlier, I am far too recognisable. And on top of that, I don't want to any more, the shame is over, I want precisely that my political work and my personal writing stand next to each other as a unity, even if I am not yet capable of integrating them into *one* style, *one* book.

They aren't defenceless, says Eric, but then I hear myself defending Anna and Ton. Because I am bitter, I say, I give a wrongly drawn picture, because I can write, because I have some journalism experience. Anna hasn't. What can she do? Write letters to newspapers? And Ton? I will give them other names, but I can't leave out the political background altogether, it is too essential. Perhaps there will be only twelve people who will recognise him, but you can be sure that those twelve people will be important to him. You have no idea of the paranoia of politicians, I say, how scared they are of looking silly. How often Ton pulled away his hand if we walked together somewhere and I saw someone approach whom he knew. I can't be a little bit honest and a little bit dishonest. Then Eric says, give them three pages to give their version. Leave them blank if they don't want to write anything. I need to think about that. I feel fine. An and Eric and Hanneke say it is OK. Hans also. There are anyway four good people who won't get angry with me.

I simmer through the next day. What exactly am I frightened of? Sit. Think, or rather let my feelings surface. What is the worst that can happen to me? Not that Anna or Ton will be angry with me, or the others. I have lost them already. I don't write *in order to hurt them*. I write about *my* experiences, *my* bitterness. I am scared of the disapproval of my friends. Etie, who, when I wrote something about Anna, said, should you have done that, can you do that, without giving her the chance to defend herself? I am scared of Etie's disapproval, not of Anna's.

It is *my* story. It is completely true, because they are my *experiences*. It is fiction, because they are *my* experiences.

A recording of a moment in time. A year ago I would have written it differently. A year from now also. Meanings shift. What I think are relevant experiences now might later seem to be unimportant. It should be a kaleidoscope, instead of a flat book with square pages and straight sentences. Colours that shift over each other and so become other colours. Sentences like circles, like spirals. Experiences which, when looked at through other experiences, become darker, or even lighter.

If only people didn't take the printed word so much more seriously than if I just told it to them.

Part Two
The sexual and other revolutions

Left Out, my Sister – don't you see? Goodbye to the illusions of strength when you run hand in hand with your oppressors; goodbye to the dream that being in the leadership collective will get you anything but gonorrhoea.

Robin Morgan, *Goodbye to all that*

The moon and sixpence

I am obsessed with theatre. Not the fashionable kind, but living theatre made by small groups, connected to real life. I search, go with Paul to the Theatre Terzijde where I watch rehearsals. Try to make myself useful, keep books of cuttings for them, duplicate, send letters. It is clear I will have to choose, the people who work there work day and night, mostly without wages, sometimes drifting from friend to friend or enduring a minimal existence on an unheated houseboat. I am the only one with a child. I want to finish at the Social Academy. To participate half-way isn't possible. Try to find another function in the group. I notice that Annemarie is the only one who comes forward with material, who decides what themes will be worked on. Can't we talk more often about political subjects, learn things together so that we are less dependent on you, I say to Annemarie when she complains that the group is so dependent on her. But she doesn't care much for that, I don't have the feeling that she wants to share her position with members of the group. And, as an outsider, I don't have much say, don't take the same risks as the others in the group. I become sad seeing Paul always around, just as beautiful, untouchable. I withdraw. And shortly afterwards Annemarie walks out of the group and everything falls apart. I search.

The womanly way, being involved in something via a man. A theatre festival in Amsterdam. An American play, outspokenly political. I am breathless, follow them around, go again and again to the experimental theatre at the Mickery. After the performance go up to speak with the director who also acted. Eli. Small and mobile, almost ugly, but I forget that when I see him

69

acting. An appointment in the Stedelijke Museum, the next day. An hour later we are lying on my bed making love, passionate fumbling, with our hands under each other's clothes. We don't take them off because Armin is due from school at any moment. At night I go with him to the Mickery, look for the fourth time at the production, proud that I know Eli, proud that I can go to him after the show, can touch him, can take him home. We make love, strange, a different body from Jonas's, who was a head taller than me. Eli doesn't know my body, doesn't know how it works and makes no attempt to find out. Used to theatre groupies, come and then turn over, get sex where you can find it. I am already satisfied that he wants me, don't think about afterwards. Eli gives me his London address when he leaves. And a few days later I receive a letter. He is much more affected than he thought by the meeting with me. He misses me. Can I come to London? I go, after I have found someone to look after Armin for a week.

London, I drown in the city, I hold tight to Eli. He has no time to show me round, is in the middle of rehearsals for a new show. I follow him like his shadow, attend rehearsals, go with him in the afternoons and evenings to other shows. London is bursting with theatre, showy plays that run for six months, out of the way theatres with more artistic pretensions and the off-off Broadway, the fringe, the political theatre in basements and empty factories. I see two shows a day, shows I don't understand, theatre where they try to involve the audience by throwing water at them, even by tying them up. In one week I see three shows where people take off their clothes and two where the audience is pulled onto the stage to dance with the actors.

I follow Eli, eat with him twice a day in restaurants, sleep with him in his rented room where the gas is always off because it runs on sixpences which are always used up. I buy all the books I can find on living theatre. After the performance we sit in an obscure restaurant that looks like a barn which has settled against a house. Run by a couple, she English, he from India. The Moon and Sixpence. Chips and curry. Hamburgers with rice. They know Eli, cook him pancakes when they see him come in. I laugh at Eli because of his need for sweetness. My Jewish heritage, he says.

A double life. In Amsterdam I am Armin's mother, student at the Social Academy. In London I am Eli's girlfriend, who walks silently behind him. The director of the basement theatre in the Tottenham Court Road, where Eli works, can't even remember my name. Amsterdam! he calls if he wants to say something to me.

In Amsterdam I am busy with finals. Difficult in my one room which is also the room where Armin plays. A restless child. Always busy with balls and marbles and sticks. He isn't allowed to play on the street because of the traffic. I try to keep my fingers in my ears while I learn for an exam. Take them out again because I can't hear what Armin is up to. Who puts the poster from the toilet into the fire. Or washes a sandwich under the tap in the kitchen so that the kitchen sink is blocked and overflows. Until I come running and see that he is busy mopping up the water with a couple of cushions while the tap is still running. Jam on the walls if he makes his own sandwiches. The cat box turned over if he walks through it when he is shooting arrows. Now and then I hate him because he can't ever sit still. Subdue my aggression until he lies in bed and I can, at last, almost exhausted, study for an hour before I fall asleep over my book. Almost attack him when he jumps out of bed because he is hungry and can't sleep.

But I make it. A final essay paper on 'formative work with young people in industry'. Mrs Meulenbelt, says the head of department, do you know that Gorz, whom you so enthusiastically quote, is a marxist? I hardly know what a marxist is but if Gorz is one, I also want to be one. I receive an extra project, to set out in ten pages why I am left-wing. I do so gladly because in the meantime I am confronted with Vietnam and hurt my nose when I am trampled on during the protest march to the occupied university.

I am given a position at Paradiso, an underground-culture youth centre, where I am taken on before I have finished studying. Begin with high hopes, the integration of politics and sub-culture that I myself believe in, becoming steadily more left-wing

71

and at the same time enslaved to the theatre. It must be possible, I think. Projecting my own enthusiasm onto the Paradiso public.

As Eli's position in London improves and I become more left-wing in Amsterdam, our relationship deteriorates. Eli doesn't direct at the Open Space any more, but has been promoted to the Royal Court, not actually mainstream theatre, but it can no longer be called underground. We have rows. He thinks me immature with my left-wing fanaticism. Thinks it serves me right that I narrowly missed a blow on my head from a policeman during the occupation of the university, I should have stayed at home. I try to explain to him my anger when I see a couple of students being beaten to the ground after they have been caught in the doorway of the university library. How I could see the sadism, the hate on the faces of the police from the other side of the glass wall which I was pushed up against. And how I almost grabbed a stone during the Vietnam demonstration when I saw how the police with motor bikes with side-cars rode into the march from the back. He did not understand. And your show then, I say, desperately, the show through which I had learned to know him, a strong indictment against America, against capitalism. But that is *theatre*, he says impatiently. Theatre isn't the same as politics. Why do you perform then? I say. What do you live for? To make good theatre, he says. Would you also direct such a musical, I ask, referring to one or other cash success with names of stars in lights that blink on and off. Naturally, if it is good theatre. I wish I could have directed *Hair*.

We leave it there. But the next time I am with him, at New Year, the break comes anyway. Eli is again directing a new show. I have been to the rehearsals, read the script which I don't understand. In the afternoon we are in the city with Eli's friends, an Italian-English director who attacks Eli because he is doing an anti-semitic show. I don't interrupt. At night we sit after the performance with other friends. Not the kind of friends he had when he lived in a cheap rented room, but more chic. A young woman in an expensive dress, with expensive perfume and carefully made up face looks at television. Typical, she says, when she sees a strike reported. Wanting money without working for

72

it. I look at Eli but he says nothing. His next girlfriend, I think. At night when we wait in Trafalgar Square for midnight and his friends are at last out of the way, I ask if it is true about the anti-semitic play. Somewhat, he says, it is slightly anti-semitic, but it is a good play and after all you should show different points of view. Eli, I say, you are Jewish yourself, how can you do that? It's a good play, he says, tight-lipped, it's well-written, it has rhythm. Why don't you stop criticising, what do you know about theatre with your half-baked lefty ideas, when will you grow up. Do you think I will get far if I sit crying every day about Vietnam? Do you expect to improve the world with a few demonstrations?

I give up. Say no Eli, yes Eli. Creep silently to the other side of the bed. Pack my suitcases early the next morning when I wake up. Where are you going, says Eli, in a small voice. Away, I say. Put the keys on the table. Drag my suitcase to the underground because I have no more money for a taxi. Sleep on the boat train I have so often taken from the Hook of Holland to Amsterdam, no one expects me. Armin is still with friends when I get home. I cry for the first time when I lie in bed.

Again there is a hole in my life. I work in Paradiso, but that isn't enough. I feel incomplete, without direction. As if I don't quite exist, as if I am waiting for something. I miss the link with the theatre that I had via Eli. Was I in love with him or with the world he opened up for me? Looking at theatre isn't enough, I want to be there when it is being made, I want to belong there.

In Paradiso I feel like a stranger. Twelve o'clock I go to work, work through till five. Rush home, shopping, Armin. Then at quarter to eight open the doors for the public who stream in all at once by the hundreds, on peak days there are one and a half thousand. A pack in which I can no longer distinguish people any more. They dive into the dark halls, music so loud you can't talk, light show in the half dark so you can hardly see each other. At one or two or three in the morning, kick the last clients awake, look under benches to see if anyone is still lying there, pull the last one out by a foot from behind the stage. Go home, deafened, fall asleep and wake groggy the following morning at seven to help Armin go to school. Fall asleep again and wake just in time to go to Paradiso again. Mondays and Tuesdays, when I am off, I tidy the house, take the washing to the launderette, do the shopping, clean the cat box. I see almost no one except the people in Paradiso, and Bahasj who is a singer and also has strange work hours. A night life. Sometimes I am aware that I haven't seen daylight for days on end, except the ten minutes to and from home.

We are told to politicise. The golden age of Paradiso and the sub-culture is already over. The creative avant-garde has long since moved somewhere else. Those who come in are the junkies, the young men who have nowhere else to go and on Mondays, when we are closed, hang around aimlessly in the doorway, the school children and curious tourists. They get what they want, pop noise and light shows that become steadily more complicated. Drown in it just like their fathers do each evening as they stare brainlessly in front of television with their beer. A colourful decor with nothing behind it. An illusion of contact.

Now and then I try something. Get a group together that wants to publish a newspaper, another group that wants to make theatre. I work with ten people in the attic above the racket of pop music and the Mickey Mouse films that are projected back to front. Am called down because there must be supervision over the thousand others. A luxury to work with a handful of people when down below the dealers forget that they may only deal if they aren't seen and that they will be thrown out if they try to call out in the hall, who still wants to buy shit. I try to project films in a small room, but it is impossible to get anyone interested, and half the audience come to lie on the benches and snore themselves to sleep.

I can't do it, catch dealers. Have no contact with them. Fucked up chick, they say, if I walk around watching that they don't sell speed and trips and other bum stuff. Almost throw a dealer out whom I have been watching for a while when he openly gives a dark cube to a tall dazed young man. Then it turns out that it's only liquorice.

I try to influence the programmes in the big hall, get into trouble with Piet who is in charge of artistic direction, when I am showing a film about Vietnam and he, because of his ideas on the 'integration between sub-culture and politics', turns off the sound and projects a light show over it. I try another way. See if I can't get the audience to do something. I don't care any more what they do. I have long since dropped the word politicise, no longer choosy. If only they did something. Begin by stopping the sound now and then. Screaming from the hall. If I put on the light a few visitors freak out. (Hey man, I'm sitting here just having a blow, you know, when, when, when suddenly the light goes on, you know, you can't do that, you know.) When a young man comes stumbling in with an elephant on his stomach that we have to lift off, I have for the moment had enough. It is dangerous to experiment. I get a blow on my nose from a junkie, who is waiting in front of the women's toilet to give himself a jab, when I try to direct him to the men's toilet because I need to piss. I learn that you can only push a junkie aside after he has had his shot. Almost no one turns up for a demonstration for legalising soft drugs. When I try to organise a visitors' council who will help organise the building, only the dealers participate, the hippy middle class who want to keep their grocers' concessions safe. The big boys don't come to Paradiso, they haven't the slightest interest in the legalisation of drugs, have long enjoyed the situation as it is.

I feel dried out, empty. I become cold from the poverty of contact in the place which is called the centre of the new scene. Only enjoy Wednesday evenings when there is jazz and I can draw beer for normal idiots, a simple task that seems meaningful in comparison with my fruitless attempts to do something other than hanging about comforting those who have flipped out, kicking people awake early in the morning.

If I have time or am not lying in bed exhausted, I visit theatre productions with Bahasj. Take the bus to the Mickery theatre, or the university theatre. Another theatre festival. Groups from England, the United States.

The first thing that strikes me are his eyes, dark, intense. *Finnegan's Wake*, by Joyce, with musical flowing sentences. Badly

75

acted, with a stiff American who tries to look ten years younger and therefore looks twenty years older. But the dark eyes of – Shaun, I read on the programme. I want him, I say to Bahasj. Stay around after the performance when there is a first night party. Go to him, Shaun, who has stayed after I have seen him wave goodnight to one of the actresses with dark hair. Tell him I thought it was a good play, badly acted. Ask why they gave the dreadful American the main part. You're telling me, he says with a grimace, she's the wife of the director. From close up his eyes are even more beautiful. Laughing, self-conscious, penetrating. We grin at each other. I want to see you again, he says, but I must go now. Come to me tomorrow, I say, explain where I live. Are you sure you are coming? I ask. Yes. I give him the big enamel ring I wear. Say that then I'll know for sure that he will come, to bring it back.

Dream about him at night, on heat.

The next day when I come home from Paradiso I find the ring, with a note. I can't come, he writes, circumstances, circumstances. I write a note to the theatre, that I will be there again that night, will sit in the front row. He fluffs his lines when he sees me. A little later a boy from the theatre sidles up to me, one of the actors is waiting in the passage for me. Shaun. Nervous. I have only five minutes before I'm on again, he says. I want to see you but I can't, he tells me. Tomorrow another performance, the day after back to the States. Why don't you come tonight after the performance, I ask. My girlfriend, who is now on stage, her solo. I look, the woman with the dark hair. I bow my head. Perhaps I can put off my return flight, he says, go a week later, I'm still on holiday. But I have no money for an hotel. You can come and live with me a while, I reply. Time is up, he must go on stage again. I can't see you tonight, he whispers, I promised my girlfriend. . . . Then suddenly we have our arms around each other, hungry searching mouths. Christ, Jesus Christ, he says. Flight. the rest of the performance I can barely look at him, butterflies in my stomach, shaking knees, flames in my cunt. Go home after I have seen him leave with the woman with the dark hair, he still looks round, helpless.

The next day he telephones. Onion? Listen. I'll be there in a few hours. I'm staying. I dash around the house, tidy up, clean sheets on my bed, buy a bottle of wine, look breathlessly four or five times at the clock. Wait paralysed until he rings the bell, walk in a trance to open the door for him. Where he stands, in his ordinary clothes, a plant with yellow flowers in his hand. No luggage I see immediately, understand there is something wrong. I have come to say goodbye, I can't stay, he says. Walks behind me to my room. I can't do it, he says. Dayle has become hysterical, she doesn't want to go back alone, she's heard from someone that I saw you. I can't let her go alone, we're engaged. I hang against him, don't know what to say, know only that I want him to stay. Madness, he whispers, while we cling to each other, we don't even know each other. Jesus, what must I do with two crying women, but his hands say something else, my body becomes fluid, I feel the blood beating in his body, the same rhythm as my own. We can't let go of each other, I bury my face in his neck, his dark hair, the smell of another body. I haven't experienced that for a long time. When he looks at his watch it is an hour later. He jumps. How long does the bus take to the airport? About an hour. I run with him to the air terminal. The bus has already left. He telephones the airport, by the time he has found anyone who can help him the passengers are already on the plane. I stand muttering spells that it is too late, that he will stay. He gets his fiancee on the line, I hear her wailing. Listen, Shaun says, listen Dayle, listen baby, Dayle calm down, I'm sorry. Sure I love you. I just missed the fucking plane, Dayle. . . .

Go and stand somewhere else because I don't want to hear it. Then he comes over to me. You may have me, it is decided for us, I'm staying. He turns out his pockets. Six guilders thirty. No clothes except those he is wearing. We go home where we open a bottle and look at each other silently, sniff each other, touch each other carefully with the tips of our fingers.

Summer. Armin has gone to a children's camp, six weeks' freedom from motherhood, for the first time. After a week the alarm clock inside me stops ringing, I don't wake up with a start at seven in the morning any more, stop thinking Jesus it's already ten to four Armin is coming home from school. Shaun has written Dayle an express letter. I don't know what it says, know only that he is staying for the moment. Now and then he asks me if there is any mail for him, but nothing arrives the first weeks. We sleep, make love, sleep. Begin the mornings with a joint, are stoned the whole day. Shaun looks at everything with the eyes of a child, as if he is at a fair. We borrow bicycles and ride stoned along the Amstel river. Make love in the grass. I begin to see with his eyes, the eyes of a city person who isn't used to seeing ordinary green grass. He picks flowers, sits entranced looking at a windmill, gets ecstatic over cream cheese. Journey of exploration over each other's bodies, my fingers travel over the dark curls on his chest while he grunts happily, rolls another joint, fantasises over the films he will make when he leaves university.

Days in which we don't bother to dress, camping on the bed until one of us, after the nth joint, is overtaken by an unconquerable, overwhelming desire for chocolate and we draw lots which of us will throw on a few clothes to walk across the street to the dairy. He talks lyrically about my bum, he wants to make a film about it, it is the most beautiful he has ever seen: more beautiful than that of. Dayle, the name is seldom mentioned. I don't even begin to talk about it. He gets a letter. Is depressed for a day. Says she has forgiven him and asks him to come back. He writes a letter back that he tears up. I fish the pieces out of the wastepaper basket later and piece them together. Dayle baby, I love you, I'm sorry, I made a mess of it, I'll be back soon. But he doesn't send the letter. Stays.

When I work he drifts around outside, comes to visit me in Paradiso, where he acts as if he doesn't know me and keeps looking at me from a distance, follows me around. He fishes up other Americans, one also lives with Bahasj now, Bill, who plays the guitar, 'while my guitar gently weeps'. Shaun finds an old recorder which, after a day's practice, he takes with him on the street, with Bill and the guitar. Comes back at the end of the day with three guilders fifteen, honestly earned, which he solemnly hands over to me. He has written to his grandparents for money, but they won't send him anything, only a return ticket.

78

I bought you a present, he says one day. Lets me look, two little orange pills in a folded bit of newspaper. Acid, the best, Sunny Explo, let's drop it.

I hesitate a moment, but not for long. Have read everything about LSD, know what you must do. Shaun says he has heard from other people that these are good, not rubbish. Bill will be our trip master, someone to keep the link with reality, who will watch out we don't do strange things. Who can help if we have a bad trip. Shaun has tripped before, Bill too. We make plans for the next day, know that it lasts six or seven hours, perhaps longer. Fetch shopping so we don't need to go out. I'll make meat fondue with sauces. We turn off the doorbell. I had wanted to tidy up first, but forget to do it the next morning. We put out records we want to hear, choose a book of pictures by Escher, a reproduction of Hieronymus Bosch.

I feel nothing, I say to Shaun, who is already sighing, fascinated by something and calling wow, surely I am too rational for this. Let it go, says Shaun, let it go. I feel nothing, I say, while I look at the orange cat who becomes longer and longer, a sort of giraffe with the head of a cat. I hear myself giggle. Realise vaguely that cats shouldn't have necks one meter long. You have to remember it's all in your head, Bill has said. I try to put the cat together again, sure that I must be able to make his neck shorter if it is only happening in my head. Then I let it seep through to myself that it is really happening, let myself go with the wave, float with it. See the books jump in the bookshelf. I look breathlessly around me. The room is busy changing. I haven't tidied up. This gets through to me. I suddenly see how the dirt floats ten centimeters above the floor and along the wall in waves like the sea. I wade through it to the mirror, see curls of dust make a glistening trail of footprints behind my heels, kneel in front of the mirror, see deep green cat's eyes that scare me, scared that I will sink into them as into a pit from which I will never emerge. I tear myself away, become immediately distracted by Shaun and Bill who stand next to each other and look like pashas from a film with their dark Jewish heads. When Shaun says something it stays hanging in a balloon above his head; a comic strip. I laugh,

laugh, keep on laughing. Then sink away into the yellow flower that Shaun brought with him and which still lives. It lives now truly, becomes bigger, glows. Laugh anew when I realise that it is true what all the books on drugs say: I am the centre of the universe, I am everything, while I am at the same time extinct, nothing. A truth like a bullet.

I try to get to the kitchen where I hear Shaun calling wow, to tell him, a journey through the room which keeps changing colours that become so vivid that it seems to me they will catch fire, carefully putting down my feet which have developed webs for swimming which is to the good because in all kinds of places the floor has become fluid and I have to walk round caves which open up suddenly and unexpectedly in the walls. Shaun stands in what was once the kitchen with a tomato in his hands, a shining, burning red coal. Can we eat this, he asks, are you sure we can eat this? Lets the tomato fall; dying on the floor in a pool of blood. We can't eat that, I say, pointing at the steak for the meat fondue: square blocks of dead animal which I push under something with a fork so that I don't have to see them. Cheeseface, says Shaun to me, we'll make cheese. We laugh uncontrollably over that. We decide to make cheese from the cream for the sauces, beating it until it curdles, throwing in salt and vinegar. Screaming with laughter when it doesn't make anything, want to take it to Bill who is allowed to eat it. Stand on the threshold to the passage, the blue linoleum has become a heaving ocean, the walls a cathedral, we won't get through there. Go back to the room, shuffling hand in hand, a journey that seems to take hours. Stand in front of the print of Hieronymus Bosch in which we walk together, yes, yes, yes look at that, yes, round the pond, between the other naked people, then out again. Shaun lets go of my hand, puts on a record of the Iron Butterfly, music that I can now see in waves of changing colours. We lie on the bed, no longer able to talk, to move. I sink into Shaun's hair, a glittering jungle into which I must be careful not to fall. Look at him and see him become older, become grey, develop a wrinkled skin. A darling old man. Then I see that he hasn't become older, but younger, a baby. A wise, old baby. Light comes out of his eyes, he is all eyes, his chin disappears. I see what kind of person he is, a visionary, not someone who acts. He looks at me, sees glistening green cat's eyes, hair that curls and lives like snakes. Medusa, a witch. Soothes the snakes, they lie down. Everything divides into colours, into patterns, an orgiastic kaleidoscope, *one* big orgasm that makes it unnecessary to touch each other. Music that lets me glide over it, I must go with the wave, if I go against it, it will hurt me.

Then it ebbs slowly away. The colours become less vivid. We end our trip separate from each other. Shaun engrossed in the etchings of Escher, I looking at him, from a distance, warm, satisfied. The final clashes of colour. The last books move back into their places. We are exhausted. Before we fall asleep we show each other how we walked through the Bosch print, wordlessly. Precisely the same path, I haven't done it alone, we were truly together. I think that I will never again look at things in the same way as before, that I have learned how to see.

Another letter from Dayle, which I read when Shaun is out walking with Bill. Please come back I need you I want to have your baby. I don't tell him that I have read the letter, say nothing. The summer is almost over, Shaun must go back to university. His grandparents send him a return ticket that he must use within a week. He goes away for a day, with the bicycle. Comes back, says he has thought it over, that he has no choice, that he must go back. To Dayle, to university. I cry silently, under the shower, on the toilet where he doesn't see me.

We paint the balcony purple. Shaun, who has never said that he loves me, writes te quero on the wall before the purple paint covers it. I understand enough Spanish. Two days before Shaun leaves, Bill brings two trips with him. No, says Shaun, but I want to, persuade him, want to do something intense with him just once more. Bill leaves. In Bahasj's room are Americans whom I don't know, don't like. Carelessly, no trip master. In the morning we share the first trip, not the same as the last time. It is grey outside, it stays grey. The colours don't return. It isn't LSD that makes you see, it is a trip where you talk, feel. Shaun goes to the toilet, I'm going away, he says, I'm letting you go. I stay sitting in the room. Hear only what he has said, *I am going away*. I become scared, cold. I want the colours back, the warmth.

I take another half trip, become panic stricken, have I done something wrong. Find Shaun back in the other room deep in conversation about the States, what he will do when he gets back, the hamburgers he has missed, films that he will make. I don't belong there, three strange Americans one of whom looks like Shaun. I go back to my own room, where I try to write something on a piece of paper, spirals appear, a few words. Go back to my wardrobe to look for black clothes, a black shirt, a long black dress, that I put on. Sit in front of the mirror when Shaun returns, a widow. Onion, he says, onion, come to bed. But his skin is grey and cold when I touch him, his hand heavy and lifeless. I feel cold tears on my cheeks, don't notice that I am crying. Onion, says Shaun, it's no use. I have to go back. He falls asleep. I am too wide awake, the extra half trip I have taken needs to work itself out. I look at him, his sleeping body. It looks as if he is dead. A marble statue which has the face of Shaun, whom I knew. I go to sit on the roof on the corrugated iron plates behind my window, among the cats who sniff at me curiously. Pain, a cold pain, cold. I remain there until the sun rises, grey, through a layer of cloud. I am chilled to my life's centre, stiff from sitting, creep in next to Shaun who turns round, mutters something in his sleep. I shudder. No warmth comes from Shaun's back. On the paper I find the following morning I read in my own handwriting in cramped desperate letters: you are still but a whisper on my way.

We don't talk much. There isn't much to say. We buy clothes for Shaun from the money his grandparents sent when they knew for certain he was coming back. He buys a shirt for me from India, black and red with gold thread. We pack the things he has slowly collected, the Escher etchings I have given him, the bag I made for him from an old piece of cloth from the Waterlooplein flea market, the film cameras he bought with my money to film the cats on the roof. I take him to the airport, don't wait for him to leave. He is gone.

The next day I have to fetch Armin from the same airport, coming back from his camp, chattering happily. I play mother, listen to him, laugh. No time to mourn, until Armin is asleep and I lie alone in bed and the pain nails me to the bed as if I am being flattened by a steam-roller. Pain in my wrists, hands, belly. I toss and turn, looking for Shaun, addicted. Withdrawal pain. The first. The first time that I have not chosen loneliness myself.

A letter from Shaun. Onion, he writes, in childlike square letters, I have never been able to tell you, I thought that I could not say it because I was not free, Onion I love you. I am now with Dayle, I must finish something I have begun, Onion, I promise you, if I have made a mistake I will come back. And there follow, with steadily increasing intervals in between, the letters in which he writes that he is married, that he is living in a commune with Dayle. Sends a cutting when he has won a prize with a film. Says again that he loves me, that we will see each other again, that he knows that for sure, but never writes how, when. And from his letters I learn that we are steadily becoming different people, I a political animal, he busy with films for television which have nothing to do with politics.

Gordes 5

Manuel is delivered by Hans's estranged wife to whom he is still married because there is no point in spending money on a divorce. Manuel is a couple of years older than Armin, taller than I am, but they get on well with each other, especially in the water.

I sit by the swimming pool almost every day now, a lazy routine too pleasant to break. At first we pretended we were only going to stay a few days. We didn't want to belong with the tourists who let themselves bake brown every day in their lazy fat, definitely not, because it is also a semi-chic, semi-progressive tourist trap, not even an ordinary proletarian place where you would be forgiven for spending your holiday. Jazz in the background, or pop. Swimming pool on the edge of the valley, beyond it I can see for miles.

I write at one of the wobbly tables. The blue exercise book is almost full. Lie in the sun if my words dry up, letting myself fill up with new ones. Swim lazily. I can just manage a length of backstroke.

Petite bikini girls with new breasts and untouched illusions, next to whom I feel clumsy and old fashioned. Each day the same ritual. Two of the macho young men drag one of the bikini girls to the water to throw her ceremonially in. She screams, but defends herself only symbolically. All the men in the pool look on grinning. I hate them because of their thinly disguised triumph, the show of power of a kind that reflects even onto the small, thin men. But I hate the girl as well, that she doesn't just kick such a youngster in his balls and jump into the water herself – if that is where she wants to be.

I am surrounded by my men of different sizes. Hans, my best friend, Armin, my son/my other best friend, Manuel. I have to arm myself against their demands for attention to be able to write. Armin is the best trained, years of practice. Hang on, I say, I am in the middle of a sentence. OK, he says, without sitting and sulking. And from the way he takes it for granted I become almost frightened, he has so often let himself be pushed aside because I need to work, to study, to sleep. Bahasj, the woman who lived next door to us when I had to work a lot at night, told me much later when she hoped it would not hurt me any more how Armin often cried in secret when I was gone. While he had said cheerfully to me, go on, I don't mind, to my anxious questions.

New people in the swimming pool. A well-built man in minute tiger trunks. A Wagnerian woman with a shiny black bathing suit. Both well-preserved, they hold in their stomachs, the fat still firm. We guess unkindly that they are swingers. The circus with the bikini girls begins again. There is a new girl with them, a fat one, also with new breasts, but with already substantially fewer illusions. A tease, a nuisance who jumps in next to the pretty girls so that the hair they try to keep dry is splashed. She shrieks, shows off. I know exactly why she does it.

Anja, calls Armin, and entices me into the water in which I first stand up to my cunt, shivering, trying to get used to it. Then he splashes, pulls me in. We have an understanding that he may in turn splash me and leave me alone. One moment youthful, one moment old and shivering. I swim after him, try to catch his slippery wet body. He scratches me by accident. I swear. Does it hurt, he says, where, and kisses it better, just like I used to do for him. Jesus, how I love the boy.

The bath superintendent is the most beautiful man I have seen for a long time. Nothing of the macho muscle show you associate with the words bath superintendent. Small, compact, delicate, muscles just under his skin, a devastating line of hairs between his navel and his faded bathing trunks. He walks like a cat. He is self-conscious. Fond of the children to whom he has to teach swimming, whom he never barks at, but supports in the water if they are tired. The only bath superintendent I have seen who doesn't like water. He stands shivering in it up to his navel when he has to teach an unwilling girl. Once or twice a day he dives himself, when the pool is almost empty, supple movements like a seal, and comes up again glossy, glistening. Perhaps he can purr.

Sexist thoughts.

He is called Nicolas.

The turn of the screw

I can't live without someone who belongs with me, without a man. Even if it is only for a while. The times I am alone are drab, colourless. I endure them waiting, waiting for – still the prince on the white horse. No, not marriage, I know that

85

already, institutionalised loneliness that has nothing to do with this need for – passion, fire, colour.

When I am in love I live in another world. I embrace it, live his life. Breathe and drink theatre if he is a theatre person. Live politics if he is in politics. Am only interested in art if he is a sculptor. I don't understand how other women can do without, how they can live alone, or with a colourless husband.

The only way that I can get rid of the withdrawal pain when Shaun is gone is with a new love. I look for it where I most expect to find it, in the theatre. Even in the winter I take the bus with Bahasj over the frozen winding road to the Mickery theatre. A one-way ticket. We count on being brought back, or taken along, or to stay. I make a pact with Bahasj that we may leave the other alone only if either of us finds a man we want to go off with.

Matthew looks like Shaun, the same dark moustache and dark eyes. But no warmth comes from him, we can't laugh together. My body feels like betrayal, will not join in. He doesn't even notice, used to women like tram stops on the way to somewhere else, not to stay with longer than is strictly necessary. I am glad when after about three days, he is gone.

Bill is sweet and superficial and cheerful, but I find nothing in him of the intensity that I seek. But Bill is from Bread and Puppet theatre, a big group of happy people who live together. Later the temptation to go after them, but no, Armin, and on top of that Bill isn't right.

No more so than Tom and Jim and Bob who follow. It seems like all Americans have the same dark curls, the same droopy moustaches. Reproduced in series. I fuck them in series. It seems like Amsterdam is full of Americans looking for free bed and breakfast and a cheerful string of one-night stands before they return to the States, their girlfriends and fiancees and their college where they can boast to their friends about the fantastic broads in Europe. Anyway I've done my best to keep the myth going. I should get a prize from the National Tourist Board.

I keep myself stoned in order not to feel the pain, almost anonymous bodies who stay outside me, however many tricks we perform with each other. Far from my centre. Or now and then, momentarily close, unexpectedly. Bob, whom I bump into as a spectator at the Mickery. Oh well. Dark eyes, dark hair, the droopy moustache. A narrow, tall body. A lazy sculptor who makes plans for soft objects, pretzels three meters high, irons of soft rubber, the kind of objects that Oldenburg exhibits in the Stedelijke Museum a year or so later. But Bob is too lazy to do anything with his ideas. A cat that only wants to lie in the sun, stoned, and to make love. A supple body that makes no extraneous movement, he says not a word too many, is completely taken up by the needs of his body, so egotistically set on pleasure, shameless, guiltless, without reflection. I flow with him, waves of erotic warmth, nothing else, but that. When after one week he has to return to the States, he buys with his remaining money all the beautiful things he can find for me, an African chain, a cloth from India, flowers, a jumper for Armin. Promises that he will be back in a couple of months, that he will look for a studio in Amsterdam where he can at last make his soft objects.

But in the letter I receive from America there is nothing about that, only imaginative descriptions of what our bodies did with each other, what he would like to do, flames in my cunt as I read it. I save money to go to New York. Just a few days before I am to leave he moves to San Francisco. For that I don't have enough money. Then a final letter, confused, about heroin and the man with whom he makes love. He sends a rubber heart and a cunt made of sandpaper. I no longer wait for him.

What's his name, Armin asks me in the morning as he looks over the top of my sheet. As if it is a stray dog that I have brought with me. I have had enough of Americans. If they can't make love well I don't know how to get rid of them. Think in the mornings, what am I doing with this strange body in my bed. That wants to be fed as well. And if I again feel something of the old warmth, I want to keep him. Continually the withdrawal pains when it is over. Looking for a new substitute to fill the hole in my soul. It doesn't have much to do with sex.

Michael has no dark curls and dark eyes. On the contrary. He is big and drinks too much, which you can see from his stomach, and he is already becoming a little bald. And he is completely crazy. He doesn't come from the States, but from London. In his passport next to 'profession' is written 'environmentalist'. He makes theatre, not as stories in which you can lose yourself, but as environments that force people to behave differently. The first time I saw him in the Mickery with his group they were doing a piece where they reversed the roles of black and white. A shocked visitor who found it all too coarse was tied to a pole. A woman who suddenly finds one of the actors sitting on her lap beginning to make love, nearly cries while her friends sit paralysed next to her without daring to do anything. It is after all *art*. The actors are auctioned off as slaves. The Mickery audience, always ready to experiment, participates happily. As a result they have to go through the entire interval with the actor they have by chance bought, handcuffed to them, looking subserviently up at them. Afterwards I talk to him, Michael, interrupted by visitors in evening dress who come to tell him that they have found it very fascinating and to ask what he actually meant by such a play. We grin at each other, comrades, while he says that he had no intentions, that they must work out for themselves what they think about it. Impolite. I think he is attractive. Drink too much gin, he too. Your wife on the telephone, calls someone. He returns, more gin. We carry on grinning. Bahasj has already gone, driven off with someone. I have forgotten to ask myself how I will get back to Amsterdam, I should be back home with Armin who must get up early tomorrow to go to school. I make plans with Michael to try to get his group a booking at Paradiso. I tell him about my work there, how difficult I find it to make that audience react. Did you see the audience here, he says, I don't really want to work in this kind of theatre at all. The only thing you can do with people like this is shock them. That's what they come for. A monthly helping of sensation. They want Laura, whom I work with, to take off her clothes. And instead they get me, a man, naked.

We laugh. I like him more and more. He also needs to go to Amsterdam, someone drives us. We sit silently against each other, a little dizzy from too much gin. I say he can come home with me, but he hesitates. No, he says, in a friendly manner.

88

Asks where I live so that he can write to me whether he can come with his group to Paradiso. When I get out I touch his face with my fingertips only. Fall into bed, happy that for the first time someone does not automatically fall over my body, a little sad that I am now lying alone. Happy that plain friendship is apparently also possible, without sexual strings. I am not used to that.

When I return home the next day from Paradiso, with a lingering hangover because of the gin and the lousy situation at my work, Bahasj says Michael was here. I find a bottle of gin and a letter. I am coming tomorrow at five.

I have not been able to talk to anyone so easily for a long time. We laugh about the same things. Make love in between because it is fun and also it fits. Talk further. He leaves the next day for London, there are a string of performances booked. I say goodbye to him, a little sad, a friend who is leaving. Don't think I will see him again, he with his life there, wife, two children, his theatre. I am here with Armin and my work.

I am surprised when I walk into Paradiso the next day and someone tells me, there was a telephone call for you, from London. Then an express letter. Michael writes that he wants to see me again, that he hasn't stopped thinking about me. He telephones, his voice in the distance between crackles and pips, asks if I will come to London. I can't do that, I say, your wife . . . I'll write you, he says. His voice is lost in strange noises. I sweat, so scared of telephones. I receive more express letters. You are the first with whom I have wanted to share work and life, he writes. It has always been the one or the other. I must see you. Do you remember the first evening, when I didn't go with you, he writes, I now understand why. I didn't want to lose you. I didn't want to be someone for one little night, I wanted more from you, I need you.

When I stand with my suitcase at London airport he isn't there. We have deliberated for hours over the phone about how we will see each other. A conference about art in London, an excuse to go. Can you arrange it? I ask three times, are you sure? I'll fix it up beforehand with Victoria, he says. I don't think she'll mind.

89

And even if she does mind, there is nothing to be done about it, I must see you.

I have already waited half an hour. I reflect that I can't phone him, that I can't go to his house when I don't know if he has arranged things with Victoria. I am almost certain that I must take the plane back when a name which sounds like mine is called out. A message from Michael, will I take the bus to the terminal in the city. When I am once again waiting there, he stands behind me. We stand self-conscious, arms around each other. I had forgotten his smell. We have been with each other for hardly a day, the rest of our relationship by letter and tele-phone. I did not know what your eyes looked like any more, your ears, he says.

We must first eat, he says. London, the same carbon monoxide smell of London. We take the underground because we are both poor and have no extra money for a taxi. A Greek restaurant in Soho. I remember it from when I was there with Eli. Michael has suddenly become quieter. When we have finished eating we look at each other. What now? I ask. You know, he says hesi-tating, that conference. I've been chosen as chairman. That means we don't have much time. And? I ask, with the feeling that there must be more. Victoria is secretary to the conference, he says. We will have to work together during the weekend. I feel a cold stone in my belly. Have you talked it over with her? I ask. No time, he mumbles. I only returned to London this morning, I haven't seen her yet. She isn't home tonight. You can sleep at my house. Tomorrow morning we must perform at Trafalgar Square. You can come with us then. Tomorrow eve-ning the conference begins. We'll see. I go with him. Hand in hand, Putney, swans in the half dark of the Thames. There are friends of mine staying, he says. I'll tell them you've come for the conference, don't let them see anything, about us, they are also friends of Victoria.

His friends finish off the gin I bought for him. I ask where I am to sleep in the hope that he will come after me. The feeling that I can't bear it another minute like this, he chatting with friends about people I don't know, far away. It looks suddenly so unreal, false. I want his body next to mine, to give me back the feeling that something is happening between us, that we

90

aren't sitting opposite each other like superficial friends. I try to catch his eye, but I see nothing when his eyes turn towards me. In the orange room, in the strange bed with a weird, bumpy mattress, I lie shivering, waiting for him. I hear him clattering about, talking, walking up and down the stairs. I need to feel his skin against mine, his hands on my body, I want to hear him come, his satisfied grunt afterwards, laughing. That necessity a physical pain, quite different from the melancholy thinking about him when we are far apart. I can't bear it, *one* wall between us and still untouchable. I fall asleep in a turmoil.

The next morning he wakes me with a mug of English tea with milk. I search for his body under his clothes, to hold on to, but he is defensive, whispers that we must get up. The others are already awake, waiting for him, we are being picked up in half an hour.

A grey London day, drizzle. They have been hired by an action group to improvise something on the steps of the church of St Martin-in-the-Fields while the members of the action group hold a twenty-four-hour hunger strike to draw attention to the Third World. Michael has thought up something with buckets of spaghetti which he throws among the fasting people who are pleased at first, then begin to shout that it has nothing to do with politics. Michael puts down rows of sugar cubes on the pavement so passers-by have to walk carefully between them or step on them and then are accused of having no respect for food. All the while the fasting action group abuse Michael. Whose side are you on anyway, one of them calls out. On the side of the sugar cubes, calls Michael. Meanwhile Laura stands on the other side of the street, naked under an open raincoat with bare feet on the wet asphalt. Another actor tries to pull her away by a rope around her neck and in the end ties her to a lamp post. No one is clear what this has to do with the Third World, probably an idea of Laura's, who sometimes, in the middle of the show, stands on a step just to call out cunt, cunt, cunt, or who rides around naked on a bicycle, preferably if that has nothing to do with anything. I stand watching, shivering, from the cold and rain and too little sleep. Look longingly at Michael, who is totally absorbed in what he is doing and has probably forgotten me. His body, which I don't find at all beautiful, but for which I am longing so dreadfully, a warm place in bed close to him.

The pub afterwards, where it is at least warm and where I can stand close to Michael to feel a little of the warmth and to smell him in secret. But always the other actors are with us, who ask nothing about my presence, but who obviously mustn't know anything.

The conference is a disaster. Michael still further away on a platform behind a table. I can't understand why everyone is getting so worked up. Next to him a dark woman who must be Victoria. In the break she stands near me. She seems friendly, not glamorous. I don't dare go to her. I haven't seen Michael for hours, except in the distance. Five o'clock, we have arranged to meet, but it is already six and Michael is still busy chairing the meeting, which appears to be about extremely important business. I go up to him, with my face as neutral as possible, while I try not to look at Victoria. He whispers, in an hour, outside, wait for me. Two hours later, he comes out. It's dark. I don't know this part of the city, office blocks, dead at this time of day. He doesn't even touch me. A white face. I'm sorry love, he says, I can't do anything with you tonight, the meeting is continuing, I must still fix up something. With Victoria? I ask. With Victoria, he says. It was not how I planned it, I couldn't have predicted this.

Where must I go, I say, suddenly completely alone in a hostile part of the city, no one to help me. I have rung friends, you can sleep there, this is the address. I try not to cry. When will I see you then, I ask. Are you coming there tonight? I'll try, says Michael, I can't promise anything, I'll ring you. He stops a taxi for me. Opens the door for me. Have you the address? Have you money? I nod, dumbly. He forgets to kiss me.

The next morning my aeroplane leaves. Without my having seen him.

Bahasj, I say, what is wrong with us? One of the evenings that we sit together and talk about our lives. Jasmine tea, peppermint tea. One of my long monologues. What do we do wrong? Perhaps expect too much, perhaps what we want just can't happen. If you don't want to marry, this is what you get. We can choose: we become wives, housewives or we are forever the loose girl-friends, throwaway chicks. Second choice, without rights, outlawed.

I let Bahasj read Michael's letter. 'Love, I can't explain to you what happened. I became confused. I do not ask if you can forgive me. I am not suited for the kind of relationship you want. PS. If I am in Amsterdam again can I drop in on you now and then?'

No, I write back.

And then sit writing to myself to sort it all out, to unravel the ragged pieces. I don't understand. I am unhappy in Amsterdam. Victoria is unhappy in London. Neither of us gets what she wants. There is something fundamentally wrong. But what? Is it just that I always choose the wrong man?

Problems:

a All men are rotters;

b I have a radar for rotters;

c They become rotten through me.

I can't puzzle it out. In any event it is clear that I can't allow myself to care too much for the men with whom I mix. If I want to play the game, don't want to go to pieces, I will have to do it differently. Not commit myself, like them. Be off before it is too difficult, stop before it would be too painful to lose him. Jesus, what an instruction. How do you avoid that, falling in love with someone. Why wasn't I born with a built-in thermostat I could keep set permanently at luke-warm.

Work. Everything is going wrong in Paradiso. Always more dealers, always more junkies. On Saturday night they freak out three at a time. A young man almost jumps from the balcony. Addicts queue outside the toilets to give themselves shots. The drains are permanently blocked by the cotton wool they use. I am scared I will be set upon outside, given a hit on the head by one of the big dealers who want to revenge themselves for the fact that they are thrown out. A couple of jiu-jitsu heavies are appointed to keep an eye out for this lot, but that doesn't help much. They can't distinguish hash from speed, and the dealers who bash each other's heads in with chair legs if it appears they have cheated each other aren't planning to ask for their help. Plain clothes men who look like plain clothes men make an occasional raid, but it doesn't help. Everyone spots them long before they arrive with their beige raincoats and floppy felt hats. They are ridiculed, get a glass of beer spilt over them, 'by accident', someone stubs a cigarette out on them. The inspector complains that every time they have been in Paradiso they need to have their raincoats drycleaned. And they catch nothing. After a raid we find a few hundred guilders worth of stuff under cushions and in the urinals.

The staff co-operation is not going well either. An unlikely composition, the staff. Four co-workers who on paper have the same status. Piet, the ex-junkie hippie looks after the programmes. He earns twice as much as me. Just because he asked for it. We can't communicate with each other. Piet doesn't like women who have opinions. If I wear a red suit to a staff meeting he walks away, gets bad vibrations from me. You must be more humble, he says to me, you are too stuck up. Piet likes humble women. His humble woman looks after his two hippie children, while he fucks around with other humble women in the attic, doesn't come home for days.

Emiel who does the business is quite a different person. A beer drinker, non-smoker, an ex-military man who, when he is drunk, can boast about the blacks he has shot down in Indonesia. Emiel also likes humble women, also has one at home, about whom he talks sentimentally, how good she is as a housewife, every morning his clean underwear on the same chair, his shirt perfectly ironed. Emiel actually wants to be director of Paradiso, but he doesn't say that out loud because the ideology is that we are a team in which we are all equal. But he will never deny it if he is addressed as director. And if we go to an important meeting he gives me the portfolio with papers to carry so that I look like his secretary.

Evelien, the third staff member, is actually the secretary. She makes coffee, strokes the men on the cheek. Calms arguments. Says to me I should manipulate the men more adroitly, when I sit once again swearing, simmering with anger, after a staff

94

meeting. They are just like children, she says. You must give them what they want then everything goes much better.

We need a social worker who is able to make contact with the public. Who can evoke enough trust in the junkies, to whom they can go with their problems. Jonas applies and is appointed. He succeeds where I didn't. With his narrow white face you can't distinguish him from the customers, he understands them better than I do. I ask him if it isn't going to be difficult for him, after the relationship we had, to work with me, he says no, goes silently on with his work.

Another new policy in Paradiso. Stricter with dealers, more attractive programmes to attract a different public. I look for young people who have come together from left-wing organisations who can set up something in Paradiso – from the Red Youth, The Fourth International, the Socialist Youth – who thereafter spend their time arguing with each other. Have another fight with Piet, who, contrary to the undertakings, deliberately puts back the light show and once more drowns the place in pop music. I consider whether I should resign, but decide that I should continue to try. Then the conflict comes anyway.

Michael comes to Paradiso with his group. The old feeling in my belly. It isn't over. We work on his programme. He throws hard boiled eggs at the audience and if they don't react and remain passive, raw ones. Succeeds in hitting one of the young men. Emiel is furious. Sees the whole audience soon in revolt, in action, and us with only three staff members to keep the lot in order. He prefers them passive, consumers, less of a headache. Michael and I stand and drink a beer afterwards. I am full of things I would like to say, questions, but I am silent. Izzy, one of the regulars, walks by. Sees my crippled face and says you love him, right. Yes, I say, abashed. Do you love her too? he asks Michael. Yes, he says, while he looks at his toes. Now that's just fine, says Izzy. Why are you both acting so depressed. Are you coming home, I say to Michael. He nods.

Three days. We make no more appointments, no longer talk

about the future. The rules are clear to me now. As long as I don't try to pin him down or get clarity, he doesn't go away. He phones me, at four in the morning, from the bar. I am five minutes from you, I think I am coming over, he says. And does come, eventually, two hours later. I don't become happy any more. Sure that this is the last time, that I can't count on anything. The evening before he leaves he comes to find me in Paradiso. We stand with our arms around each other staring blindly at the light show. I should walk about, keep order, but can't get it together. Everything is going fine without me. See Piet and Emiel, but don't take any further notice. With our arms around each other we walk home, forget to fuck, fall asleep.

When I get to the staff meeting the next day there is a rumpus. Emiel is furious. Piet also. Your behaviour yesterday, says Emiel, don't you understand, as I ask amazed what is wrong. Do you think that the public will still respect you if you stand in the middle of the hall making love? Now they think you are a slut. I stare at him. Think of Piet and his girlfriends bouncing in the attic, Emiel's dirty jokes, the way in which he pinches my bum, or Evelien's. Think of all the naked girls who may give jolly performances on the stage, a light show over their naked bodies. But Emiel takes a high-minded view. He has phoned up the members of the management committee, who arrive bewildered at this hastily called meeting in the conviction that I have had a complete orgy in the middle of the floor. Which, for that matter, would have been a nice change.

I explain that I had only stood in the hall with my arms around Michael, but I have no desire to defend myself any more. It has been clear for a long time that I don't agree with Emiel and Piet about anything, that we can't work together. I am tired, empty, broken. The members of the management committee don't know what to do, have had their doubts for a long time about the way Paradiso is being run, but it is clear that no new crisis can blow up without the risk that the whole place will go to pieces. Then I had better leave, I receive a charming letter of dismissal, that it wasn't my fault. Jonas said nothing throughout, was present in silence. He votes neither for nor against me when my dismissal is talked about. He has had his revenge.

Gordes 6

I wake, almost dreaming still, the kind of dream where I can see all the details, can dream a complete house with all its rooms, can read the books on the shelves, know the past of the (unknown) people who appear in it. I can dream landscapes, sometimes cities. I can decide, in a certain dream, to go up a particular staircase in a particular house, to meet someone. I hope, in my dream, that it is a likeable person, but you never know. And then the surprise. Sometimes it is a self-conscious student who does not expect me, who trembles so much from nervousness that I must help him with the buttons on his shirt. This night it was a musician, not a very good one, in his thirties. Everything became plush and rust-coloured except my crocheted bedspread which was also there and had the colours of the rainbow. A man, whom I would have never found attractive in my waking life, smooth greased down hair, holding onto his stomach to hide the fact that he drank too much. Certainly not the prince on the white horse, but in this kind of dream I can't be too demanding. He announced beforehand that he would probably take much too long to come and handed me a rubber which was good because as I had (in my dream) not expected to make love, I had (in my dream) left my diaphragm at home. It was in the middle of a restaurant. We built a nest on one of the tables with rose-pink sheets. We helped each other with the buttons and zips on our clothes. The waiter objected. There were people waiting to eat and all the tables were occupied. I wanted to take him home with me, remembered that Armin would be coming home at four and someone else with whom I lived (Jonas, Hans?) so I arranged to meet him the next day in my house on the canal where you could see the water through the chinks in

97

the floorboards. We dressed ourselves again while the waiter showed a new client to the table, a lady with a thick layer of gold eyeshadow under her eyes. Then I woke up. Sometimes I have an orgasm in my dream, wake up as it ebbs away, feel the last wave still in my cunt.

Not my revolution

Once more a hole in my life. Except for the trip to the employment office and social security I have nothing to do. Look after Armin. Too weak and listless to start anything. I lie in bed for hours, recover from a chronic lack of sleep.

I don't see any of my lovers any more. Michael definitely vanished. Bob has not answered my last letter. From Shaun I receive his annual letter that he still loves me and that we will see each other again. Perhaps he is coming to Europe again, he writes, with Dayle, whom he has now persuaded not to be plagued by petty jealousy if he makes love to other women. He doesn't write whether she also makes love to other men.

I arrive at the strange discovery that I have almost no friends. No one left over from the time at Paradiso whom I still want to see. And because of my idiotic work hours I had no opportunity to meet friends anywhere else. Bahasj, in the other room, is the only person with whom I can sit and moan about how depressed I am.

All the people who have walked in and out of my life. I have kept no one. Is it possible to be friends with men? All my contacts were via sex and that always went badly after a while. Now my work has fallen away I belong nowhere. Uprooted.

I won't find anything in the sub-culture, that's clear. In spite of the fact that I read nothing in the time I worked at Paradiso, hardly a newspaper even, all the same it has slowly penetrated through to me that there is a lot wrong with the world in which I live. I have no contacts with the student movement, left groups. But I feel that is where I belong. How do I get into the movement?

As always, the theatre. A piece about the States which I sit sadly watching. America, where I have never been, but whose paranoia I know almost inside out via the lives of all the Americans who flee to Europe, go underground for a while, fill up in order to fight against it again. A thin man speaks after the performance about the oppression of the blacks in the States, the setting up of the Black Panther party and the persecution of and sometimes murder of its members. A solidarity committee has just formed. Money is needed and people who can help type, duplicate, sell newspapers. I am impressed, give my name.

Meetings, I belong somewhere again. A small group of people, journalists, a publisher, a few are black. Hanna, the girlfriend of the tall thin one, does the typing, keeps the administration together. We publish a bulletin, import the Black Panther newspaper, organise lectures. I read everything about the Black Panthers which I can lay my hands on, spend days writing addresses, duplicating, doing up parcels in the publisher's basement. I'm alive again. I've no doubts about whether what I do is meaningful. Films arrive from the States, I accompany them to lectures in order to speak the translations. Each time with a knot in my throat from emotion, the anger of the blacks that breaks through, the passion, pride, strength. Huey who describes the day when the blacks will rise and take back what is theirs. Up against the wall motherfuckers, this is a hold-up, we're gonna get what's ours. Am bewildered when I hear and read how the offices of the Black Panthers in the ghettos are destroyed by the police, how the food they have collected to give the children breakfast, is seized. A few are murdered, shot dead in their beds by the police. The press publishes only reports that the Panthers are shot dead in a gun battle that they themselves began.

The first lecture that I am allowed to give by myself because no one else has time. I hear my own voice, passionate and indignant. It works, people sign up to sell the newspaper, want books, ask what they can do. I continue to give lectures, sometimes with Marcel, who is a black man from Suriname and who, after my piece about America, talks about how we in Holland are still responsible for what happens in our old colony. We go out two or three times a week, by train or car, carting books, newspapers. Duplicate. Talk with Hanna who does the biggest part of the work behind the scenes, practically unnoticed. It begins to dawn on me that Hanna and I do the lion's share of the work. The journalist writes the pieces for the bulletin and the publisher occasionally parcels up the newspapers. The others come in order to meet, to make decisions.

Fall out with the Cineclub, my first acquaintance with left name-calling. We are accused of élitism, we are bourgeois because we give lectures to schools. We should be on the streets, say the Cineclub boys, making action. We offer to work together. They on the street if they think it helps, we on the distribution of the newspaper and continuing to spread information. But that isn't the point. A demonstration is spoiled by the Cineclub boys who suddenly develop vanguard tendencies and begin to run in front of the march, stared at in bewilderment by the action groups of black immigrants who walk at the front and who don't understand what the little band of white boys screaming through the megaphone are up to. Hanna and I go as delegates to the Cineclub to talk things through, to decide with them what to do. *We* take the decisions here, says one of the boys from the Cineclub, and a vote is taken. Twenty boys, Hanna and I are two. That is democratic centralism, says the leader, satisfied. We leave. Shall we rape them men, says the youngest boy, who could be around fourteen years old.

We continue with our work, the newspaper is distributed in ever-increasing numbers. The Cineclub plot together. Turn up in force at an international conference with freshly printed Panther shirts to accuse the Committee in public. The conference decides then and there that the Committee is disbanded and that we can no longer speak for the Panther Party. The Cineclub takes over the distribution of the paper and the bulletin which then, after one issue, never appears again. The distribution network disintegrates because the newspapers are no longer delivered on time. But that doesn't bother the Cineclub, who are already after something else. Cardboard workers, Moluccans, it doesn't matter as long as it moves. I must look closer to home, I now understand that. No perspective in the support of a group that barely needs us. You must organise in your own country, said one of the Panthers who visited us, clear up your own shit, we can look after ourselves.

And I also find it difficult to find a place in the black movement, where I don't belong.

Leroy, from London, black militant theatre, Black Pieces. I turn off him when it appears that he only fucks with me because he enjoys letting his friends see that he has screwed another white woman. I only sleep with white women, he says proudly, as if with that he has climbed a step up the ladder. What about his play about Black Pride and Black is Beautiful, I ask. Listen, he says, I act in those kinds of plays because I must earn my bread. Only *one* nigger can play Othello in a year. And is hurt when I don't want to any more. Didn't I satisfy you baby, he says, and whispers in my ear all the things we can still do. But I don't want to any more. Even have doubts when I see how macho the Black Panthers act. Show of force. Bill, who fucks one of the women on the committee and then afterwards boasts that she was a bad lay. Stories about Stokely Carmichael, who has said that the only position for women in the black movement is horizontal. I don't feel at home, but I have difficulty in saying why. I understand what racism is. But the word sexism isn't invented yet.

They must solve their own problems, make their own organisation in their own way. I join the MLS – the Marxist Leninist Student Union – the kindergarten class of KEN – the Communist Unity Movement of the Netherlands, at the same time as a couple of students who have been thrown out of the Vietnam group when it was blown up by an American who afterwards was shown to be in the pay of the CIA.

A completely different scene. No longer the lively meetings of the bourgeois intellectuals screaming at each other, but the strict

101

discipline of comrade students who try to look like workers. I change my clothes to fit in. Not the colourful clothes that were even too smart for Paradiso. Sturdy jumpers, preferably darned at the elbows. The boys have short hair, the girls pull it severely back with an elastic band or cut it short, no paint on their faces.

Solemn, we seldom laugh. We study. Mao, Lenin. Marx we can only read later, pronounces the comrade from KEN who leads our study. We hear that we may become members of KEN later, where the true workers are, if we have proved by our studies and practical work that we have let go of our élitist position and have true solidarity with the working class. I imagine workers as big, well-built men who look optimistically into the future in blue overalls. The masses as a whole lot of workers looking into the future. We have to give out pamphlets at factory gates and on the docks, sell the *Tribune*. Later we may question selected workers.

I try my best, do my homework. Notice that I'm not allowed to put too critical questions when I get for the nth time the piercing eyes of the chairman fixed on me and the advice to reread Mao's *Against Liberalism*, which is specially written for people with a bourgeois background like myself. But surely I am not automatically middle-class because my parents are middle-class, I stutter and then swallow the criticism. Perhaps they are right. Perhaps it is élitist to want to discuss things instead of swallowing them whole. A luxury to hold a deviating opinion. You can't afford that, you have to make the revolution. The workers should have the leadership, not me. The workers are in KEN. It is obvious therefore that we carry out the instructions that reach us via the chairman.

I am bored stiff at the study meetings, but dare not say so. No one laughs. No on ever talks about himself. No one is interested in what I do outside my work for the MLS. A split life. At home Armin and Bahasj and the cats. Luckily none of the comrades ever get the idea to drop in. I would definitely not be approved of by KEN if they saw my room, the books I read, the cushions on my low bed, the incense and pop music and jasmine tea, left-overs from my sub-culture life.

I hide my last remnant of hash in the blue transparent box

behind the quickly growing row of Mao and Lenin. From now on just beer, more proletarian. My room doesn't look at all like that of Comrade Linda, who will probably quickly be admitted to KEN with her bare writing table and one folding bed with only a blanket as a spread, a plank with books, a poster with the heads of Marx, Engels, Mao, Stalin, Lenin on the wall. I daren't ask what Stalin is doing among them, who seems to me to look considerably less charming than the others.

A sober love life. None of the comrades looks very caressable. For months no more fucking except with one of the men whom I have kept over from the Panther time and who comes round for an hour once a fortnight. Introductory conversation. We have little to say to each other. Into bed, one half hour. Out of bed again, back to his wife. That was very nice, he says without fail when he leaves. I ask myself why I go on with it. Talk it over with Bahasj. It isn't for my pleasure. The feeling that I'm not completely alone. That there is someone who thinks I am worthwhile. The comforting feeling that I have at least somewhere a man, even if no one must know it because he is married. Better than nothing. At a party where I turn up by chance, I come across Frits, the popular young man from my class long ago who always went out with the beautiful girl. I take him home with me. He hangs around. I ask myself if I find him attractive. We can't talk about anything, the anecdotes about school are used up long ago. He makes jokes about my work with the marxist leninists which quickly cease to be funny. He compares me to his mother who was also a lefty and who gave him too little attention. Says poor boy to Armin when he has once again to go to bed alone because I must go to a meeting. But doesn't offer to do anything together with Armin.

Making love. I don't know why I don't enjoy making love to him. Tell me that I have a beautiful prick he asks while he waves it in front of my face. You have a beautiful prick, I say obediently, but with little conviction. Because although he has a beautiful prick, nothing happens to my body when he is busy with it. No flames, no colours. (O Shaun, Michael.) A pattern starts which becomes silently established. Frits comes on the weekend. During the week he is in his own house. His shaving things in my bathroom. I cook for him on the weekend. After the film. Once we drop in on his friends, whom I find boring, who make boring jokes about left-wing demonstrators, and about women.

Why am I doing this?

Wouter is at least left-wing. He is in love with me, or at least tries to convince me that I should go to bed with him. Why not, he insists. Because I already have two lovers, I say finally, with the idea that now he will definitely piss off. So, he says. And carries on. What do they have that he doesn't. I don't know either. Silence, no arguments against someone who is really nice and obviously needs it so badly. A service for a friend. Then Wouter is also someone I can't get rid of, because from then on I have to find new arguments each time why I don't want to. So I am stuck with three men – one in the week and one for the weekend and one for reserve in between.

Why aren't I happy, I ask Bahasj, who doesn't know either and at that moment doesn't have even one lover to complain about. A political goal, three lovers who are all attractive, a model of progressiveness in these times of the sexual revolution that seems to have taken place. What more do I want.

O Shaun.

Michael.

While my lovers think I am oversexed I feel chaste and cold. Only come sadly on my own when none of the three is there. None of them ever asks himself if I have as much pleasure in fucking him as he with me.

The dock strike in Rotterdam. Excitement among the comrades. Capitalism is finally in its last gasp. We are approaching the eventual triumph of socialism, the dictatorship of the proletariat, the masses are moving.

I collect for the strike, at the market. Walk through working-class neighbourhoods up and down stairs to collect money. Some women empty their purses when their husbands aren't looking. Other women call their husbands to them or shout to the back Henk are we giving to the strike? I imagine that the whole of KEN is now walking through Amsterdam to collect money. When I deliver the money and the tin of stew that I have also been given it begins to dawn on me that Willem and I are about the only ones whose shoes are on fire from running about. Willem the only one with whom I can sometimes talk and to whom I also dare to confide my doubts. What are they doing to us, we ask each other. How many workers are genuinely members of KEN? We have still never seen one. And will they admit us, or are we going to remain dogsbodies forever?

Then there is an attempt to spread the dock strike to Amsterdam. Our chairman climbs onto a soapbox to address the dock workers of Amsterdam. Comrades, he calls, in his most proletarian manner, but no worker takes a blind bit of notice. A student! one person calls. KEN tries to take over the leadership from the strikers. Does that by setting still higher demands, demands that they already know will not be met. Division is created, confusion. I become unsure. This is not what I had imagined by the idea that we should support the proletariat. Here the proletariat isn't being supported, here three and a half students plus a handful of workers are telling them what should be done. No wonder they don't take it.

Heated discussion afterwards. The most conscious part of the working class must take the lead in the struggle, shouts the chairman. Are you that, I ask, that handful of people in Rotterdam who work for you?

We prefer to leave before we are thrown out. Willem and I and a few other students.

We should go about it differently we decide. No vanguard pretensions. We must offer ourselves so that the workers' movement can use our skills. We have more time because we are students or unemployed. We are also in a less vulnerable position. As a group we join a small metal workers' union. Offer to look after the newspaper, to get new members, to do the work they don't have time for.

Willem and I become lovers. Having collected together at the market, walked out of KEN together, we have a feeling of belonging together. Willem with his genuine proletarian background, who now studies. I with my middle-class background who must now live off welfare, the weekly trip to the social security, the monthly trip to the employment bureau. Willem plays chess with Armin. After a meeting, sitting on the bar of his bicycle, I decide that it is time to make love. Obviously. If you have been friends for a long time with a man, this is what happens. The three lovers get the boot, I had been looking for a good reason to get rid of them for a long time. With Willem I at least have the political work in common, and common sympathy. That is more than I can say about any of the lovers. The whole sexual revolution is just one cold transaction. And a typical middle-class phenomenon.

Suddenly I am living with someone again. It isn't decided, it just happens. Good for me, I think. Regularity after all that chopping and changing, all the pain, all the difficult situations with foreigners, married men. Regularity, a simple life. One man, one woman, one child. Political work. I decide to become happy in a restful, uncomplicated way. Do you love me? asks Willem. Yes, I say five times a day. Do I make love just as well as all the other men? asks Willem. Must you ask that, I answer, you need not make comparisons. Scared that I will have to lie.

O Shaun.

Michael.

At last work again. The trip to the social security had begun to be endlessly far. The yellow letters in my letter box. Will you explain today between ten and eleven where you were yesterday at a quarter past twelve when an official called in vain at your address. The explanation that I will never have a career in cultural work if I wait passively at home. The letter back that I should keep to the rules, should stay at home so that it can be seen that I do not work illegally or cohabit with a man who could support me. Luckily Willem lives on a grant. Argument with officials when I hand in my cheque too late and have to sit waiting three-quarters of a day on a punishment bench until I am eventually given the money. Every month tell the officials at the employment office where I have applied for work. Carefully explain that I am not suited for all the work in the cultural section, that I also need something of a political nature. Don't set your demands too high, Mrs Meulenbelt, says the official, but luckily he stamps my card again and asks in a friendly way how my son is getting on. Apply for appearances sake and because I must for positions where I hope I will be promptly rejected because I know that anyway after a month I will get the sack. The fright when I am almost appointed as a youth worker in a progressive catholic discussion centre where they are interested in 'a dialogue between social reform and the regenerating task of the church with reference to modern youth', and I am supposed to represent social reform. I spread my marxist jargon thickly over my sentences so that they eventually become scared and appoint a more pliable person.

Then a job that looks like it suits me perfectly. An open centre that offers service to action groups and young people who are beginning to be interested in politics, but don't know what they want to do. Recognisable from my own experience. Has it political relevance, working with action groups that have no links with the working class? ask my comrades, but I explain that we must begin carefully and can set up a course in marxism once the centre is opened. I am appointed because I have worked with action groups. And because I have good connections with the city council via management members of Paradiso who had regarded me as one of the more clear headed people in the subculture mix-up. Good for the subsidy that is still being negotiated, thinks my new management.

An exhausting routine. Five days a week in the centre. Often at night too. Two evenings a week with the comrades. One evening study, one evening folding newspapers and duplicating and meeting with the people from the union.

In between Armin demands my attention. And Willem who expects meals and nurturing and attention. Who can hardly cook, makes so much mess in the kitchen that I prefer to do it myself, lets his clothes lie where they fall. Expects the sheets to become clean by themselves, dust to disappear by itself, the shopping to put itself into the kitchen cupboards. When I go with him to his house it is obvious why he is like that. A mother who runs around him, three sisters who grumble but still serve him if he asks for milk, for his food. He smokes a cigarette in an easy chair while his mother or his sisters or I do the washing up, make coffee. I argue with him. Say that his mother can slave for him, but that I am not planning to do the same. Grumbling, he begins to vacuum clean, vacuums carefully round the pile he has let fall on the floor, so that I must once again like a shrew go after him to explain that there is also dust under the newspaper which he has thrown down. I hate myself while I stand nagging. But the alternative, to do everything myself, doesn't make me any happier.

My first workers, whom KEN for so long denied me. Meeting with the management of the union. See with horror broken hands, missing fingers. Hear stories about backaches, nervous diseases. When we go through the card file it becomes clear that from the people who were members of the union just after the war, almost no one is still working; finished. I didn't know it was still so bad. We help carry out an action in a welding factory where the health regulations are not observed, every day the men are subjected to poisonous fumes. They can get a bottle of milk for the biliousness and the foul taste that stays in their mouths. We send a chemist in to measure whether the fumes are really poisonous. When it is proved they are, we duplicate sheets. The young men in the group give them out, less vulnerable than the welders who can be sacked. The action succeeds, machines to suck up the fumes are put in. Our first little victory. The union gets more members. The management is satisfied with us. One of the old KEN members, who was himself once a worker, the oldest of the turncoats, is elected to the management.

A man's world. I am the only woman in the union, in the group of students. I am glad I am allowed to belong with them. I don't have it easy with the men in the union. Miss, they say accidentally to me, although I have asked to be called Anja. The same double-edged reactions that I remember from the time I worked with apprentices in the adult educational centre. Sex and class differences mixed up together. A thin layer of politeness over their bitterness and suspicion because I am sitting there, a girl with a posh accent, educated, girlfriend of Willem, the student. If they had met me in other surroundings I would just be a woman to whom they might say, shall we get her men, or can I have a nice nip at your tits, bitch. The winks at Willem, sexual innuendos. Then sly looks at me to see if I am offended. When Kees clumsily makes coffee because I have refused to do it and pours mine, he jokes, it's good my wife can't see me otherwise I'd have to do it every night. But because you are here, he says, just this once. On the study evenings I try very hard. Am ashamed if, because of all the pressure, I haven't managed to read what was on the course. Sometimes I almost fall asleep while the others are still vigorously discussing until one in the morning about how far we can work with only the productive sector or whether we should also work with the unproductive workers. When we meet at Henno's house his girlfriend doesn't join in, but sits in the kitchen or in the bedroom. Asks if we want coffee or tea. Both, says Henno, and fetch some beer from the corner for later. I feel different from her. More intelligent, I join in, she doesn't.

Won't she join us, asks Willem. Oh no, says Henno, she's not interested. Let her go her own way, she likes it better like this.

Jokes about frigid women over the beer. That bitch was as stiff as a board, couldn't do anything with her, says one of the young men about a woman. And another complains about a girlfriend who won't leave him alone, waits for him at his front door, while he has made it clear that it must be finished. Hysterical, he calls her. I say nothing, behave like one of the comrades. Don't say I don't believe frigid women exist. A subject I'd rather not talk about. Willem is happy with his new status, a man with a girlfriend.

Good eh? he growls as he rolls off me. Do you still love me? I don't dare talk about it, how squashed I feel under his heavy body, how I can barely move, can only go under. I dare not say that I am far, far away from coming like that, and that the mechanised pumping is beginning to oppress me more and more. I think him too nice to hurt him and I am scared of the aggression which I sense just under his skin. His ego as fragile as a christmas bauble.

We still need to get used to each other, I think in the beginning when I am still so softened that I don't mind so much that we don't make love satisfactorily. I do it for him and I'm satisfied with that. But it becomes more and more difficult to talk about

109

it once the pattern is established, more and more difficult to admit that it was never any good. And also I have no hope that it could be different. What must I say? That he mustn't make love only with his prick? That my body is more than my cunt? I see how he holds a cup tightly in his hands, rolls his cigarette too thick and stiff, and keep silent. It is no technique I can teach him, about a touch here, and his hands there. It is the way he lives inside his skin.

A skin that is too thick and no electricity in his fingertips, I don't tremble when his lips touch my neck, *if* his lips touch my neck.

O Shaun.

I dream of Shaun, of Michael, of unknown men who are the combination of all the erotic waves that I have experienced. I daydream about Bob, the lazy sculptor who set my body on fire, drowning in all the perfumes, tastes, that our bodies had to offer each other. Bob who lived inside all of his body and who stretched like a cat when my lips make a voyage of discovery over the sensitive place in the transition between his leg and his stomach, a slow swelling against my cheek about which we have to laugh. The beast wants to go in again, he says as we swim inside each other, rock each other to comfort and come again and again loudly, almost pain. My body that I almost forget, that only exists now in senses, tremblings, scents, explored via my skin. I forget the shame of my mother-body, the breasts with which I have fed Armin. Shame that returns when one of the boys in the study group talks about a woman: the girl with the hanging tits.

What are you thinking about, asks Willem. I blush, look the other way. O nothing, I say, ashamed because I deceive him.

Difficulties with the union. Suddenly we discover that the man who was elected from our group to be on the management has become a member of KEN again. He was so strangely silent, awkward, recently. Talking again in jargon. We find out that he has had orders from KEN to take over the union, or otherwise to blow up the lot. We demand that he leave KEN or at least tell the union that he is a member. He demands from us that we

110

become members again, and obey the orders of the central committee. We refuse. Heated discussions, union work neglected. Our old loyalty to KEN stops us informing the men in the union about the strategy that is being fought around them, but when the KEN member attempts to persuade the union to throw us out when we still refuse to obey orders from KEN, we've had enough. Plotting behind their backs is not the way to win over workers to take up a more marxist position, we decide. Ben talks with one of the members of the management and explains the position. The KEN member is furious. We have played into the hands of the right-wing forces, he shouts. When Ben comes to the union offices he is almost thrown down the stairs. I'll break your legs if you put one foot inside, screams the KEN member, and we know he is capable of that.

He is put off the management, the whole group is expelled until everything is clear. The people in the union don't care much for students who fight out their arguments over the heads of members; they have better things to do. Willem and I go underground for a few weeks in a student flat when we hear that the KEN member has waited at the front door of one of the others to beat him up. Rather keep out of the way for a while. The group continues, but the fire is somewhat dampened now that we have little practical work to do. We read Gramsci, Gorz. Parts of *Capital*. Talk over the strategy of the revolution. By the time the union hesitantly allows the group to help again with the newspaper, things are going badly between Willem and me.

Shaun has sent a friend. Stands one day at the front door, just like that. Small, dark, lots of hair. Willem and he hate each other at first sight. Willem wants to know nothing about my wicked past with all those funny freaks.

John drinks jasmine tea and strokes Miepie, the cat. She stretches, lies on her back, head arched backwards, eyes deliciously closed, feet clawing with lust. The beast in my belly stirs and moans. I want that too.

But I say no to John when he tells me a little later that he feels too much for me to watch without becoming involved, that he will go away from the city if I don't come to him. And then get into a crashing row with Willem, who feels my tension and

111

is jealous. The hundredth row over the housework, but this time it is not about housework. You act as if it is just your house, screams Willem. If you put more effort into it, then it would also be your house, I yell back. Then we'll start now, Willem screams again and makes an attempt to throw away a vase of dried flowers to which I am attached. Over my dead body, I shriek, if the plant goes, you go too. Good, screams Willem while he energetically begins to throw his few possessions together. And then packs more and more slowly. While I keep silent. We have already performed this scene ten times over: Willem close to the door with his suitcase calling furiously, I'm going. And I begin to cry and persuade him to stay. Too scared to be alone again, too scared to have to bring up Armin again completely alone, too scared to lose my little place in the student group if I break with Willem. But this time I say nothing as Willem stands hesitating at the door with his suitcase and says, right, I'm going then.

It lasts one month with John. A complete mistake, but that doesn't matter because I understand that I couldn't have lasted much longer with Willem. Permanently unfit for the role of housewife, provider, one who puts herself in the background, constantly busy propping up his damaged ego. Then rather be alone, I think, however much it costs me.

John is a sadist, a real one. The first real sadist that I have come across in my life. We make love once, ecstatically. The next time he blames illness when it completely flops. Then lets me see photos of his first wife, naked and blindfolded and bound to a bed. I stare. If you don't want to, you don't have to, he says. And asks if he can't just tie me up a little bit, it is just a game. No, I say. Hit you a little, not very hard? he asks. No, I say. Then he disappears to a girlfriend who is a masochist enough to cry when she hears that he has begun a relationship with me. He can fuck women who cry. Which happens when he returns from the girlfriend and I am also crying on the bed and he promptly gets an erection. But I can't cry and fuck at the same time, don't enjoy it either. We talk it over. I have learned my lessons from the sexual revolution well. Everything that happens between two people who enjoy it is good. Where do I get the right to disapprove of the fact that he can only come if the women are tied up or crying? Sorry, I say, but incidentally I don't enjoy that. What do you enjoy? he asks, ready to do a deal, to exchange tricks. Just up and down? How must I explain that my sex has nothing to do with tricks and positions, but with –

O Shaun.

Michael.

A winter full of disasters. The cat on John's boat crawls into a box in the hold where the petrol generator is stored and is gassed. Days later we find her, frozen, curled up in the box as if she is asleep. It is freezing, I am continually cold. Opposite us a fierce fire breaks out and the next morning I read in the paper that two old women have been burned to death.

Everything goes wrong. Armin cries because he doesn't want to sleep on the boat. John doesn't touch me any more now and cuts himself off in the evenings while he smokes a roll-up and reads porn magazines. I am disgusted, but believe that I am not allowed to be disgusted. Am upset if he is critical of me, when I sit reading and don't talk to him, when he decides that I don't dress sexily enough, that my arms are too long and I don't smell good. Until it dawns on me that this has a pattern, that he is trying to make me cry because he lusts after that.

Then I go away. Go back to my own room which I change completely, take out all the blue and green. Dark brown walls and dark brown rugs. The narrow bed out, the table away after I have decided that I can eat more easily on a bed than sleep on a table. A big thick double-bed mattress with a dark brown spread. The room is twice as big now that everything with legs has gone. Just a dark brown space, books, the bed. A Chinese poster with fierce colours. A few rainbow-coloured objects on a dark brown cube. Plants on the balcony, which I also paint dark brown over the purple paint that Shaun and I once covered it in. A hole to hide myself in. A support for my back in a winter full of disasters.

What I had expected has happened: now that I am no longer Willem's girlfriend my position in the student group becomes

113

steadily more difficult. We are solemnly addressed by Ben. He says that he will give me a chance, but it is his experience that it is mostly the woman who, after a while, resigns from the group. I resolve to do my absolute best, but it turns out badly. At the centre we get the first conflicts with the management. Endless meetings at night. When I don't turn up because I have made arrangements with my student group, my colleagues and the management members are angry. If I do go to the meetings, the comrades say, you see, we knew that you were less motivated. Meanwhile Armin is in trouble at school, has called the teacher a fucking bitch. I go to talk with her and decide for myself that she is a fucking bitch. Once I forget to fill in the request form for his afterschool playgroup. Receive a letter that Armin is not admitted any more and that he must now go home at lunch time. I telephone, angry. What do they want. Must I get the sack and go on welfare or do they want Armin to sit on the pavement every afternoon? Mrs Meulenbelt, says the head of the school with a pursed mouth which I can almost see at the other end of the line, those are now the consequences of a certain way of living.

I can hardly take it any more. Dull and tired, I am often sick. Flu that no one believes in because after a day or two in bed I drag myself up again, colleagues who phone up with problems that I must fret about, Armin who must eat and for whom I must shop. I go to talk to the student group. I can't go on. Is it all right if for the moment I don't carry on with the work for the union, but still go on with the study. Ben looks mean and says that the group must have basic discussions about it. They come to visit me at the centre. Question me on my motivation. I explain that I can't go on, a full-time job together with looking after Armin, together with the work in the group. Well, says Ben, that is a question of priorities, isn't it? Obviously you give your career priority. And attempts to begin a discussion over the fact that the action groups that come to the centre have no direct link with the proletariat. I am nearly taken in by the discussion. Try to explain what I want to do with the action groups. Think about the way I myself became left-wing, surely not a conversion to marxism between one day and the next. Think about the fact that I am the only breadwinner, that I can't choose between political work and a wage, because I must support Armin and have no grant or allowance from my parents like they have. See in their eyes the mirror image of a spoiled middle-class bag who is only in the group because her boyfriend was also involved, and who is too rotten to stir a foot when necessary. Before the comrades have decided if I may continue with the study, I say that I am leaving. Actually it can't happen without a basic discussion, says Ben, but we had already expected this.

I like the work in the centre, although it is difficult and confusing. There is only money for the alterations to the café, the subsidy is still not decided. We have to make a profit, but how can you do that if you work mainly with action groups that are chronically short of money. Ask rent, says the management. Then they'll disappear again, we answer. Show films and charge admission. But even then we can be glad if we cover costs. Then it had better come out of the café, says the management, and we get a picture of a public permanently drinking beer, not the people we are aiming at.

Dolle Mina, the first feminist action group, leads demonstrations from the centre; for abortion, for Angela Davis. I go with them. Consider becoming a member but decide not to. Why should I? Big meetings full of quarrelling women; that doesn't attract me. The class struggle is more important, those in Dolle Mina say so too and I agree with them. I am already a marxist, I don't have to return to nursery school to hear that the class struggle is what it is all about. Abortion, great, Angela Davis, also great. But is it really necessary to get hundreds of women together for that? God, is it five o'clock already, says one of the action leaders, I must go home, soon my husband will be waiting for his tea. I feel that I am above such problems. I have escaped the existence of a housewife. I have no emancipation problems. I am self-sufficient, independent, have my career. (And I am unhappy, but that hasn't anything to do with emancipation, has it?)

I have read Betty Friedan, at the Social Academy. Interesting. The problem without a name, completely recognisable from my housewife past. Past. Mrs Meulenbelt, says my examiner, while

115

he lays his warm hand on my knee, there are still differences between men and women? Oh yes, I say, to comfort him. What would we do without them, he says, and gives me an A.

When the action centre is about to be opened I am unexpectedly summarily sacked, together with my colleagues. Financial mismanagment, says the committee, we had not worked in a businesslike fashion. How did you expect to make a profit from action groups? we ask amazed, but then it appears that that isn't the point. I hear that I was appointed because I had good connections with the CTM council from the time at Paradiso. And the man behind the scenes, who is formally unconnected with the centre and who hates me because I don't take any notice of him, has for a long time planned to sack me as soon as the subsidy is granted and to replace me with a more pliable person with less pig-headed ideas. When I go to the office the next day to fetch my things, I find my poster of Marx's head torn off the wall. We appeal, the subsidy is withdrawn, the centre goes bankrupt while we're eventually vindicated in the last round because no mismanagement is proved.

I walk once more, bitterly, to all the agencies. Job Centres, social services. I greet my old officials at the employment exchange. No one wants to pay me anything. A unique case because we are found to be in the right long after the centre is liquidated and no one is responsible for the five months unpaid wages. But that is impossible, I scream at the social services. Everyone has at least the right to something, everyone must be able to stay alive.

Madam, says the official drily, it appears that you have managed that.

Gordes 7

A new notebook, clean, it smells new, yellow cover. The book grows. The words flow nearly constantly now. At night I wake, whole fragments write themselves for me, complete with commas. It happens almost outside me, I am the medium. Sorry that I don't have a tape-recorder to connect directly to my brain so that I don't have to drag my lazy body out of the sun each time to look for a table in the shade, gather together notebooks, pens. Ink cartridges always just empty.

Great blank patches that still need to be filled in: Ton, Anna, the discussion group, the left-wing groups. Not difficult, but a lot of work. I make an outline, rough division of chapters, and take fright. It is a lot. Must I leave something out, can I leave something out? I have the conviction that everything should go in. I can't write another such book next year, perhaps in thirty years' time. But all jobs, all communes, all relationships, all groups of friends which I grow out of again. I shall have to select.

Hans frets. Letters he still has to write. His graduation. Thinks already about work, the first day after the holidays, staff week, when we will be together as colleagues. Don't you find it strange to be there as a lover, he says. I? I haven't thought about it. Don't see us as a couple. My job, which I shape in my own way. I want to make my own quarrels, I say, I don't want to be there as the other half of you.

But other people do see us as a couple. Are Hans and Anja coming? they ask. Where is Hans? I hear if I go anywhere alone. What do you *two* think about it? Hans is sometimes taken in by it. That's what *we* do, he says or: *we* are coming to see you at the

117

weekend. Taken over. Penetration has taken place and now we are an animal with four legs, clumsy, Mrandmrs.

I don't want to be half of a marriage. Don't want to plan my life around someone else. Don't want to have to give an account of myself if I don't want to sleep in his bed. The deadly expectations of a marriage, which progressive relationships imitate. Heterosexual codes like millstones that make me responsible now for him and what he does.

After a month or two I feel guilty if I go with Joyce and Selma to the pub and don't feel like phoning him to ask him to join us, if I don't feel like sleeping with him. At which moment is the decision taken? That I don't need a reason *to* sleep with him, but do need a reason *not* to sleep with him. When I have so consciously chosen *not* to live with someone else. No expectations, no living together just because your clothes happen to be at the same address, or because you have bought books and records together, because your mail comes to the same address.

I am too comfort-loving, I decide. So easy to fall in at Hans's place after work, to eat with the commune, to watch television afterwards, to stay the night. Armin likes it. Not having to go to my room on the Noordermarkt where the breakfast things are still on my unmade bed, the heating off. Really it needs to be vacuum cleaned. Armin's room is a pile of rubbish. It takes an hour before I feel at home, have built my nest again. I let myself slide too easily into the routine of the commune. Hans brings me breakfast in bed, toast, tea, a soft-boiled egg and orange juice. Before I know it I am half of a couple. Have to explain if I don't turn up. Need an excuse to stay a few days in my room. This was not my intention.

Ex-colleague Ed thinks he has found an ally in me because I don't want to marry/live together/be half of a couple. I distrust his fellow feeling. I see his fear of emotions, fear of commitment that rises in him after he has seen a woman four or five times. Know the pattern well now, from all my lovers, ex-lovers who were just as scared, fled when too much happened. Hear one of Ed's old girlfriends tell the same sad story that I have so often heard in different versions. Out together, make love together,

118

but don't talk about it. Don't make appointments, but drop in if it suits. Especially don't label anything, don't promise anything. Until in the end she asks, what are you doing here actually, why do you come actually? And he turns away, mumbles, refuses to give it a name. She makes demands, that he doesn't roll into her house without a word at two in the morning and without saying a word expect to get into bed with her. That she doesn't enjoy waiting until he drops in. That she also wants to take the initiative, wants to plan a weekend with him, wants to know whether he will come as he has promised. He growls, grumbles, that it isn't necessary to pin everything down all at once, to give everything a name all at once. Must you be so heavy? He says. Promises that he will go the next weekend into the country and then arrives on Saturday night at one, says that a conversation in the pub kept him, that they can still go out of the city tomorrow. Fuck off, she says, that wasn't what we arranged. Shrew, he screams, angry while he stumbles down the stairs and slams the door shut behind him. Bitches, always want to hold onto you, always want something from you, why can't it just stay pleasant. And breathes outside, relieved. Escaped. On to the next bed. Too bad, that woman was too demanding. Ed will never experience the madness, the obsessions, butterflies in your belly. To touch each other the most important thing at the moment, time meaning nothing, hours flying past when you are together, ten minutes that last years when you sit waiting, your eyes glued to the clock. Madness. Which, for god's sake, I mustn't have too often, because then I can't work, can't eat, can't sleep. But if it never happens again I will become grey, one-dimensional.

I am afraid to drown in it, a stream of emotions. I have reasons enough. But I will never become like the Eds who stand on the edge, frightened, sticking their toes in the water, scared of the depths. The fear understandable, but the Eds are not my type.

Sounds good, Meulenbelt, I tell myself when I read what I have written. And where does it get you?

An endless stream of tiresome relationships. I can't even get them all in. Discover time and again that I have left out people. Complain to Hans. I can't get my lovers in. Around thirty. He suggests that I devote around five pages, six per chapter, to them. On average. Then I will have more than a hundred and fifty pages and I've only dealt with the men. Haven't even started on myself yet. Put them in an appendix, says Hans. At the back. I'll just leave a few out, I say, filled with lust for power. I see them running to the bookshop and looking up what I've written about them. And there's nothing there. Ha!

An attack of self-doubt. What does it all add up to. Endless drivel about men, as if I spend my whole life crying or fucking. A summary. Who is interested in that except Hans who is always wanting me to make a list of the men in my life because he always mixes up the names. Hear my critics grumbling again. A summary of self pity. See the therapist making notes. Promiscuous. Superficial contacts. Compulsive repetition of behaviour patterns. Not capable of making longstanding bonds.

Shaun, tell them that it isn't true. Hans, am I superficial? But naturally Hans says no. And Shaun is far away, a film maker who has probably become fatter, who is making a career. A liberal, he writes, when I tell him I've become a marxist feminist. I still love you, he writes, but for a long time that has had nothing to do with me, only with the dream he wants to keep alive, the dream of Europe, youth, the feeling that he always has me, somewhere. I have not answered his last letter. I am spring-cleaning in my dreams.

Notebook, says Hans, come and swim.

The prince on a white horse

Attacks of anxiety about my livelihood. I'm never going to work again, I think. Contaminated by two sackings, the welfare world in Amsterdam a clique, everyone knows everyone else. I'll never get work again. See myself forever on the dole or social security. A minimal existence, filled by cheques from social security, sitting at home for the control officials, being stamped at the employment office, applying for jobs where they won't employ me and where I don't want to work.

I go underground in my brown hole. Learn once more to live on borrowed money instead of a real wage, until I get my next dole cheque. Anxiety about living. There is no foundation to my life. No work, no political shelter. My ex-colleagues continue with their studies, have their relationships. I feel uprooted. Don't understand what I live for. Still don't understand what happened. Am I really so pig-headed? Can't I be more diplomatic, shut my mouth, do what is expected of me? I still hang around with the action groups, who have now also lost their centre. But the energy is gone. Begin again. They all seem such terribly naive young fellows, without children to bring up, without fear of living. With grants or dependent on their parents or satisfied with drifting around. Not thinking about later, because it will be fine later on. I feel old, am living in the later on, see no perspective for the future to which I can strive. Jealous of the people who can fall back on a relationship.

When the need is greatest, salvation is near, says Bahasj, when I again sit one evening with her and moan. It'll never happen again, I say morbidly. Although it is statistically improbable that I will never again meet a man whom I like, considering my past. But someone who isn't married and doesn't live in a foreign country and isn't right wing and is still pleasant and goodlooking? Bahasj, we have the whole marriage market against us, I say. All men look for girls who are younger than they are. All nice men who would want to go out with women who are well into their twenties are married or live with someone. If we still want we can be mistresses for the fun, to be thrown away as soon as we want too much. If they aren't married they try to tame us as quickly as possible into domesticated animals. Or they are rotten eggs who can't do anything with their emotions, who break you after a month as if against an impenetrable wall. A wide choice, I cry with thick alcoholic tears on my cheeks. Shit.

But when the need is greatest, salvation is near and as if in a romantic plot with the violins playing in the background, David appears. Friend of one of the colleagues, taken along with us when we are so confused by all the petitions and forms, desperately thinking up new tactics, almost giving up, then the centre down the drain, then dismissal. David comes to help us, listens to the almost indecipherable cat's cradle of judicial complications. Writes a few points on a piece of paper. Now if you first explain in writing all the points in the dismissal note and then go to the employment bureau and then. . . . I sink into his eyes that cause a trembling in my stomach. His hands, delicate and trembling a little. Very lively hands. We walk along the beach to get some fresh air. David plays football with Armin. We turn in circles around each other, the area between us is electric. An elastic cord from our navels pulls us towards each other. It seems as if sparks fly between our hands when we sit drinking gin in the beach pavilion to get warm again. Sorry, he says, when he bumps against me at the exit. Minutes later I still feel the place where our hands touched, hot. Invite him to dinner the following day. Add quickly that he can bring his colleagues with him if he wants. Good, he says, until tomorrow.

It has happened again, I report to Bahasj. Completely. I am completely confused. Dazed, obsessed. Can't think of anything else. Worry that I am just fantasising, feeling something he doesn't feel. Is he married, asks Bahasj rationally. No, I say, but he lives with someone. His girlfriend has gone to do winter sports, she's not coming back yet. When he comes the next day I am almost paralysed with tension. Stumble over my feet, upset a wine glass, don't know what to say. Aren't the colleagues coming? I ask. I didn't ask them, answers David. A confession! He wants to be alone with me. We struggle through the meal. Very good, says David. I taste nothing. The bed is the only place to sit. Luckily. Armin goes to sleep. We put on a record. I wait. All my emancipated courage and initiative has left me. It means too much. I dare to initiate only when I am not afraid of a rejection. We sit silently next to each other, the five centimeters between us are alive with tension. Until I feel his hand very carefully on my hair and we fall sighing against each other, hands, mouth, skin. Eyes shut as if we are drowning.

One week. David doesn't work, neither do I, we have unlimited time. To sleep, to fuck, to talk, to fuck, to talk, to sleep. To eat. To sit in the pub and stare at each other over the gin. To talk. The days overflow. We can't get enough of each other. Listen to each other about our pasts, about silly things. David has given up his studies. Sits at home now, plays the piano and reads Wittgenstein and Hermans. Now and then a mountaineering holiday. I trace with my finger the scar on his shoulder, his weak shoulder which was responsible for his fall from a mountain. I feel the fall in my belly, a sickening feeling. Kiss away all the pain he once felt. One week. What do you live on, I ask. Lin has a job, she types, he says. A painful subject, Lin. I daren't ask further. Don't ask when she is coming back and what will happen. Leave it to him.

My unemployed status is no longer a problem. My political homelessness unimportant. Shelved for later.

One week. On Friday afternoon he says that he will leave in an hour. That Lin is coming home by train. I say nothing, ask nothing. Not even when he will come again. You need time to tell her, I say understandingly. He nods.

When he is gone, I stop living. I hardly ever leave the house for fear he will ring when I am away. I wait, for the telephone, for the ring at the door. I walk in circles or sit paralysed on my bed. Try to read, but my eyes slip mechanically over the letters without taking in anything. Even Hermans, whom I have bought because he is David's favourite writer. But when he is back a few days later and we have made love again everything is fine, pain and anxiety forgotten. Bodies already familiar as if we have known each other for years. I know all his birth marks, every hair, every spot, every smell. I know exactly what all his movements mean, every sound. I have Shaun back again, Bob, Michael. The best lover I have ever had, I say, and this time I mean it.

Heartbeats that beat together when we lie sweatily afterwards, gasping, laughing at the feast.

He comes and goes, unpredictable. I notice he doesn't like it if I ask him as he leaves when he is coming again. I learn to improvise. Dare to ask only after five o'clock if I can fetch a chop for him as well. And still don't know whether he will stay the night. Isn't Lin annoyed, I ask carefully. No, he says. We don't have a possessive relationship.

That is clear. He must in no way get the impression that I am after a possessive relationship.

He talks about his past. His ex-girlfriend, whom he liked a lot. Why did you leave her, I ask. I didn't dare go on, he says, it became too much, too emotional. And then suddenly cries, grindingly, as if he is rusty. I hold him tight, rock him, stroke him. This hasn't happened to me in years, he says, while the tears continue to fall. No one has ever understood me so well. No one with whom I could talk so easily. Everything is coming to the surface.

But will you leave me too if it gets too much for you? No, he says, I can't. When I get scared I come straight to you. When you hold me, it is over.

Then we laugh again. I am sentimental, he says. No, emotional, I say. Isn't that allowed?

He tells me about Lin. A completely different relationship from that with his ex-girlfriend and with me. We used to fuck twice a day, he says. And now? I ask carefully. I don't need to so much with her anymore, he growls with his face in my neck. We have a kind of stark relationship almost. Restful, we haven't much to say to each other. I don't talk much to her. But I don't dare leave her on her own. She is still so dependent on me. She must first stand on her own feet a bit more, begin her studies again and so on. Find her own friends.

We're not in a hurry, I say when I hear that, full of sympathy for Lin. The calm security that I am woman number one, that he really loves me. He doesn't even have to say it, I feel it in his body. And he says, if I have rung you from home I walk around all day with an erection, do you know that?

We drive in a car with a friend, a day out in Antwerp. Hand in hand, we can hardly keep off each other. Eat green herring and mussels. Slightly tipsy from Belgian beer. Almost in a trance. The first day we can walk outside without a coat. We look desperately for a place to fuck, but in the whole of Antwerp we can't find anywhere. The Maritime Museum in the harbour, finally, where at least there are dark corners and we stand rubbing up against each other while we pretend to be interested in the models or ships. But the guard sees through us, walks suspiciously behind us. Until we drive back to Amsterdam and there fall into my faithful bed and at last do what we want.

At night he goes back home. I promised Lin, he says. She's a bit upset. She can't stand it much longer. We must find a solution. I nod. I can't bear it myself any more. The transition between the ecstacy when he is here and the dull paralysis into which I fall when he is gone.

Lin rings up, she wants to talk to me. David is with me when she rings. Is that necessary, he asks. We don't have to be too dramatic about it. But an hour later she is at my front door. David jumps like a hare out of the house. You two sort it out, he says, I'm going home. Trembling I pour sherry for Lin and myself. I like her, that isn't pleasant. She has brought a paper flower for me. You know, she says with a shaky voice, I don't care if he fucks another woman, but what drives me completely crazy is not knowing what I have got, not knowing when he is

125

coming home, never knowing when he is leaving. When I have just cooked a meal, suddenly he puts his coat on again, I can't bear that. I don't like it either, I say. But he said you were used to it. He said that about you too, says Lin. We giggle over our sherry. Have meanwhile finished the bottle, I go wobbling over the road for a new one. Crazy how the tension disappears when we talk to each other. David rings up, he is hungry, is Lin coming home. No, says Lin, I'm enjoying myself, get yourself some fish and chips. An heroic act of Lin's who would not have dared if he could have got angry at her and come to me. But now nothing can happen. We are letting ourselves be played off against each other, we conclude. Neither of us dares to demand anything or to quarrel with him. Because then he can always go off to the other one. This can't go on, says Lin. He must choose. I nod. Secret thoughts. If he chooses he will choose me. He has practically said so. That his relationship with Lin is dying, that he has had enough of her dependence. That he finds himself when he is with me. But I don't say it out loud, so as not to hurt Lin I think, hypocrite.

If we help each other a little for a while, I say. Demand of him that he makes clearer arrangements. And we can both make sure that he keeps them. And we can arrange with each other that when we can't take it we can telephone. OK, she says. I don't know if it will succeed, but we can try. When she goes home we kiss each other drunkenly. It was really good, she says. Perhaps we should do it more often. I don't know if I like you, but when we sit together like this, David somewhere else. . . . Let David cook his own food more often I say, he'll become a big boy like that.

For a week or so David keeps to his arrangements. But he is sombre. It's not going well, he says, Lin can't take it. Which shows when she begins to do strange things. Jumps into bed with David's best friend, hitches a ride with a man who almost rapes her and then whom she lets get on with it after she has wheedled twenty-five guilders out of him. David gives no sign of jealousy, but looks dark. Becomes furious when she phones him in the middle of the night while he is with me. Answers curtly yes, no, no, tomorrow. Hangs up. Dives sighing into my arms. Something must happen, he says. I think that I'll go to Germany for a few weeks to work. Then we'll have more money and I can reflect for a while.

The two weeks before he is to go to Germany fly past. I walk around with a permanent leaden weight in my belly that doesn't disappear even when I have David in my bed.

The day he is going away we sit silently next to each other eating breakfast. I keep on expecting that we will make some arrangement. I want to be comforted, but David says nothing and I don't dare to ask anything. Will you write to me when you are in Germany, is the only thing I dare ask. No, he says, I never write, to anyone. And besides you will file me away in your archives just like your other lovers, with an elastic band around me. A reference to the big box with letters from Eli and Shaun and Michael.

Just half an hour before he is to leave, and David is reading the paper. I suddenly feel a mad anger flare up in me. I am raving. Is that all you want to do here, I say, read the paper? What do you want, he asks, tired. Well, we could, for example, talk. What do you want to talk about, he asks. For example what will happen next, to us, to you and Lin. You know that I have nothing to say about that now, says David coldly. I suddenly see red from passion. Tear the paper out of his hands. Go home then to read the paper, I scream. With Lin. Who takes everything from you. Not me. Good, he says, formally, puts on his coat while I look on numb. Bangs the door shut behind him.

Then the anger changes to fear. Sick with fear. What have I done, I think. Go to the telephone, dial his number. Lin, I have quarrelled with David, can you please say that I am sorry, that I didn't mean it. Can you please ask if he will phone at once when he comes home. I'll do my best, says Lin. Her voice sounds pleased.

I lie groaning on my bed, waiting for the telephone. Nothing happens. I ring once more. Lin again. I asked him, but he said nothing, she says. He is out now doing the shopping. I think he is very angry. Please will you ask again, I say, crying now. Right, she says, even more pleased than before.

I wait, wait, petrified, a bundle of pain. He doesn't ring. In the middle of the night I think that I am going crazy. I ring. Hear the telephone ring endlessly. Lin. Please, I say, barely audible. He doesn't want to, says Lin. You had better go to sleep. I hear her steps, his voice far away in the background, footsteps again, hers. I am sorry, she says, he really doesn't want to. I write a letter, that I am sorry, that I was mad, that I did not know what I was doing, that I can't do without him, that I love him. Put on my dark glasses to hide my eyes, swollen from crying, and take the letter to his house where I let it slide into the letterbox. In this way he gets it just before he goes away.

I live on valium, on drink. Sick. I write long letters. Begin to hope again. It can't end like this, I think. Not after such a stupid argument.

Itch in my cunt, trichomonas. David must also be treated. He is in Germany, I say to the doctor. Get pills for him and give them to a friend of Bahasj who is also going to Germany to work there, with a box of chocolates and still more letters. I don't get a single sign of life in return, but only half expect it. I know that he was planning to spend a weekend in Amsterdam after about three weeks. I wait, sadly. Dare not telephone his house to ask if he is there. And think, if he doesn't come, then it is because he needs more time to think it over. Carefully let it dawn on myself that it is perhaps indeed finished, that he doesn't want me any more.

And bump into him by chance, completely unexpectedly in the Ferdinand Bol market when I am shopping.

Hello, we say to each other, as if it is nothing special. Were you in the neighbourhood, I ask stupidly. Yes, he says. I have been planning to visit you the whole weekend. We walk home hand in hand. May I stay with you tonight, he asks. Naturally, I say. Our bodies understand each other. We catch up on our hunger. Tell me about Germany, I ask. And he tells me about the heavy work, the bare dormitory, that has an almost purifying effect. That he almost wrote to me, but did not dare because he still didn't know what he should say. That he sometimes missed me terribly and then again thought I don't want to have anything to do with these women, not with her, nor with the other.

Did you take the pills, I ask. No, he says. That would already have been a decision. And I thought, I don't want to make love again, with anyone, so it doesn't matter anyway. Will you swallow them now, I say. Naturally, he says. Mustn't you phone Lin to tell her that you are here, I ask. No, he says, she understands that. We fall asleep. I take him to the bus which he must catch back to Germany after we have made love for the last time, more intensely and tragically than ever before. We stand in the dark waiting for the bus. In a few weeks I'll definitely come back, he says. Then I will also have made a decision. I will let you know before I come back, I will write to you, I promise you. I laugh. Soon you will lie after all with an elastic band around you in my box, I whisper. I will write only one tiny letter, he says. The bus comes. The other men call to him. Let go of the woman, in Germany you can also screw. I don't look back again when I walk away.

Four, five weeks pass. Still no news from David. It is taking longer than I thought. One of the colleagues comes to visit. Last week I was with David and Lin on the Loosdrecht lakes, he says. With David? I ask, while I feel the colour drain from my face. Didn't you know that, he asks nervously, he has been back from Germany for two weeks.

I wait until he is gone. Walk to the telephone. Dial the familiar number. David speaking, he says. Anja here, I say. David perhaps you can explain to me what is going on. Now, he says, I thought that was clear. Oh, I hear myself say, goodbye David, and hang up.

Bahasj comes running anxiously when she hears my screaming. What is it? she asks. But I can't explain, can only moan like a sick animal, my head against the wall. Bahasj makes me tea, looks for the valium for me. Pain, pain, I can't think any more, know only that I want to be rid of the pain. I want to die, I say to Bahasj. Bahasj, I want to die. I don't want to live any more, I can't take any more. I want to die. I want to get out. I don't want any more. I can't take any more.

129

Valium, drink, sleeping tablets. I am kicking the habit, as from an addiction. Cold turkey they call it when you stop taking an addictive drug, no medicines, no substitute to soften the attacks. Raw pain, I am thrown into it, come up again. Cold, lucid moments when I see razor sharp how everything fits together. How I expected too much, have projected the whole reason for my existence onto another person. And more rationally, what a shit David actually is, playing two women off against each other, getting the best from each of them without having to be scared that he will be left on his own. The caring given to him by Lin, his bed made and his meal cooked. And then with me, excitement and sex and emotions.

I see how I have spoiled him by adapting myself to the situation acting the happy hedonistic woman who can accept it all. And drive myself crazy.

Pain that returns unexpectedly when I think it is all over, when I see a book by Wittgenstein in a shop window, when I walk into a bar where we have sat together, when someone puts on a record. A razor sharp pain stabs my belly, knives in my hands and wrists while I sit gasping for breath. How long it lasts! The memory of our bodies that could not deceive each other. It isn't true, I think, those weren't lies, my skin, blood, finger tips do not let themselves be deceived. My cunt knows better.

Recovering. Living each day at a time. One day I find on my desk *Notes from the Second Year*, feminist literature from America which I bought because I thought I should be informed on the women's movement. One of the action groups, after all.

I find a piece about love, by Shulamith Firestone. Strange, an action group that writes about love. Our weak point, Shulamith calls it, the soft underbelly of politics, hidden away in what we call private life. I read, fascinated. She is writing about me. About all hangovers after the end of affairs with men. About the sexual revolution that is indeed sexual, but not revolutionary. About how we let ourselves be used, played off against each other. All in the name of the love we need. That men also need, but they don't want to know about it. Don't want to descend to the lower castes who are us. Instead of which they put a woman on a ready-made pedestal now and then, for a while. So that they don't have to look her in the eyes.

Every man's problem, says Shulamith, is how he can get a woman to love him without having to love her in return.

Love between unequals is impossible, she says. And we are not equal. We reinforce the inequality by playing their games with them, by participating on their terms, because we are so afraid we will have to live without love. We sell ourselves cheap. We are satisfied with a surrogate because we are scared of loneliness. The sexual revolution is a trap into which we walk blindly. Previously we let ourselves be told that we were bad because we fucked. Now we let ourselves be told that we are bad because we don't fuck. An imitation of the behaviour of men that gives us nothing except the emotional poverty which men suffer from. Our need for warmth and contact canalised into boring mechanical sexual gymnastics.

Or if we, with great trouble, manage to 'psych him out', to break him open, then he runs away, in hysterical fear of too much commitment. We have had enough. There are no solutions, as long as we are oppressed, writes Shulamith. Face it, baby, face it. There are no solutions. We can choose between a few possibilities. We can banish love from our lives, which is as painful as cutting off your nose to spite your face. We can go back to the traditional games and meet ourselves again as embittered thirty-year-olds who moan to ourselves that all men are bastards. We can wait for the one man who is prepared to give up his privileges and expect that we will have to fight for a place in the queue. We can try to have relationships with women if we can, with all the arguments failed relationships start in the movement. We can build up better relationships with ourselves and satisfy ourselves, accept that sex with someone else is not for us.

I cry. For the tough way that it is expressed. There is no prince on a white horse. There is no solution. But I am not the only one who struggles with the same dilemmas.

I am not alone.

I am not alone.

I am not alone.

131

Part Three
Public Woman

There is something every woman wears around her neck on a thin chain of fear – an amulet of madness. For each of us, there exists somewhere a moment of insult so intense that she will reach up and rip the amulet off even if the chain tears at the flesh of her neck. And the last protection from seeing the truth will be gone.

Robin Morgan, *Goodbye to all that*

If you think I'm feeling sorry for myself you're right. But I'm greatly in favour of people feeling that particular emotion. It's against the grain of the fearless Protestant ethic. Yet you don't know you're a human being until you feel sorry for yourself in a very grand way. Then you look around you and see possibly for the first time how we're all in it together and then you'll feel that big cosmic emotion and that's how you discover with a certain shock that you're religious even though you've read the French existentialists on the death of God.

Jill Johnston, *Lesbian Nation: The Feminist Solution*

Women with high ideals who believed emancipation possible, women who tried desperately to rid themselves of feminine 'hang-ups', to cultivate what they believed to be the greater directness, honesty and generosity of men, were badly fooled. They found that no one appreciated their intelligent conversation, their high aspirations, their great sacrifices to avoid developing the personalities of their mothers. For much as men were glad to enjoy their wit, their sex, and their candlelight suppers, they always ended up marrying The Bitch, and then to top it all off, came back to complain of what a horror she was. . .

Shulamith Firestone, *The Dialectic of Sex*

133

Hysterical materialism

I have my hair cut short. Begin a new life. Later I read that the women in China did that – cut their hair – as a symbol of their resistance against their old oppression. Later. When together with other women I discover our own herstory, our ancestral mothers. Enough plans to begin again. But nothing to hold on to. I have no roots, I blow over. I have tied myself to, hitched myself to men. Men with whom I have had relationships, men with whom I worked, men in the left-wing groups. They have disappeared. The inescapable hangover after a relationship is over, not one of them remains a friend. From all the Americans I hear nothing more, even the yearly letter from Shaun is no longer directed to me but to a ghost, a romantic dream. Not to tell me anything, only to make sure that I am still there, as a dream, available.

I am with Carla in the Stedelijke Museum when I see that the man in the white suit who is doing something artistic in the pond with coloured flags and ropes and glass dishes is Michael. The woman standing next to him up to her knees in water is not Victoria. I look in the programme: his wife. Michael sees me, but gives no sign of recognition. A good actor.

Lucky you didn't keep hanging onto him, says Carla, with your feet in the water like that, that would never have been good for your kidney infection.

I see David in the street, in a street café. I walk the other way, don't want to meet him, a sickening anger rises in my stomach.

The comrades from my left-wing groups do not greet me when they meet me in the street: a renegade.

135

I must do something with my life. Not wait until something happens, but make a plan. Work, I must have work, but in the Amsterdam welfare world I can't see it happening. Then I must study at the university. Something to do for the next six years.

And, further, there is something deeply wrong with the way relationships mess me up, I think. The crisis after David is not something to be endured again. I have survived it, but how many times will I do that? I register at the clinic for therapy or analysis or whatever they consider is good for me. I ask myself, when I sit telling my story to a gentleman in a suit, will they find me mad enough to accept me as a patient, but they do and I am put on the waiting list.

In addition, I want to talk, to talk endlessly about what is going on with me now. What do I do wrong? Or are my expectations contradictory? The American feminist articles which I've read have awakened something in me. No accident that I needed to lose completely all my illusions before I was ready for that. My class privileges first, irretrievably fallen out of my social setting, and I can never go back, never. Not because they would not take me back as the prodigal daughter if I behave myself properly, marry a lawyer or businessman, shave under my arms and have my hair modelled by a hairdresser instead of cutting it myself. I can't go back. I see too sharply what they are, what they themselves don't want to see. I see too clearly the emotional poverty of their class, how they sit boring themselves on their expensive furniture, the anaemia of living for nothing else than the expansion of the business, the status of the family.

And other illusions: that my life would be less alienated if I made it serve a good cause. Could give myself to work for the revolution. The left-wing boys who could so easily make use of my old class-guilt feelings: the shame when a canteen waitress is too polite to me, a taxi driver opens a door for me, not having the courage to complain if I am shouted at by a shop assistant because I think that she is actually justified. Taken up in the battalion of women who sacrifice themselves for others, who think that they are emancipated because they don't make coffee for their husbands, but for their comrades, who think that it doesn't matter if you fuck against your will with a radical because that is the way to belong, or to fuck against your will with your husband because otherwise he gets so bad-tempered.

I can't bear it any more, the split between talking about the oppression of others and the systematic way my own problems must be ignored. I am being broken by it.

It is no accident, I think later, that I was sensitive to the women's movement only when I had nothing more to lose. Not one dream left to hide myself behind. No more class privileges. Failed in my work. Put out in the cold by the political groups from which I had expected most.

I have resisted a long time. Cherished the illusion that I had avoided my mother's fate by not fitting into the norms of marriage. My attempt to emancipate myself as an individual had to fail. Not strong enough to become a career woman, looking down on other women, living without warmth. The choice between housewife and 'free woman': the choice between two unreal ideals. The choice between hanging and strangulation. I am no longer prepared to pay the high price of the loss of my own ego that happens in almost every marriage. But I am not strong enough to keep myself together as the outlaw in a male dominated society. I am unprotected against the cold, the emotional poverty, the illusory progress of throw-away relationships.

I look for women, hesitating at first, just because I need them. I admit, I look for them as second choice, because I had not succeeded with men. Because I am broken by relationships in which I always have to choose between sex and intellect, between adapting myself to male expectations or just becoming invisible.

Women. In the beginning I realise I hardly know any women. I don't believe in women yet, have for too long felt superior to my kind. I have hidden myself from them. My clinging to men and looking down on women is nothing other than contempt for myself. My blindness about that is nothing other than a symptom of my own oppression.

And now? I know only Bahasj. The Women's Association is too much of a ladies' club, for that I am too left-wing, too much a political animal. Dolle Mina, the first feminist organisation, drowns in party programmes dictated by men and slogans about the class struggle. Not much room to find myself.

I look for women. Talk with the wives of ex-colleagues whom I had first ignored as appendages of their more interesting husbands. I harp about David endlessly, about all my relationships, about my feelings of belonging nowhere. They listen! And tell their own stories. Marri, who is struggling with her jealousy when her lover disappears to another girlfriend. And feels she shouldn't, that she shouldn't be jealous because we live in an age of sexual fun and games, and Marri, says her lover, didn't we say that we would leave each other free? And Ellis who gets angry at parties when her lover stands chatting up little girls, and thinks to herself that she has no right to say anything, fun and games right? and in addition if she looks in the mirror at herself she thinks she is too fat and how can she blame him if he is attracted to small delicate innocent children, even if she doesn't understand how he can pretend to be listening to their chitter chatter while actually he is peeping at their tiny tits. Fay comes back from America, Fay whom I got to know long ago at the Social Academy, where we had little contact with each other. She says that in America small groups of women are coming together to talk about exactly those kinds of things with each other. An idiotic idea. Ridiculous and attractive. Perhaps we should do it here too, we say, giggling and nervous. Do you know women here who would want to, asks Fay. Marri, Ellis, Bahasj. Willem's sister, who is also in despair about a relationship that has turned out badly. Fay also knows someone else who might join. We feel conspiratorial, a little ridiculous. We can always stop if nothing happens, I say.

We condescendingly call it our ladies' club.

We have looked at each other uneasily. Talk about what exactly we will do with each other. Read books? Will it just become interminable hot air. If it doesn't get down to anything, I'm leaving, right, says Ellis. And Fay's friend Nel says she hopes wè won't only slag off men.

Marri knows how we should begin, she has heard of a similar group that has already taken off and that it started with each telling the others their life stories. But we don't need to make any more plans because imperceptibly we have begun talking

138

and we can't stop any more. Experiences tumble over each other, hardly patience to let each other talk. Apparently we are all about to burst. All our difficulties with relationships, sex, jealousy, loneliness. To live with a man or without. More relationships or certainly not. Children or not. The men at our work. The men in the left-wing movement. Other women. Our mothers. Strange things are happening to me. A warm feeling in my belly. I cry when I see Marri crying. I become angry when Ellis tells us about her lover and when Fay tells what a mess she is in. I see the faces around me when I tell them about David, Shaun, Michael, tense faces, they are right in it with me. They recognise what I am saying. They understand me. Late at night, when we say goodbye, laughing in the doorway, touching each other, saying to Marri, think about it, you just send him away, right, and Ellis, if it gets too difficult for you then ring up, and I walk home warm and confused, almost glad to be alone again so that I can calmly chew over everything that has happened to me, reflect on that strange warm feeling in my belly. Almost as if I am in love. Was that what we so often talked about in the left groups, this warm glow inside me?

Solidarity.

I am not alone, I am not alone.

I am given an appointment by the clinic. The introductory talk to see how mad I am. I turn up at the address I am given in a letter. Wall-to-wall cream coloured carpeting, plexi glass, little tables with expensive books about Mexico. One carefully chosen etching on the wall. A skinny man who shuts his eyes tightly now and then to put me at my ease. He does it so often it can almost be called a nervous tic. How is your living situation, he asks. I begin to settle down into it, to explain to him what it is like, together with a child in one and a half rooms of a house, the toilet that has almost fallen through the floor, the ceiling that is coming down, but he cuts me short. That wasn't the point, only an introductory question. Then the real work. Pictures about which I must tell a story. Ink blots about which I must say what I see. I only see bats but so as not to disappoint him I make up other things. I am given a long list of questions to take home. Am I afraid of spiders, do I ever hear voices, do I ever have black stools, do I ever feel myself attracted to persons of the same sex. I fill in the questions with Bahasj, both of us screaming with laughter.

Then the real conversations. Again a man in a light grey suit, correct, with a tie. Again art objects scattered on small tables. I speak formally to him. Notice I haven't done that in the last few years, I no longer mix in such circles. A nice man, youngish. I ask myself what he has experienced in his life. Not much, I guess. I try to explain what I have come for. That I want to find out why my relationships with men are so difficult, why they end so traumatically. What I can do to get over it. He translates it for me. What it is really about, he says, is that in your contact with men you have the feeling that there are disturbances operating. Yes, I say, hesitating. And think, no. Disturbances? David, say that isn't true. Nothing disturbed in what happened between his and my skin. It was afterwards, when it became too much, when we overflowed with emotions. But I lack the language to make it clear to this man. I have the feeling that he is asking the wrong questions.

Back to my youth. Did you compete a lot with your younger brother, he asks. Yes, no, yes, how can I answer that? I sense worlds of unspoken condemnation behind the words. The wrong question. Why doesn't he just say what he thinks? Why doesn't he just ask me what he wants to know. I sit full of stories about my own life, which he doesn't touch with the questions he puts. Yes exactly, he says when I talk and makes notes. Do you have difficulty reaching a climax when you are having intercourse, he asks. Yes, no yes, that depends. . . . (And think, must I explain that fire under my skin when I make love to Michael, whether we have an orgasm or not. And a mechanical orgasm with Jonas which means nothing more.) What is that, a climax, I want to ask him. What does it mean to you, I'm sorry, to you, doctor?

For three long sessions I try to find a crack in his mask. To draw a reaction from him. The third time he smiles when I tell him an amusing story from my youth. Hoorah, he is alive. I am working harder on him than he is on me, I think as I walk home. And talk about it with my women in the discussion group. How can you talk about emotions with a man, about pain. Have you never had a good talk with a man about emotions? asks Ellis.

Oh yes, I say, when they are naked. But this man, so stuffed into his suit. Take it off, says Marri. But I shudder, must not think about that putty coloured upper-class skin that would then appear. He has definitely got those pyjamas with grey stripes, I say. How can I talk about difficulties in communicating with men, with a man with whom I can't communicate?

It would be a year, I reckon, before I could reach the level of communication I have with my women's group after only two or three times. All my energy to entice him out of his tent, to warm him up, as I have learned to do with the men I have known. He should pay me, not me him.

I write a letter to explain why I am not coming any more. Get a telephone message back that I have not yet returned the questionnaire and that they hope I won't be needing it any more.

Endless talk about sex and about relationships.

In any event a relief that I am not the only one who has difficulties there. Talking about David. Why is it that it so often turns out like that: David who couldn't go on any more, Michael who suddenly got confused and vanished.

Do you know what is so idiotic, I say. That it was so different from the relationships that just fizzled out because they didn't work out, because we weren't on the same wave-length. Because we were, David and me. That was what drove me crazy, why I couldn't carry on, it was so good when we were together and still the sudden decision to stop it. I am surely not crazy because I know for sure that it was good? I mean, could your body deceive you so? What can you trust then, for God's sake?

Did you make too many demands, ask Ellis. We go into it. I don't believe so, I say. I didn't ask him to leave Lin. He could come when he wanted, go when he wished. How can you make fewer demands?

You know, I say, as an image suddenly becomes clearer in my head, an image that has haunted me for a while. I had the feeling he was scared. And Michael too. And Shaun. No, not about the demands I might make, about the emotion, too much emotion. Not mine, but their own. Is that possible, I ask the other women, is it possible that they are scared of their own emotions, is it

141

possible that they are scared of us because we awaken the emotions in them?

Is it true that they are scared to love, that they channel all their warmth into mechanical sex, run away if they don't succeed? Pieces of the puzzle fall into place. I begin to see patterns. My amazement at the men who desired me although I felt nothing for them. The men who ran away because they did feel something for me which they could no longer deny. The whole sexual revolution a trick to get us so far that we will play the games. That we should believe it when we are told that we are too old-fashioned to distinguish sex from love. Naturally our old conditioning, to find sex safe only when there is marriage in the bag. But for us, as we are now, that is no longer acceptable. We do not look for commitment, but we don't want to feel split, don't want to cut off warmth from sex. Fuck with someone we don't even like. My body refuses service, will not let itself be misused. While in my head I still think that *I'm* the one who is crazy, that I am behind the times because I don't know how to control my emotions. Because I can't take it like a man. Slowly I begin to see what happened. The men who came to me because they found me attractive, perhaps precisely because they sensed the warmth in me that they themselves lacked. And at the same time they are afraid of it. Tightrope dancing is what we must do, to keep upright in the situation that is so contradictory. And suddenly I understand the rules better. How we are being trained, step by step, to be available, but to ask for nothing. Let him decide when he's coming round. Never talk about – a taboo here heavier than sex – love. But to give it, all the same, without speaking. Why do we allow it to be done to us? I ask amazed. Do you have a better idea? asks Ellis.

We aren't crazy, I say. Or if we are, we are all in it together.

But is the conclusion then that we can't have anything more to do with men? asks Marri. There are still examples of how it can be otherwise, says Ellis and we look at each other hopefully. But we can't think of many examples for each other of how it can go well and we have, after all, enough experience. Marri has in the meantime broken with her lover after a long struggle and eventually her ultimatum: her or me, choose then. He has vanished, comes back now and then if he has difficulty with his new girlfriend, but Marri doesn't enjoy comforting him any more. Willem's sister, Susan, is also without, just like Bahasj and me. Fay flirts with a refugee Spaniard, but it isn't from her heart. Ellis still with her regular boyfriend. Oh, she says, it goes. A little bit monotonous, calm, you know exactly what you've got, faithful. I am jealous, I say to her. When you get home you have a warm bed, I say. But you can go your own way, she says.

I become depressed from it, freedom, certainly. It is a hollow freedom. I know too well what I want, I say. I have experienced it, even if it was short. The feeling with Michael, truly the feeling that you are sharing something real with each other, sex so unbelievably more intense when you know that you also share other things outside the few hours in bed, the feeling that you are the same kind, what do you call that.

I don't want to accept that that is all over. I go miserably home. To my own empty bed.

When I get home, the telephone rings. Ellis. I just wanted to tell you, because you were so jealous of people with secure relationships, that I have just got home and the room is a pig-sty, his clothes pulled out of the cupboard, shaving things in the washbasin. The master is clearly out on the spree. I just mean, a warm bed when you come home, did you say? We laugh, I am a little less miserable when I go to sleep.

I haven't completely given up. Sjef, from Antwerp, left-wing, that is something at least and he looks terrific in his drainpipes. Within an hour I have seen it all and with the freedom that you get when you have the feeling that there is nothing to lose and it can only get better, we lie under the astonished gaze of a friend of Sjef's – who was actually the one who had his eye on me – making love on my brown bed. My neglected skin begins to flow again. He makes love enthusiastically and we can also laugh with each other. When he returns to Antwerp I feel wonderful. A little in love, but not too badly. Perhaps it is possible.

But when I go to Antwerp it is less cheerful. Actually we talk badly with each other. The cynical jokes that he makes irritate me when it appears that they are a standard reaction. When I tell him something about the women's group, he jokes that away also. What nonsense, women's oppression, he says. Has never seen a sign of it. Perhaps because you don't listen to women, I say, viciously, just as you don't listen to me. Look, he says, I fancy you because you are a fine female, but you mustn't mess my head up with that kind of difficult stuff. And when we later stand at the bar, he eyes up all the women there, caresses old girlfriends on the bum, with one eye on me to see if I notice.

But at night in bed he is warmer, as if his warmth appears only in that one hour, when making love. The next day he is cool again, stand-offish.

In Amsterdam we quarrel. Why? Perhaps because I have said to him that I think he is unpleasant to women. That I can't understand how he can split his life so, the comradely conversations with his friend with whom he doesn't make love; his sex with the women whom he subtly plays off against each other. That, unless he fucks, he doesn't dare expose himself. That he doesn't listen to me.

He rings me from Breda. Little Meulenbelt, he says, you are really a fine female. If you quickly catch the next train to Breda, you could go with me to Antwerp and we could have a great weekend. I go, dumbfounded by so much explicit affection. Maybe he has understood a little of what I was on about. But when we are in Antwerp I see it is a complete disaster. As if he must make up for letting me see so much emotion, he does his best to keep his distance and to seem as cynical as possible. In the pub he acts as if I don't exist, hangs onto all the pretty girls, excluding me. Listen mate, I say angrily, I didn't come here to see how well you can chat up women, I'm taking the next train back. Then he thaws out a little. Says it was just a joke, asks if I will stay, that we will have a good time soon. Until the last train has gone and he knows that I can no longer get away and he opens out all the stops on his unconscious hatred of women. Fuck off, I say, I am not offering myself to give you the chance to react against women. You can do that with the women who haven't yet seen through it. I thought you were nicer says Sjef, not one of those aggressive, frustrated bitches. I take the first train back the next morning.

And think on the train that it is true. Frustrated, terribly. And furiously aggressive also. Incurable. No longer the fine female, without problems and sexy and pliable, which I used to think was the highest form of femininity. And it also becomes clear to me that this is what is waiting for me if I don't play the games any more. Unconscious aggression now openly expressed. Men who forget as soon as I don't behave like a stereotyped woman that their mothers taught them to be nice to girls. The first thing I must learn to put up with: that they won't even pretend that they like me.

The discussion group is a warm place in the week where we can come to lick our wounds. It is as if I look at everything differently. A painful clarity because I see a lot I'd rather not see. It scares me sometimes. I notice that I become steadily less able to go back to my old life and don't know what I will get in return. Construction, so much more difficult than destruction.

Meanwhile I haven't completely forgotten Marx. I find that my training in marxism still shows too many gaps and join a trotskyite training group where I am, in any event, sure that I can study in peace without being immediately sent into the factory which the maoists do to new recruits. Once a week we read a section from *Capital* at Karel's house who teases out the argument of surplus value while fiddling with his socks. His wife makes the coffee, that I notice at once. There are two other women, one is the wife of one of the young men, and as such is usually ignored. The other comes on her own and is allowed to type Karel's work onto a stencil in her free time. The young men don't have time for that.

The work is thorough, that at least. Long drawn-out discussions between Karel and two of the cleverest young men, that a product *IS* use value and *HAS* exchange value and one of the clever young men comes along exuberantly with the discovery that Marx himself made a mistake on page such and such. I feel properly stupid. Dare not ask questions out of fear that it will show. I notice that the other women are the same. Where did you buy those trousers, I whisper to the woman who is sitting next to me. Made them myself, she whispers back and we go on about clothes until we are discovered and keep quiet, ashamed.

Karel questions us each week on the chapter we had to read.

145

After I have once or twice waited nervously in case he should ask me anything I say something about it, that he never asks the women anything. He does so the next time. First let's see if one of the ladies can give us an answer on that one, and naturally I can't do so immediately and sit sweating and red-faced waiting until the hilarity calms down. After that I am glad no questions are directed at me so that towards the end of the evening I can fall half asleep and escape into dreams. I have no contact with any of the people outside the study evening. Most of them know only my first name, don't even know what I do. Only Karel's wife asks me how I manage with my child when Armin phones one time because he has had a bad dream. But I decide that I must persevere, that it is good for me to read through *Capital* at least *once* thoroughly and on top of that I am making love a little with Thomas, who began the study at the same time I did, and with whom I sometimes have a drink afterwards. He says of himself that he is a late developer and has more or less thrown himself into my arms to learn it all. Thomas, who says he is crazy about the emancipation of women. Three weeks go well, until he informs me that he is travelling to Berlin that weekend to fetch his regular girlfriend with whom he is going to live in Amsterdam and confesses that he selected me because I seem such an excellent supplement to his girlfriend who isn't yet so emancipated and in addition is not so in control of her emotions. Before me he had already had another woman in mind who was a very good musician but wasn't a marxist, and that was of course more important. Perhaps you need to get used to the idea a little, says Thomas when I stare at him in amazement and he doesn't understand at all when I say that he can clear off and that I have no desire to go with him to the pub after the class. He still tries to placate me with a beautiful edition of *Capital* bought in Berlin and invites me to come and meet his girlfriend. I refuse. A year later when I run into him, he tells me that he is very disappointed in me because the emotional pieces that I wrote don't reach the political standard he had expected from me.

They are just like little men from Mars, I say in my women's group that is now called a women's group and no longer a ladies' club. As if they are talking a completely different language.

Gordes 8

I am miserable. The mistral is blowing. I am annoyed with Hans, who is walking around with what I call his Jesus-on-the-cross look, having made up his mind to leave me in peace but in the meantime not letting me out of his sight. I feel his eye on me, sticky, when we go for the day to Avignon. Avignon, where I would have gone with Anna, if she had not left too soon. I walk around the castle, try to act as if I am alone. My melancholy is so much more bearable when I don't constantly have to take into account the people around me, but I feel Hans's eyes riveted on me, across the group of tourists also wandering around the castle.

Back in the camp Hans cooks a meal for me while I sit writing. French and Belgian women look curiously at us, a mixture of envy and disapproval. You hardly ever see French men cooking here, at most they lay a piece of meat on the barbecue while their wives wash clothes, peel vegetables, scrape out pots. Twice a day they rush to prepare an enormous meal while their men go fishing or sleep or stand around on the grass with their games of boules. Drink pastis with their friends. New French women sit at the sidewalk cafés, a couple of young ones from the city. What do I have to complain about, when I see how all the women look jealously or curiously out of the corners of their eyes at Hans, who sits peeling onions and pours a glass of wine for me.

While all I do is write.

I struggle with the transitions in my book. See at night, when I am still awake, a logical division. Chunks of the past, a piece of

Gordes at the breaks which are easy to indicate. My special cycle of around three years. The break of my pregnancy – out of my social setting. Three years marriage. Break. Three years Jonas. Break. Three years sexual revolution and Marx. Then another break, after David. Then the women's movement. And then the break after Anna. Always beginning again, always the experience again that the bottom has fallen out of my life. Return to GO. You can't even collect 200.

But when I am busy writing, the different sections don't turn out to be so logically distinguishable from each other. I see that after my 'conversion' to feminism, I still flirt with men just as curiously as I did before. I get the inclination to conceal that. In my memories the transition to the women's movement is irrevocable, I distinctly break with an old way of living. And I still think that. But meanwhile I notice that, for example, the affair with Sjef belongs in an earlier period, and yet it was when I was already in the discussion group.

How do I indicate the change, how do I describe it, without falling into boring mystical language. My conversion. My revelation. A completely different way of seeing. Another level of living, a slow process of de-conditioning, with bursts of clarity and then again a falling back, confusion, what is it all about? Another level of consciousness in which I have found myself, while my behaviour still changes only slowly. How do I describe that, my existence has another quality, which is not so easily seen in the events of my life. And then, how do I describe the women's movement? The discussions through which the scraps of my life fall into place like pieces in a jigsaw puzzle, the lines of my past become visible. All the meetings, parties, conferences with women, more difficult to show in a book than the relationships I had. My language is inadequate. Everyone knows the rules of man-woman relationships. Emotionally recognisable even when stereotyped. But how do I describe the first experience of solidarity, the warmth in my belly more real and tangible and physical than my being in love, without falling into exalted language. Sisterhood. It sounds so old-fashioned, like nurses, nuns, oldmaids.

Hey, stop.

148

There is something wrong. Because I'm not sitting in Gordes now at a marble table in the sun behind my notebooks. I am sitting in Amsterdam behind Marjan's typewriter in Boujke's room. It is becoming complicated. The way I am writing now is different from six months ago in Gordes. There I let my associations run free, wrote down only what offered itself in the flush of rosé and sun, without worrying about how the book would look, without thinking whether it would really become a proper book. In Amsterdam I have to arrange the material I collected through free association in Gordes. Those parts I left blank because I thought they would be easier to fill in when I was typing, have turned out the most difficult. I fooled myself. Peak experiences are easier to write about than slow processes over years, with continual backsliding. And it was precisely the peak experiences which surfaced in Gordes.

It is also different, writing in between all my activities. Days stolen between meetings and classes and essays. Telephone calls that disturb me, letters, meals that must be bought and cooked, Armin, people who want something from me. I sometimes take hours to find the old colours again which came to me so effortlessly in Gordes.

And then extremely prosaic negotiations with the publisher that disturb my concentration, poison my mood. After I have sent my first chapters in so bravely, sweating, a letter from Carlien gave me courage. Then I heard that it was indeed good, that it would be published, and now I hear that I still won't get a contract. What is happening? First trouble with the publishers who did not keep to their contract and put a sexist jacket on the Dutch edition of *Our Bodies Ourselves*. Sueing them and still saving something of the book as it should have been cost me more energy than all the work that went into writing it. Then the trouble with the socialist publishers, the SUN boys, endless back-breaking talk to get through to them that we will not allow the content of our work to be messed about, that they are not capable of editing feminist work.

And now trouble again with my third publisher. No one can explain to me why I can't get a contract. Mieke comforts me and Carlien brings me sherry and then I do get it by not giving in

149

and mumbling something about rival publishers. I have won, but go away with a nasty taste in my mouth. I don't like fighting. Always the temptation to make concessions, let *Our Bodies Ourselves* have a commercial front cover, let the SUN boys do what they want and cut out everything that smells of radical feminism and quibble over every line about whether it is relevant to the class struggle and the scientific development of marxism in the Netherlands.

I get furious when my feminism and socialism book appears and I read the lines on the back. There should have been: 'The women's movement's goal is not contrary to socialism but it broadens the struggle to the areas that have stayed too far out of range: the family, the sphere of reproduction and personal relationships.' And instead there is written: 'The women's movement should serve no other goal than to strive for socialism, they should broaden the struggle to areas that until now have been too far out of range: the family and social relationships inside and outside the workplace.'

With a few words we have again been incorporated, made subservient to the class struggle. An oversight, no one meant to do it, it just happened, they say.

I am sick to death of it. Must go after them again to make sure that at least there is a piece of paper inserted which makes it clear that I did not say this. I get my way. That we do win each time is only because feminism has good market value and all the publishers lust after books on women, all the better if there is also sex in them. I feel like giving up.

The letter from Hanneke from Eindhoven pinned to the wall. She sends me twenty very long and ecstatic country kisses because I am writing this book. Letters from An and Eric to encourage me, a present from Hanneke and their photograph of the balcony in Gordes. Tears in Leni's eyes and Ria throws her arms around me and the letter from Mieke from my women's group and Nurith who rings me up and says she thinks it is fine and that she now understands more about me. Armin is proud of me and has asked only if I will change the word boy into young man. I need all the warmth to go on with it, now that I am back in a world full of people. It is so much more difficult

150

than in Gordes. Their criticism comes out of solidarity and I can use it. I scrap two sidewalk cafés and a few helpings of salade niçoise when Mieke says the Gordes pieces are really full of them, and with all that pastis. Reflect on what Marjan says, that all the men stick in her throat after a while. I decide to leave them in, I also feel up to my neck in them, but that surely is what it is about. And each reader can easily skip what she doesn't like. Not a very pretty book. I won't make it prettier than it was.

Back to Gordes, before it gets completely out of hand.

I find it again, my miserable mood, when I decipher the black letters on the yellow writing paper. An inexplicably depressed mood. Everything is irritating. Hans who looks at me. The water supply at the camp site has broken down. The toilets overflow, muck up to their brims. Irritating Dutch people next to us. A bellowing child gets a blow from her father who screams do you want to lose your other good tooth as well? I soften the sharp edges of my irritation with wine. You are much less irritable than you were this morning, says Armin. I'm a bit pissed off, I say. And sad. You are sometimes like that too. Yes, says Armin, then I go for a walk and it is over again. A wise child, my son. Write some more, he says, and picks a flower for me which I put into a coke bottle next to me in the last bit of mineral water because the water supply is still broken.

At night in my tent I look in my diary and notice that I am just about due to come on. Premenstrual tension, that's what it is.

Mother isn't coming

It surely seems that it is becoming a movement.

It begins with a phone call from a woman who says she is also in a women's group and do we want to come over to meet them. A group that has walked out of Dolle Mina, the first feminist action group, because they aren't allowed to talk about their own experiences there. More women like us! We are not only seven crazy women, there are eight more idiots at least. And then we hear of two more women's groups in the Women's Association who also came together in spite of accusations of sexism because they don't allow men in their groups. How sensitive to the accusation we are still. We are man-haters because we enjoy being together in a women's group once a week. As if people who work with young people hate old people; but that is an argument I discover much later. For the present I have no other argument than that I need it and it feels good. And I try to avoid the occasions when I have to justify why I am in a group with women. The few times when I am so careless as to tell someone I notice what an angry reaction it arouses in men, what a fearful reaction in women.

A party with the other crazies. I am dragged there with difficulty. Only used to the women in my group, so many all at once I find creepy. But when we are all sitting there, in the attic at Marjan's house, I get over my fear and talk excitedly with the other women. We are all concerned with the same things, all come to the same conclusions. We must do this more often, we say. And give the names of all the women in our neighbourhood who have heard of the women's groups and also want to belong.

The women who left Dolle Mina begin a women's newspaper.

Collectively we print the next one, write about our own experiences in the discussion group, our experiences outside it. It's the first time I write something, except letters. We read the pieces over to each other, give advice, but don't criticise. And all the pieces are printed, there is no editorial board to judge whether something is good enough or not. All the articles are unsigned, on principle, because it isn't relevant which women had what experience, which woman writes better than another woman. A pleasant anarchy. Suddenly duplicating is fun, not alienating. It is our own product, no one else's. We are proud of our first papers, first a print-run of two hundred, then three hundred, then steadily more. All the time new groups join us. It is no longer possible for us all to meet at someone's house.

What happened to us has a name now. Consciousness-raising, we call it, this other way of seeing through which our whole life is turned upside down, through which we begin to understand our past differently. And we call it de-conditioning. Because while we are becoming conscious of the way women are treated in our world, we see at the same time that we have not remained undamaged, that our self image is imposed on us, that we keep ourselves small because of the standards which we ourselves have internalised.

We talk about our bodies in the discussion group. Each woman says what she doesn't like. Then we notice that no one is satisfied with her body, not even those we thought were really beautiful. I am too fat, says Ellis, I feel like a kind of fat lard cake. Marri talks about her head, which doesn't please her and her thin hair that she can do nothing with. Fay tells us about her thick calves that no one had noticed. And you? someone asks me. I draw a deep breath. I have a laundry list. Actually nothing pleases me. I have no back to my head, I say, starting at the top, and I have a strange nose and I have always wanted an interesting narrow face instead of these cheeks, and I have terribly ugly teeth and – I hesitate. My weakest point. Hanging tits, I say bravely. Not one of you has such ugly breasts as I have. They fed Armin and then hung down. Do you find that terrible? asks Marri, who thinks she has a terrible head but beautiful round breasts.

153

Only if I have to undress with someone new, I say. When you know each other it isn't so bad any more, but that first moment of taking off your bra and then thinking . . . Let us see, says Ellis. I try to talk it away, that there are also times when . . . Let us see, says Ellis. I don't dare, I say. We'll help you, says Fay and takes off her bra. Marri undoes mine when I have taken off my jumper. You see, she says, you are really lovely. Idiotic, actually, what we find pretty and ugly. Do they feel good, says Ellis. Yes, I say, soft, a soft skin, a warm weight in my hands. We can learn to find ourselves beautiful, we say to each other. Stop looking at ourselves with men's eyes. Learn to believe ourselves beautiful as we are instead of always thinking how we ought to be. No one satisfies the standards, no one. Only one-and-a-half models and a film star with a face lift.

For the first time we must begin to let ourselves be seen as we are instead of hurting each other further by pretending we are more beautiful. We can leave off our bras. If all women did that we would get rid at once of the breast complex. I'll not wear it any more, I say bravely. Put my jumper on again. In any case now no one need be disappointed because the wrapping promises more than there is, I say. It is much more important how you see yourself, says Marri.

On the way home I feel them moving softly under my coat, they have become cold and unfeeling, like unwanted children. As if they aren't a part of me anymore, as if it's their fault. I must learn to live again in my whole body, like when I was a child.

Sexuality, a subject that often returns. Our first experiences: for almost everyone, rotten. Our first orgasms. Marri, who as a child of seven, eight masturbated regularly. Ellis who came for the first time after hours of sweated labour with her lover. Nel who, like me, thought she was frigid because she didn't come when fucking. I think back to all Toni's correctly executed sexual acts that left me cold. When did you come for the first time? asks someone. With Jonas, I say, no, that isn't true, before that once in the bath with the hand-shower. The unexpected electrical shock which I concealed from Toni, scared that it would be a spur for him to more experiments, rebukes.

I had accepted that I was frigid, after Toni and I had written a letter to an agony column. The reply came that we should practise patiently and that many women suffered from frigidity who were conventionally brought up. I read booklets about the vaginal orgasms which I ought to have. Why didn't you tell him how you wanted it? asks Nel. I didn't know how I wanted it. I thought I had a distaste for sex, for the porn magazines that Toni read, for the rubber dildo he ordered by post with which they promised him his wife would get exploding orgasms. I confused my distaste for Toni with distaste for sex.

And how are we now, asks Ellis. I think of my sad orgasms which make me feel lonely. I had that, says Marri, but not any more, now I have real pleasure in them. I think it is because we have this amazing idea of Sleeping Beauty who lies snoozing until the prince comes to kiss her awake. That sex is something you must be given, not something you already have. Still isn't it better with someone else? I ask. But you can also make it good with yourself, be attractive to yourself. After all, the relationship with yourself lasts longest of all. You'd better become good friends with your body. It is like buying a good bottle of wine for yourself, and not only because people are coming to dinner. Or like rubbing some lovely soap into your body, for your own pleasure. Or once in a while buying expensive chocolates and eating them all by yourself, says Ellis, who always gets very excited by good food. We are really stupid, I say. We always sit waiting until we are given something. We can just as well come happily as a present for ourselves instead of waiting until we feel lonely.

We must reclaim our own bodies.

I buy a ring for myself. Something I would never have done before: then I waited until someone gave me one for a present. A symbol, I am married to myself. I must look after myself well. I feel strangely happy when I come out of the shop, I've spent too much money, on an impulse, while Armin needs new shoes and the towels are in rags. I drink an espresso in town and order a big piece of cake to go with it.

Sex, the conversation continually comes back to sex. We are amazed that we have so many terrible experiences to report.

155

Making love, is meant for pleasure, right? But how many of us fuck because it is expected of us, because it is worse not to?

You know, says Ellis, I really hate myself, I think I am such a miserable bitch if I say no, especially when we haven't fucked for a whole week. And sometimes it is suddenly marvellous after a good quarrel or if we haven't seen each other all weekend or if we have once again had a good talk. But for him that doesn't seem to be enough and how can I then hold it against him if he goes for other women? Those who like to fuck more often?

While we talk more reasons come up, why we fuck when we actually don't feel like it.

Because otherwise there will be an argument and that will take hours and you will get too little sleep and the next morning you will both be in a shitty temper.

Because you don't want to be a miserable bitch, like a Dear Miss Lonelyhearts who writes that her husband always wants to.

Because otherwise you will begin to wonder whether the relationship is still any good.

Because otherwise he isn't kind to you, and because you have a need for warmth and that leads automatically to fucking.

Because you can't just go sociably with someone to a film and afterwards to the pub and then say to him, you know I really only wanted to talk.

Because we are scared that otherwise we'll start belonging to the group of sour, strait-laced, frigid women that we've heard about.

Because you want the feeling that you still count, that you are attractive.

Jesus, I say. How often do we do it for his pleasure, instead of for ours? And how difficult to make that distinction. We don't even know any more what we want for ourselves. We are never in a situation where we can find that out. Either we belong to a man and then it is just three times a week and no complaining. Or we are alone, completely without. Or we are assigned to the loose mob, and then there is absolutely no question that you can take someone home with you and then still have any say in what you'd like to do.

How often have I made love to a man not because he was so

persistent and I didn't dare to say no, but because it was actually the only way to get through to him emotionally. Because afterwards you can talk better. Because bed is often the only place where he lets his facade fall just a little bit and acts ordinarily vulnerable and tender. Sometimes. I have to break him open like a nut to get to the soft kernel that otherwise he would keep invisible. It is just a deal, I say. We pay with sex to get warmth, they pay with warmth to get sex. And once in a while both are there, once in a while a celebration, ecstasy.

Why should we actually do it for less than that?

Because otherwise your relationship breaks up, says Ellis. It isn't allowed. If you live together, that is the contract, that you are responsible for each other's needs. If you don't do that he disappears to another and you can't even blame him for it. And, anyway, once you have started it's not so bad and you sleep better afterwards and if he is satisfied everything goes a bit better.

How sad really, we say.

Nel has said nothing for a while and sits fidgeting. I have a problem, she says. I don't really dare talk about it. A pause. You know, she says hesitating. Look, from just fucking I don't come. And with Fred it was like . . . he said his last girlfriend did come . . . and then I began to pretend I came. And later I understood that it was nonsense because vaginal orgasms don't exist at all and I am not frigid because I can come very easily if I do it alone, and with my last boyfriend it was also fine if he just used his hands, but now I'm in a fix, because I can hardly say to Fred that all those times I just faked it, and I can also not tell him any more that he isn't doing it right. I've done that often too, says Fay, if it lasted too long. And me too, I say, because it is such a fuss to explain and sometimes they are the kind of men who can't take it if you say to them that it isn't going so well.

Who else? asks Nel. Everyone has faked orgasms, except Marri who refuses pointblank to play-act and never has. You only hurt yourself, says Marri. And the women after you. If you don't educate a man at once properly, he'll never learn. If three women

157

have told him that he is a fabulous lover then he thinks he doesn't have anything more to learn.

We stare at each other. We are crazy, we say. And promise each other that we will never fake again.

At the women's conference we take a poll and then it appears that *three-quarters* of the women have at some time pretended to have orgasms. Long live the sexual revolution, shouts Ellis. Goddammit. We have sympathy with a man if he can't have an orgasm, we feel guilty if he is lying in bed with such a poker when we don't feel like it. We think his pleasure is more important than ours. We have been crazy. We have been idiots.

Sexuality, what is it actually? A need for warmth, for a body, to be seen and touched. And a lot of that I now get from my women. I learn to ask for it. I learn to give warmth to other women.

The need for orgasms. I learn now that I don't need to be given them by someone else. I can make beautiful orgasms, I am my own best lover. As Eskimos have many different words for snow and Arabs for all kinds of camels, so we should have many different words for orgasms. Orgasms like slides with a cool pool at the end. Orgasms like warm woolly waves with colours and strange associations, with eating almond cake on the train, where does that fantasy come from? Orgasms where you think you will remain in them, never ever come down again. Disappointing orgasms, over in one spasm like a sneeze at the wrong end. Orgasms that surprise you like a small boy in a doorway who shouts boo.

And then the need for ecstasy, for peak experiences. For all the clichés that now and then come true, melting into each other, becoming one. They exist, but rarely, like mystical experiences.

How we have learned to stuff all these needs into that one small hour with one person and are almost always disappointed because the hole in our soul cannot be filled with these ritual gymnastics, a jam sandwich can't satisfy that kind of hunger. We are all of us cheated, all of us. I learn to distinguish my needs. A need for warmth and for orgasm and yes, for ecstasy, but that is a scarce commodity. Sleeping Beauty wakes up and doesn't wait for the prince any more. Darlings, she says, when I need you, I'll call.

A christmas holiday together with a few other discussion-group women and their children in a rented farmhouse. Christmases are unendurable if you are not a proper family and each year I can't ignore it yet can't make a proper christmas. Half-hearted attempts to get something cheerful going with Armin, a christmas tree that is unravelled by the cats before it is properly christmas. Bahasj gone to her family, Armin and I listlessly with our plates in front of the television.

But in that too, I'm not the only one. All single mothers with children find it just as terrible. Visits to the family, duty calls that don't make you any happier. And so now we are a group of women sitting in front of an open fire while our children are playing screaming games on the bunk beds, out of ear-shot luckily. This is the first time I talk with other feminists who have children. The women in my own group are all my age, not many of them had a child at seventeen.

A few days ago I nearly threw them off the balcony, says Corry. The others laugh. My mouth drops open. Can you say that aloud! And for the first time I talk about years of guilt feelings, my eternal guilt feeling that I don't give Armin enough, that he doesn't get enough attention. But no child ever gets enough attention, says Annet, if they were to get it only from us . . . That is also impossible surely? Naturally you will hate your child now and then. And certainly they'll feel your guilt. They have a radar for it. And then they do exactly what is necessary to drive you round the bend and still demand your attention when you have absolutely none to give. What does yours do, asks Corry, mine refuses to eat. Armin sits for hours fumbling with his clothes just when I have to go out, I say. And going to sleep? asks Corry. He has no problem with that, I say, but I think that is because of the time I had to go to work whether he slept or not. I was bursting with guilt, but could do nothing about it, I had to work. I was at home full-time for the first years, says Corry, but you still get that guilt feeling. I had to lock the bedroom door in order to read the newspaper properly. While they stood on the other side banging because they had to piss or were thirsty. I really had to learn that I must close my ears tight and that it is really not so bad if once in a while they did piss in their pants. Now and then I hate them. They hate me too. It's just like a marriage, we are too close to each other, we know exactly how we can torment each other. It's nobody's fault. And look at it this way. That child of yours, hasn't he turned into a good fellow?

Armin, in the distance, with red cheeks, hanging upside down on the beams, running around outside. With a bit of space between us I notice suddenly how much I love him, a feeling I hardly know while we are so crowded together, so dependent on each other, I on the space he allowed me in order to study and to relax, he on the attention I gave him. I nod to Corry. He is actually a fantastically nice boy, I say. But I am so obsessed with everything I do wrong that I can only see the mistakes and think that they are my fault. If he is late for school it's my fault, if he has rolled in the mud before school and arrives like a pitch black pig, it's my fault, if he has made a piccalilli sandwich instead of jam as he should and I get a telephone call from the school that he has wrapped his sandwich in a newspaper instead of the prescribed plastic bag, it's my fault. I feel so guilty that I can't even talk about it except with you, I say.

Esther cries. She's Astrid's daughter, Astrid is a paediatrician and advises other mothers on their problems. Each night there is the same performance. Esther will not go to sleep, starts crying and wails until her mother comes to her. And each time Astrid in the end gives in, even though she would advise other mothers to let her cry, to let it pass over. The crying of your own child works directly on your nervous system avoiding your brain, so much worse than when you hear another child cry. And however much we say to Astrid that we don't mind, in the end she still goes. To Esther's delight, who thinks it is a wonderful game and sits on Astrid's lap with a triumphant grin until she falls asleep. Now you stay here, says Annet to Astrid the next day when Esther once again begins her act. And a bit later we hear the noise stop, it doesn't return. What have you done to her, asks Corry, have you hit her on the head with a hammer? Oh no, says Annet, I looked deep into her eyes and said Mother Isn't Coming.

I had heard about Annet before I saw her, one of the very first feminists here. Annet, who against all the social rules left her husband and left her children with him. At a time when everyone condemned her for it. He just looks after them better, she says, I am not such a good mother, the children think so too. Annet, whom I had imagined to be a big, dark woman, unlike this skinny chain-smoking bundle of nerves. You know, she says, when once again I am talking about my difficulties with men, you must feed them emotions by the teaspoonful, they can't swallow so much at one time. You have to begin on the outside, just like with children who learn to dress themselves by beginning first with something easy, not all their clothes at once. Where did you get that from? I ask. From a text-book on the feeble minded, she says.

I am completely fascinated by Annet, who has a kind of radiance in which I bask, she helps me to understand things I didn't see before, she articulates emotions where I had no words to describe them. When she is away, it is immediately a little emptier, less exciting. I feel in my back when she has entered a room, without looking.

And I notice with a shock that she makes love to Astrid, naturally, under the sleeping bags zipped together in the attic where we all sleep. I hear them whispering, laughing softly. Am I jealous? No, I decide, when Astrid goes and I suddenly, inexplicably, become nervous, imagine that she will want to make love to me next. And I will have to say no. Because I don't want to. But she doesn't ask at all. Am I relieved or disappointed? Emotions for which I still have no name. (Lesbian? Me? Are you crazy!)

And when I leave I talk about it once more. How scared I sometimes become of the process in which I am involved. Friends whom I lose, so many men with whom I can no longer associate, perhaps with none any more. We lose so much, I say to Annet. We burn so many boats behind us. And we have no idea where we are going. We also get a lot back, says Annet, and smiles.

But do I genuinely believe it? Can you survive on bits of

161

solidarity, like small plants that still need a lot of water and can still, at any moment, blow over? Is that a substitute for all the dreams that we have had and that are now irrevocably broken, not to be realised ever again?

Gordes 9

Here the cats lie in the shade, not in the sun. They are thinner, wilder. I miss my cats who allow themselves to be stroked if I get the urge to do so. There are so many cats who have populated my life. To whom I have always wanted to give beautiful names like Katzenbach and Katzenstein, and who were invariably christened Pussy or Kitty. Why don't you throw those animals out, says one of the lovers. Because I will live longer with them than with you, I say.

The cats live an underground life in my house, a different level of existence from mine. Not so servile as dogs, who smell like dogs and impose themselves and always want something. Drip, I say to a dog who sits looking at me, doglike and humble, slobbering at my knee.

The moon, low and orange. Lethargic from the meal. Moths that destroy themselves flying against the gas lamp.

Armin and I have a good time, the two of us. I do an imitation of Pie, the cat, a fat fake Siamese with half a tail and white paws who thunders clattering and stumbling down the stairs when Armin calls him for dinner. The most inelegant cat I know, skidding nails on the linoleum, almost failing to make the corner in his greed, and how foolish he looks when it turns out that Armin has teased him and his meal isn't ready yet.

Armin lies in his tent rolling around with laughter, we can tell each other endless stories about cats. Armin makes a light show on the tents with pocket torches and coloured balloons. Luckily not yet too old to play now that I am at last learning how to.

An and Eric and Hanneke are coming to eat tomorrow and I am busy with preparations. I like cooking for my friends, food in France is not yet as plastic as in the Netherlands. Choose paté, let vegetables slide one by one through my hands, onions, tomatoes, fennel. Peaches and melons sold individually. Cutting melons open to fill them with port. Chicken with head and feet still on that must come off, something I would not have dared to do until I thought that it was hypocritical to eat the bird, but not to dare look into its dead eyes. Cooking the chicken in wine, onions, carrots, fat cloves of garlic. Finish off with crème fraîche. I can hardly be torn away from the food counter in the supermarket. Each time I come home with different spices. Harissa for the couscous, spices for the paella and the bouillabaisse. And stand lusting after fish dishes, salad baskets, wooden spoons until Hans pulls me away with him and reminds me that the money is almost finished and on top of that the car is crammed full with all our tents.

Hans and I are still a little uncomfortable. He tries so hard to leave me in peace that he hardly dares ask if we should go anywhere. Relax, just stop thinking, I say. Take a holiday from me, just do what you feel like. Or go out somewhere with Armin and Manuel for the day.

Triangle with unequal sides

Are you coming with us to the de Pieter café, says one of the women from the work group at the end of the evening.

We have worked hard at the university, seven women and three men, two of whom are nice and homosexual and the third nice and timid. We have received permission to do a thesis about the position of women in this society after a fuss about whether we could indeed show its connection with the class struggle. That is just what we are going to do, we say. But that isn't enough argument and therefore we produce a small paper which says the same thing in their jargon and so we may work for a whole year on women.

I don't know, I'm tired, I say.

The women's movement slowly fills up my whole week, open evenings where we meet new discussion group women, the meetings of *The Women's Newspaper*, writing articles, preparations for the conference. My women's group is now disbanded, after a year. We want to do other things, the consciousness-raising process continues of itself, no longer able to be checked, contained. During duplicating, meetings, we continue to talk about our own experiences. And then there is Armin, I still remain mother and housewife in between my studies, and in addition there are all my other activities to earn a little money to add to my grant, five hundred guilders extra. Per year. This is less than a month's minimum wage. To support a child who eats more than I do and wears out more clothes and must go on the school outing and must buy presents for friends and a bike to ride to school. And his shoes are always being broken at football.

Come on, says one of the women, we won't stay very late. Just *one* beer, I say.

164

De Pieter, where I never meet anyone I like except the people I have taken there myself. But I have slowly learned now to have fun with the women with whom I work, I forget the men around us until they become aggressive. Having a good time with women in a pub is against the rules because you came, after all, to play the ritual games with men and if you don't fancy that you can expect questions: are you all lesbians, ladies can I offer you my services because I love to see lesbians making it with each other, I don't have anything against it if I can join in too.

In de Pieter, Josje's lover stands talking with – where do I know the fellow from? A political meeting, I remember, when I still worked in the action centre and he came as a well-known lefty big-shot to see if there was a chance to save the place. Ton. Didn't he wear a wedding ring then, I think, while I look at his naked hands. He doesn't look married, I think.

I go over to stand with them, give Josje's lover a friendly greeting, say hello to Ton. Weren't you with Dolle Mina in that action centre or something, asks Ton. Wrong, but not so wrong anymore, and we get on well. Talking about his political work, about what has happened to me since the break up of the centre. I talk about my feminism, as a test, know at once where we're at. With previous experiences I kept back the information a little out of fear, and then got the cold shoulder later: god do you also belong to those angry chicks ha ha now you really don't look the type.

But Ton is not at all hostile on first impression, even interested, and as much as we can with the jukebox blaring we have a pleasant conversation. One o'clock, de Pieter is full up with people from the bars in the neighbourhood that have shut and I stand close up against him. Not at all unpleasant. Feel his arm around me. Come, I think, don't let the poor boy do all the work and when Josje and her lover are pushed over to the other side, we start to kiss. As far as that is possible in the squash.

Then de Pieter also closes. Come along, says Ton quickly when he sees me hesitating whether I should go home. Okay, next bar, Okshoofd, a terrible disco which I haven't visited since I was completely cured of the subculture and of Americans. Music so loud we have to lip-read, which I learned to do well in Paradiso, but not Ton, so we kiss instead. I want to go home, I say to Ton, who takes me in his car, a luxury. My friends only have bicycles. Hey, listen, I say to him, I would like to take you home, but someone may be waiting for me there who has come back from holiday, so that can't happen, but I want to make a date for another time. Tuesday, eleven o'clock, in de Pieter. A true feminist, says Ton, when, with his hand under my clothes, he discovers that I don't wear a bra.

He really does come when on Tuesday at eleven o'clock precisely I am nervously waiting in de Pieter and thinking that it is nonsense to make such a date with someone I hardly know. The attack of courage that came over me when I saw him the first time in de Pieter has now completely deserted me. Always the same, as soon as I really like someone and it depends on his reaction, the initiative slips out of my hands and I can only sit waiting, tense and dependent, for him to do something. But he comes and is at least as embarrassed as me, the rituals are not so easy for him either, he confesses, which is a most attractive proposition: Ton, who is well-known and gives lectures in front of full halls and who sits here a little shyly toying with his beer glass. He is wearing a red sweater and luckily has no tie on. I like that.

Are you coming home with me, I say. I'm not such a good lover, the first time, he whispers in my ear in the car and that too I find excellent. It isn't a football match, I say, and then it goes well and I like him. We talk in between making love. He is married after all, that is not so good, but he says he has an arrangement with his wife whereby they leave each other free. And I think, it must be true otherwise how can he go home at three o'clock? When he climbs into his clothes I find it sad, I would rather have fallen asleep with him and woken up together in the morning, but I don't have any choice. I'll come over on Saturday, he says, is that all right? I nod yes with a sleepy head, forget to ask what time Saturday, fall happily asleep with a body warmed by loving between my sheets that smell unmistakeably of fucking.

Saturday morning I clear up the rubbish in my room which was not so visible on Tuesday night in the lamplight, but which in the glaring morning light is indeed rubbish. Armin is staying with a friend which makes it even easier. With previous lovers, who mostly came at night when Armin was already asleep, there was no problem, but one way or another I have the feeling that with Ton it will be more than night visits and if it is at all possible I put off the scene in which Ton feels he must be extra nice to Armin because he is chatting up his mother and Armin senses this in his bones and looks ironic and only gives one-syllable answers because he isn't about to make it easier for the fellow than is strictly necessary.

When I rush out to do the shopping I impress upon Bahasj that she mustn't forget to open the door or answer the telephone, and I return and Ton is not yet there. A nuisance that he didn't say what time he was coming.

There is nothing more to do. House tidied. Shopping in. Bahasj leaves to go to her parents. I roll a cigarette for myself. Try to read, but don't succeed. Another roll-up, pour a glass of wine which I put off drinking because I don't want to taste of alcohol as early as five o'clock. Consider whether I will phone him to ask what time he is coming, but that seems to me to be pushy and the last thing I want is to appear overdemanding. And on top of that I don't know how his wife will take it, in spite of the freedom he says they give each other.

Around eight. I have a dirty tobacco taste in my mouth from all the roll-ups. Go and brush my teeth once more. Did Ton say he would come in the evening? I'm not hungry, food in the fridge for two people, in case. . . . At ten, eleven o'clock Ton is still not here and now I am really nervous. Goddammit, I think, soon he has just forgotten. And then: don't get excited, perhaps he'll still come. I try to stay calm. To think, what does it matter. But it doesn't help much. I want something with Ton, I think. I don't meet men every day who are both left-wing and nice. And attrac-tive. And who also fancy me. Twelve o'clock. This is crazy, I think, I must go to bed and not think about it, but instead I walk around in Bahasj's room in circles while I look outside to see if his car has come. Then walk again to my room where at least I don't have to prick up my ears at the sound of every car which comes around the corner. But waiting for the bell to go is

167

worse and so I go back to Bahasj's room and walk around again. At two o'clock I go to sleep angry and then lie sleeplessly tossing and still listening and imagining ten thousand reasons why he hasn't come. Goddamit. And now it is also much too late to ring him up, I should have done it sooner. They're all rotters, that's clear.

In the morning I wake up grim and determined. No sitting and waiting. Ring him up at once, if his wife doesn't like it – his problem. If he finds it too demanding, OK, finished. And I repeat to myself all the things that we have said to each other in the women's group a hundred times. We don't have to comply with rules that we haven't drawn up. We make our own terms whether they are progressive or not. No one can force us to satisfy the expectations which we ourselves haven't approved. Let them think us a nuisance and dominant and unattractive if they want to.

Ton speaking, says Ton. Hey, listen here, I say, I thought we had arranged that you would come round yesterday. Oh, says Ton, how awful, didn't I say that I *might* come? And I did try my very best but I just couldn't get away, the room was full of visitors and I kept on thinking when they've gone I'll go, but they didn't leave and then it was too late to ring. And I wanted to see you terribly, dearest, it was so good with you. Can I come over in a little while?

I am already melted.

A meal at a Yugoslavian restaurant then walking hand in hand along the Amstel river. We act as if we're about fifteen, says Ton, we look like we're in love, what am I saying, we are in love. That this could overtake us in our old age.

Precious hours. Does your wife know you're here? I ask Ton, don't you quarrel about it? We live quite separately, says Ton, I have my own room, but we do get on and the children. . . . The children. I haven't seen them yet, but at awkward moments they have flu or must go to the dentist, just when I was counting on one of the stolen hours with Ton. A father who cares about his children. It is impossible for me as a feminist to make objections because he can't come round then. I miss him when he spends a few days with his children at his in-laws. Live again when he is back in the city and we continue with the brief hours snatched together, sometimes eating a sandwich together in the city. The few quiet hours after the end of one of his endless meetings, until it is five in the morning, the magical hour when adulterous husbands put on their clothes again, can say to their girlfriends that they have stayed the whole night, to their wives that they still come home at night.

One solitary time we take the car to Bergen where we walk along the beach and sit in a plush restaurant drinking brandy and talking about marxism and feminism or peacefully sit next to each other working, I at my studies, he at his political work. I don't know many women with whom I can talk about my work, says Ton, with whom I can sit working without boring her. How happy we are with each other.

Talk in the car on the way back about all his plans, research that he is still going to do, books that must be written, theories that have to be worked out. Work with action groups. There is so much to do.

On the car radio something is said about alimony becoming higher and new divorce laws. I'll have to go through that in a while, says Ton soberly. My heart skips a beat. Boom. But I say nothing, say nothing, say nothing.

We make wonderful plans, all the things we want to do together. But reality exists in odd hours. Do you know that we already know almost everything about each other except whether we eat our eggs hard or soft boiled, I say. We have fucked endlessly with each other and never slept with each other. Except those occasional rare hours now and then which don't count when Ton falls asleep and I wake him around four or five to go home. I don't even know what your children look like, I say. Or how you live. You can come round when she isn't there, he says. But I

169

shudder and refuse. I would feel such an intruder. Her domain. Her children.

And time and again I take it when he comes hours late, because the meeting ran on, because it was necessary to talk in the pub afterwards. You know, he says, the most important decisions are taken in the pub after the meetings. And over a beer I can find out much more than by sitting in a meeting. It is just part of my work. That is the consequence of being in politics. And I can hardly tell them, gentlemen, I must go, my girlfriend is waiting for me. Why not, I ask, don't they say sometimes: I must go because my wife is waiting for me? But it is a weak argument because most wives of politicians are trained through the years to keep meals warm and not to count on anything. And I am not even his wife.

Then a chance. Darling, how would you like to go to Paris for three days over Easter? Three days, jesus. And Paris, which I have only once driven through. Do you really mean it? I ask. Does your wife approve? I still have to tell her, he says, but it will be all right, anyway she was planning to go with the children to her parents and we had already arranged that I wouldn't go with them. In Paris I will become completely dependent and unfeminist, I say, because I can't get a single word of French out of my mouth and I'll wet my pants if I have to order anything in a restaurant. And then later you'll have to come with me to London, because in London I am big and strong.

Paris, three days, a sea of time we fill with nothing. A back-street hotel with flowery wallpaper. Ton doesn't have much money, but always more than me. We do everything that people in love ought to do, saunter hand in hand and look at the houses, look at each other above glasses of wine. Walk for hours around the cemetery of Père Lachaise where the communards of the Paris commune were shot dead and I listen gratefully to Ton who tells me about it – my knowledge of history a big hole, which as I was expelled from school during the French Revolution, was never filled in. Sleeping together in a big squeaky bed – reminding us that we are committing adultery. A luxury, so much time, to be able to breakfast together.

170

The last day in the Bois de Boulogne. We sit in a fin de siècle restaurant in the sun between azaleas and gardenias or whatever the pastel coloured flowers are called and look at old ladies eating pastel coloured cakes and poisonous-looking deep green or deep red drinks out of long-stemmed glasses. We are silent. For the moment, enough said. Ton reads a French newspaper.

On the way back he asks why I am so quiet. I can hardly speak. Then he says it himself: because it is so difficult to go back to an occasional hour after this. Yes, I say, you have understood it so well, and then the tears roll down my cheeks. I wipe them away impatiently, that isn't part of the bargain. I know he does his best, that he is married. I surely knew when we began that I couldn't expect much?

What would you really like? asks Ton. Let's tell each other for once what we would truly like. Without promising each other it can happen. And then see.

No marriage, I say, Ton you must believe me. I am not trying secretly to make a marriage out of it. Also no living together, that's the same thing. I know I mustn't do it any more, that it isn't good for me. But jesus, wouldn't it be good for once if I could go spontaneously to you, if you didn't have to put on your clothes again half-way through the night, if we could also occasionally stay a few days with each other if we felt like it, if we didn't have that tug-of-war on the weekends or on public holidays, if I could just get to know your friends.

Ton nods. I know, he says. If you knew how much I would like that too. Perhaps I should think about living alone, then at least we would be equal. Perhaps, perhaps, it isn't so easy to take such a decision, the children, and I don't know if she would agree. I must have time to think it over.

I am already less sad. At least I am not the only one who finds the situation difficult. And if I know he is also trying to find a solution, I am patient. Better not to make over-hasty decisions.

Back in Amsterdam we fall back in the old pattern. More difficult after Paris where we had such a good time, where we could sit so peacefully reading next to each other, could talk about the same things. We're like Sartre and de Beauvoir, says Ton, joking, but Sartre didn't have to go back to his wife and children at five in the morning. We write letters to each other all the time, he pushes them through my letter box at night and I deliver them to addresses where he has a meeting or where he goes for his work. Just don't send them to my house, says Ton, even if she does know about it, it still isn't easy for her. We musn't make it more difficult for her than is necessary. Meanwhile I have piles of letters. Save them, says Ton, for Part 23, Correspondence, MTW. The last weeks before the summer holiday fly past. Women's groups, women's conferences, papers on women. Ton and I have known each other five months. In the summer we won't see each other for a month. He will be in Yugoslavia with the family, I am going for the first time to Femø, the women's camp in Denmark. In the summer I'll have time to talk it through quietly with her, says Ton. I can catch her better then than now between all the meetings. And I'll write how it goes.

OK, I say. And think, if he doesn't live separately I must finish with him. I can't carry on like this.

Femø. A small boat takes us the last part of the way, the car stays behind. As we approach we see a few women waiting. Is that them? Open faces, they laugh towards us. Feminists. Other women don't smile so openly at women they don't know. One American, two Danish women. They help us with cases and sleeping bags.

A big grass meadow, two enormous olive-green army tents. This is it, says the Danish woman, there is still room in tent six on the other side. There is the toilet and there is the office and the rest you'll easily find. I spread my sleeping bag on straw, smile shyly at the other women. A big American is next to me with a small toddler and a baby of six months.

Anarchy. Almost nothing is organised. Each day a different tent is responsible for the meals. There is one tent with teaching aids for play groups because the Danish government insisted on it before they would give a subsidy. There is one tent in which we hold discussions if it is too cold outside, and have parties in at night. Discussion groups have been formed and if someone wants to suggest a topic they pin up a letter on the wooden wall of the toilet. One hundred and fifty women, a lot. I walk around, I don't feel at home. Am embarrassed by radiant faces, faces which smile at me for no reason. Ten different nationalities.

Women who speak only their own language. Little boy children manage to communicate with an international pow, pow, pow among the tents and fall over the ropes and run to their mothers to be comforted.

The second day it is hot and one by one all clothes are removed. First the sweaters. When it becomes hotter, everything.

The third day we have almost all burned a bit and then women walk around in strange combinations. A T-shirt above bare buttocks. One woman wears only wellingtons and a big flower in her hair. I look, look, at all these naked bodies. A woman of fifty who lets her long hair hang loose, two women who are at least eight months pregnant rub each other's bellies with suntan oil. We decorate each other with chains which we crochet, with shawls, with flowers. Women walk hand in hand to the beach to swim. And in tent five where the lesbians have found each other, they make love, if they don't make love outside in the sun.

In the evenings, after walking together on the beach, or alone, having seen the sun set, we dance in the big tent. Janis Joplin. Freedom's just another word for nothin' left to lose. I feel my body becoming looser during the dance.

Dancing alone, or with two other women, or suddenly in a big circle. Unused to not waiting to be asked first. I become a bit nervous when I see a small French woman who looks like a dyke smiling at me. I know she sleeps in tent five. Oh help, please no advances, and I move to dance at the other side of the tent.

The next morning I am in a discussion group with her, Elvi, and I find her extremely nice. A friendly clown who wears a funny cap. Together with her and Jean (the biggest woman in the camp who wears army boots and gives karate lessons at the other end of the camp), we walk to the only bar on the island. I talk with Elvi about my being scared of her. You tink ze lesbians all walk around to grab ozzer women, she says with a heavy French accent, and laughs. You tink I want you when you not want me. I am not like ze men. My fear is gone and I now dare to enter tent five where actually only two are making love and when I notice that they are not at all ashamed in front of me, I think why am I behaving so crazily and I look at them

173

and think that it is really very beautiful and sweet and moving to see women who love each other.

My body becomes supple, my face opens up. I forget what I look like. There is no mirror in the camp, on principle. No place where I hold my daily inspection, working out once again what doesn't suit me. I forget what I find ugly in myself. Know only what feels good, cold water against my sun-warmed skin, the wind against my cunt. I notice I look at things differently. That I don't automatically look at the older women with a calculating look, too fat, hanging breasts, but that I see how they walk, chin in the air, strong backs and broad swaying hips which I begin to find beautiful. The new women who still turn up every day are easily recognisable. By the awkward, stiff way they walk without clothes, by the way they constantly and carefully look downwards, calculating, belly, breasts, legs. By the stiffness in their shoulders and a shy smile if you look openly at them. At night we sing: women over forty, throw away your corsets and your rollers and your sleeping pills. Join us – with us you are beautiful.

A Danish journalist in the camp is making a radio programme. Only recognisable by the tape recorder she carries on her naked body. An interview with a small Danish girl. How do you like it here, she asks. Oh, wonderful, says the girl. Only I think men over seven shouldn't be allowed. Because you can't do anything with them. They only tease and fight.

But I am not completely happy. Because every morning I see from afar the post van ride onto the meadow. The postman no longer eyes the naked bodies and the women also forget after a day that there is a man walking through the camp. Within a matriarchy all shame falls away. I wait for a letter from Ton that doesn't arrive. Every morning new tension. Now there must be one. Nothing. A letter for you, calls Elvi, but not from Ton, from Armin who writes from his children's camp in Norway. 'Dear Anja. I have stayed with a real family. That was great fun. I'm fine. Bye. Armin.'

And each time the post van leaves I find a quiet place and huddle into myself. If he just wrote one letter to say it can't go on any more, I think. Better to know that it is finished than this undermining waiting. And I consider whether I should be the one to grasp the initiative. But I dare not come so close to a decision. It is still possible, I think. Seven, eight days. No letter, nothing. I imagine how the conversation is going in Yugoslavia. Perhaps screaming arguments. Perhaps a great reconciliation and the decision that Ton must break with me.

Perhaps he doesn't have the guts to write that to me, just as David didn't dare. I go swimming, alone, float on my back, sun in my eyes, until it is over and I am happy again and can enjoy all the women around me and can dance to Janis Joplin with the certainty that there will be a letter tomorrow.

The camp is over. It has become cold and we walk around shivering in wind-cheaters and wellingtons. It rains and the whole place is a big mud bath. The mothers with small children have already left. We eat sitting close to each other, plates on our knees. I decide with Elvi and Jean and some Dutch women to stay a few days in the women's house in Copenhagen before we go back.

A few days of radiant pleasure. Because Ton doesn't know that I am here and no letter can come and so I don't sit around waiting. I should never have given him my address, I think too late, then I could have had a real holiday.

I immerse myself in the bookshop in the women's house, in the literature, in English and American articles. A whole week without words, as if I hadn't eaten for a week. I make notes for articles I want to write. A true intellectual, says Elvi, who doesn't understand why I bury myself in the books. Feminism is something you live, you don't have to read about it. I laugh at her.

In the civilised world all the differences that we had forgotten in Femø are clear once more. When Jean and Elvi and I walk to the bar we notice how we are stared at. Jean, big and coarse and strong, Elvi who has to trot along to keep up with us and continually calls wait for me, it isn't the Olympic Games. And I, a size between. Dykes, obviously. And for the first time I think look then, when we are stared at and I stare back. Bars are unpleasant, drunk men all around me, I shudder when an arm around my waist turns out to belong to a fat drunk Dane instead of Elvi. Piss off, pig, I say in Dutch, because except for the word for women's liberation in Danish which is kvindebevriellse, or something like that, I don't know any Danish. When for god's sake we visit a gay bar it doesn't get any better, all the smart young men with small bums and well-cut hair who look disapprovingly at Jean who stamps through the hall in her boots and at my breasts which bounce around under my shirt when I dance. The waiters are rude and in an excess of disaster we overturn a vase of flowers. We are leaving, we've got too big for this kind of occasion, I say, and we sway sadly across the street, arm in arm, singing the International in the wrong key with the women's words. I am already homesick for Femø. An unreal refuge, a dream which can't exist, a premonition of a society which is still to come, an island where we could experience for a little while what we might have been if we hadn't been brought up as women in a society made for men, could feel what might perhaps, later, later, happen in another society. But not now, not yet. And after a day or so in Copenhagen, my face is closed as usual and I have looked again in the mirror and discovered that I still have a peculiar nose and ugly teeth.

With a beating heart I open the front door. Cats rush forward to be caressed, wait, first look for the letter from Ton that must be in the post. No letter. Jesus. Now, that's it then and I prepare myself for the familiar period of recovery which must follow. And then two days later, when I no longer expect it, it arrives.

Darling, he writes. You are never out of my thoughts and now that I haven't seen you for all these weeks I am aware of how much our relationship means to me, how far we have gone together. And I remember your white face when we said goodbye, I was also afraid that day that it was the end, but now every minute that passes proves that I can't and won't live without a relationship with you, the decision is taken after all. I am going to live on my own in Amsterdam.

Bahasj, who has seen that there is a letter from Yugoslavia, comes to ask what is happening. Sees the doubt on my face. Bad? she asks. I don't know, I say. He writes that he is going to live alone, but somehow I don't believe it. Something doesn't fit.

Read the long letter through again. Absolutely nothing about the relationship with his wife, strange. One sentence between the others says that he wants to keep on his study in his house. As if that is quite usual, to leave your wife and children and still keep on your study. I don't understand it. Something doesn't fit.

Which is demonstrated when I get a letter a day or two later.

My darling, writes Ton. Since I wrote the letter a week ago to tell you my decision, things here have taken a stormy turn. First a confession: after I had been very depressed on the journey, I told her that I intended to live alone. I have only told her in vague terms about you because I didn't want her to think that the decision was forced on me by you instead of being taken independently by me. Then she found a letter from you and after a day of violent crying on her part we have been able to talk everything through. I have at last told her the whole story and to my shame, her reaction was so much better than I could have imagined. She says that if you and I truly love each other we must find a solution as three adults together. And aside from that, in any event, the following agreement: we have complete freedom in telephoning and I can now also be whole days (plus nights) with you. And all completely open.

What's happened now, asks Bahasj. I'm going crazy, I say. Now he isn't going to live alone after all and now it turns out that she had only heard something vague about me and now we get permission to see each other and everything above board, I thought it was already above board.

Now I really do get stomach ache from nerves.

Ton rings when he gets back. Listen, darling, he says, I'll be with you tomorrow between one and two, then we can talk. Tomorrow, I say cynically. A whole hour? I thought now we were allowed to do everything. And I really think you need a longer time to explain everything to me. I hang up when he begins to stammer complicated excuses, the tensions at home, and not to go so fast all at once and he has other appointments tomorrow. Fall crying into my bed. Goddammit, more of the same shit. Worse off, compromises hasty meetings. I must stop it, I think. This will drive me crazy.

When Ton comes round the next day I am cynical, distant, but he sits there like a small boy who has done naughty things.

How did it happen that I thought she did know and now it turns out that she had no idea how things stood? I didn't tell you that I would tell her everything, says Ton, that wasn't necessary surely, it would have given her unnecessary pain and . . . And that living alone, I ask, what difference does it make that she now knows everything and didn't at first? I haven't yet decided that I *won't* live separately, but if we can now arrange everything so that we really can see each other and that I can also stay the night then I don't need to live separately and the children . . . And we don't want to live together anyway so what does it matter if I live there or alone . . . She wants to talk to you, she wants to come round tomorrow, it is still possible that it will succeed without us needing to force drastic changes, says Ton hopefully. I let my head hang. Anticipate endless situations. uncertainty, tensions. I should now say fuck off because you ruin everything, but I only think it, not brave enough to take that step.

Gordes 10

A whole day alone, what a luxury. A lot of fussing around the tents before they are all in the car. In a final exaggerated attack of motherhood I demand that Armin wears a pair of trousers without a tear in them. Protest, as usual, because Armin isn't the least bit interested in how dirty or torn his clothes are and what does it matter as long as I'm not around to be ashamed of him.

A day alone. I exult at a day without having to talk. But here in France it isn't easy to sit alone next to the swimming pool. M'mselle, M'mselle a couple of fat men sitting next to me, try to draw my attention. Shift up steadily closer to me when I ignore them. The newly arrived men who hold in their stomachs when they walk past, the older ones who know I'm not public property but private property because they have seen me with Hans, don't take the trouble. Hiss as I walk past. Not meant personally, pure routine.

I hate them because they disturb my thoughts, force me to behave crossly, to be sullen and tense. Make it seem attractive to put myself back under his protection when Hans returns, while I was so happy to have a whole day to myself.

I eat alone. There are no other women who eat alone. I am, therefore, asking to be picked up.

I hide myself behind a noisy French family with lots of children.

A woman passes with blonde frizzy hair and big owl glasses. Breasts loose in her black bikini, chin high, she lets the oily stares of the men slide off her, unmoved. Flames in my belly. An image of Anna on my green sheets flashes before me. Why do I suddenly find this woman attractive when I feel nothing towards all the smooth women's bodies which go past? It is her attitude. She doesn't try to please anyone, is not ashamed of her body, but lives easily in it. Hangs shamelessly over a chair without bothering whether she is sitting elegantly or if there are rolls on her stomach or if she has hidden her cunt neatly behind her crossed legs. I think she is beautiful and wish that I was as relaxed in my body.

I am too conscious of my body in this environment. When I have forgotten it, the men evaluate it and remind me of it again. I begin unwillingly to compare myself again to the other women and it depresses me. My soft mother breasts, skin that is no longer as smooth as a few years ago. A few stretch marks on my hips that are almost invisible except to me. A few pounds too fat. Past my prime. I know that is nonsense, when I live among women my standards are different. I stop looking at myself with men's eyes, but the confidence and pleasure in my body vanishes when I am back in the ordinary world. My joints promptly become stiffer, I walk clumsily and woodenly. I blame myself that I allow myself to be influenced like that.

My skin is suddenly peeling. Scabies, says Armin, but I know that isn't true because I have already had that.

One of the sad groupies who hung around Paradiso when I shut the building. No place to go. May I go with you, she asked and I said OK, for *one* night, you'll have to move on after that because I have a friend coming to stay. She scratched continuously, but said it was psychological. And at night when I woke up she sat next to my bed staring at me with cat's eyes and said she wanted to make love to me because I looked like Janis Joplin. I made love to Janis once, she said, but I pushed away her head which she wanted to stuff into my armpit and pretended to sleep. Unbearable itch a few days later when I had eventually got her out. Shrieking, clinging to the doorknob, crying that no one loved her and that everyone kicked her out again. I felt a heartless bitch until I noticed that she had taken a few of my best clothes with her and the itch began. Which I shared with Michael.

Miss Meulenbelt, said the doctor, now you can see that God meant us to be monogomous otherwise he would not have created sexually transmitted diseases and I said nothing, took my ointment and for three days Michael and I rubbed it joyfully into each other.

My skin glistens again and smells of oil. Brown in the turquoise water of the swimming pool. When I look in the mirror I am satisfied. Untidy red hair and eyes that look greener now that I am tanned. No longer the wrinkled grey face of before the holidays when I had worked too hard. I think that I look tasty and well-cooked and I make my eyes glisten by putting black Indian stuff around them and wear something green and blue so that I look even browner when we go to town to eat.

What have you done? asks Hans at table. Written about Ton, I say. What exactly did you see in the man, asks Hans, that you could bear him for as long as two years. I have to think hard about that. I think I saw in him what he might have been, I say. Another kind of man was always on the point of breaking through. I only saw him properly when he was shown up for what he was and I no longer looked up to him. When I felt equal to him. I think that he was at his best with me, was less under

180

pressure from the competitive morality around him, less afraid of failing. For me he didn't have to go any higher to prove he was someone. With me he could live all his boyish dreams, all the plans he had for his life. Until I became too critical and refused to function only as a kind of dream haven far from the bad society. I began to look more and more like his wife, who constantly pulled his feet back to reality. Two critical women, that wasn't the intention. He had chosen it all so carefully: his wife the rational pillar of strength, his support. And next to her, me, who didn't see through him and admired him. Until I didn't do it any more. Then he just looked for another woman who made him feel big.

Jan's wife once wrote me a letter, how could I as a feminist dare to break up marriages, grab another woman's husband. I have never broken up a marriage. On the contrary. Through me the people have eventually begun to talk to each other. I filled the hiatus in their relationship until they no longer needed me. I should really be paid by the hour as a professional patcher-up of marriages.

That is indeed a pretty rationalisation, says Hans. A gigantic rationalisation I concede. Marriage bureau Meulenbelt, not a bad idea, says Hans. Pity I get so little out of it, I answer bitterly.

Armin says he wants ice-cream for afters, no cheese.

Divide and rule

When I open the door, she stands in the doorway. Anna, Ton's wife. What did I expect? Once I have seen her, I no longer know, but surely someone different. Harder and sharper. From Ton I have received the image of a reproachful

181

wife with whom he did not have much in common. Because he created that image or because I myself wanted to believe it? I had expected everything, but not this plump childlike face with soft round eyes and the shy voice. I had hardened myself, ready to withstand reproaches, to defend myself. But she doesn't attack me, only says softly, I am Anna, may I come in?

Would you like coffee? I ask, clumsily, at a loss for words and stand rummaging in the kitchen while she sits on my bed and looks around her and murders a paper handkerchief between restless fingers. Sorry, she says when she almost knocks over her cup, I am terribly tense, so much has happened recently which I haven't worked through. Yes, I say, and we sigh together.

What an idiotic way of making your acquaintance, I say. I have known about you for so long, almost six months and yet I had imagined you to be quite different. Six months? asks Anna, shocked. I count back, no, I say, five months, but you knew that, hasn't Ton told you that? I knew nothing, I say, that can't be, that isn't possible, and I think feverishly back to all the events from which it was clear that she did know. All the times he only went home at five o'clock? Then he said he had stayed talking with Harmen afterwards, says Anna, after the meeting, he often did that. And now and then I did think is unlikely, but I thought it would be so childish to check up on him. And the time he fell asleep and never went home at all? Then he said he fell asleep in a chair at a birthday party and that they let him sleep, which was such an unlikely story that it never occurred to me that he had made it up. And Easter in Paris then, I say. She is white and her hands shake. Anna. I never knew that he was in Paris, she says. We are silent. Thoughts spin round in my head. God-almighty, I say, he has made fools out of both of us. Anna, believe me when I say that all this time I thought you knew and that you didn't mind so long as you didn't notice too much. Certainly I believe you, she says. It's not the first time that he has had a girlfriend and hasn't told me. In Yugoslavia he suddenly confessed to a few others that I never knew about. But I had no idea it had gone so far between you. The other times he stopped when it went too far, but when I read your letters I thought I was falling into a pit, I thought the bottom had fallen out of my life. And now I hear from you that he hasn't even told me half of what really happened. Tell me everything now, I want to know everything, she says. He was planning to live on his own. No, she says, I don't believe that. Ton live alone? He isn't able to look after himself for a day. And did he think that I would look after the children on my own?

He was planning to keep his study. She laughs cynically, hurt. And did he think I would just take it? I let her read his letter. She shakes her head, unbelieving. He lies to you, she says. I don't believe a word of it, Ton is completely unable to live alone. That is news to me and now a completely different image is built up from the one Ton always portrayed to me. Not Anna who was so dependent on him and therefore a reason why he didn't dare leave. Ton is dependent on her.

Have you ever seen him cook a meal, asks Anna. No, I say. And tell her of the image I had. Ton sleeping in his own room. . . .

There is no bed in his study, she says. We still sleep together and I haven't noticed anything in all this time, I mean, when he comes home late at night and he still wants to make love . . . In any event it proves he is virile, jumping from one bed to the other, she says sarcastically. I am bewildered. How can someone do that, such a double life. How could he keep it secret for five months, from both of us?

And the first of May, labour day, I say. I am continually reminded of new incidents. I had arranged to meet him in Frascati and then I saw him standing next to a few people, was it you. . . Yes, she says, I remember that well, when a strange girl came up to him and said, wait a while, I must go to the toilet, I'm coming in a minute and I asked him, what's it to you whether the girl needs a piss and then he went red and suddenly was in a terrible hurry to go somewhere else, that must have been you. I thought that it was someone from before.

And to me he said that you didn't feel well and so he had to leave suddenly, I say.

What madness, she says. It could have come out ten times over. And now I understand his behaviour in Yugoslavia better. He was so irritable, made a fuss about everything, found fault with the children, as if he wanted to engineer a break. And when I didn't rise to it – when I found the letters at the end of the holiday, that was no accident. If he really didn't want me to find them he would have hidden them better. He didn't dare take a decision, he certainly hoped I would do it when I found the letters, that I would go away, or demand of him that he would let you go.

What a coward, I say.

What a child, actually, says Anna.

We look at each other. Almost friends in our misery. Anna, I say, whatever happens, I won't lie to you. Nor I to you, she says, crushed. I had wanted to hate you, but I haven't succeeded, she says. But I am also not planning to accept it all. He must leave the house for a few weeks. I can't think now. Everything makes me giddy. You have had months to get used to the fact that I exist. But I heard it all this week for the first time. That is fine, I say, and Anna, I promise that I will not see him in the meantime. That he can't come running to me now because you put him out. Is that OK? She nods. We must keep contact with each other. Talk again when I am a bit rested, she says. I can't at present put two words together properly. I'm going home now to tell him that for the moment he must go some place else. That I will still have to see if I want to go on with him after all this.

But in the event everything happens differently. When Anna rings the next day she says she has found Ton at home with a heavy attack of angina and a high temperature, that the doctor has been and that he is now on penicillin and can in no circumstances be allowed out of the house.

Itch in my cunt, just like after David. Psychological, I think, too symbolic to have the same again. But when I go to be examined at the clinic it is indeed trich again. I get pills for Ton. I want another bottle of pills, I say, for his wife. She must go to her own doctor says the old pig who is the boss around here. What nonsense, I say, you always know with these things that by definition it is about more than two people. And if she has infected still more people I suppose they will also want pills from us to keep us in business. Anna, I think, with other people? I laugh. Impossible, I say. There are others who claim that, says the doctor. And I explain to him how things stand, how bad it is for everyone already and she please mustn't as punishment

184

have to sit in the waiting room as well. . . The man is unrelenting but the nurse has winked at me behind his back and when I leave she gives me an extra package. Don't tell anyone, she whispers, otherwise soon there'll be a queue.

Two weeks no fucking, none of us three, at least that is a very peaceful idea. I arrange to meet Anna at the Central station, half way between my house and hers. Hand over the pills. Come and have a cup of coffee, she says, it is so idiotic on the bridge like this. A happy second meeting. Girlfriend hands over pills for venereal disease to wife.

How is Ton getting on? I ask. His angina is better, she says. But he is in a terrible state, cried when he saw how bad I thought it was, all that deceit during the last months. I think that he is scared of losing me. And you. I notice that he also thinks a lot of you, she says, while she stirs her coffee rather sadly. He has never let it go so far before.

In a few days you should visit us, she says. Because he is sick now and I also see him. Then you can look at the house as well. Or have you already seen it? she asks, suddenly unsure. Sorry, but I hear new things each day that I never knew about. No, I say, I have never been in your house, I didn't want to.

Don't go, says Bahasj, when she sees how I delay nervously on the day I should go. It seems insurmountable. Visit to the married couple. An optimistic letter from Ton doesn't convince me. He's jubilant: everything will be different, and: I am so rich with two such amazing women. I see myself sitting there talking to Ton with a cup of tea in my hand while Anna looks on unhappily from the other chair. Jesus. Ton the patriarch – husband – is that the same Ton as the one in Paris and walking along the Amstel. I must go, I say, grimly, I can't escape it.

We drink tea. It isn't easy for all three of us to make conversation. Ton coughs nervously. Their younger daughter stands in the middle of the room, five years old, staring at me with big brown eyes. Gives no sign when I ask her name although I've known

185

it for ages. Stares. Show us your beautiful drawings, says Ton. No, she says, cool and determined. And stares. You are right, girl, I think, strange aunties who make love to your dad, not to be trusted.

I'll take her for a bicycle ride, says Anna nervously. I walk through the house with Ton. The couple's bedroom with the table where Anna works. Ton pulls me to him on the bed. No, I say, and walk out. Ton's study, big desk, books. Teenage room of elder daughter, playroom of the younger. Functional furniture, a lot of red and green, drawings by children pinned onto the wall and Petje has drawn a big cat on the wallpaper behind the sofa.

You don't believe it yet, says Ton when I sit close to him on the sofa, that it can now be different. No, I say, I don't believe it and then Anna and Petje come stumbling back inside. Anna confused with red cheeks and windswept hair says sorry, I wanted to stay away longer, but I kept on seeing you sitting together on the sofa, I can't get used to it. Do you want more tea? she asks, but I refuse, say that I am going home. Ton waves to me when I stand at the bus stop.

You could easily have stayed for a meal, he says when he rings me in the evening. Anna had cooked extra food for you.

The first big conference for all the women's groups and for women who want to find out what it is all about. Months of preparation, workshops on motherhood, appearance, sex, marriage or no marriage. Naturally I want to be involved in everything but I choose the one which is most important to me at the moment. The workshop 'Divide and Rule', about triangular relationships

About ten women. Half of them are wives. The other half are 'the other woman'. One woman has a husband and a boyfriend. Another is both wife and girlfriend. Sara and Willemien share the same man. Couldn't you bring Anna with you. No, I say, I don't believe she wants to have anything to do with feminism.

According to tradition we are each other's rivals, but while we talk together we don't feel that. Isn't it strange, we say, that it so often happens, a man in the middle, a woman on each side. And both the women unhappy. How does it happen? Why do we accept that?

We are much more tolerant, says someone. We accept what men wouldn't put up with even for a week. Is that true for you too? we ask Elizabeth, the woman who has two men. I am not the only one for either of them she says, otherwise I think they wouldn't accept it. It began because Piet had a girlfriend and he said to me you also have the freedom to start something. And when I really did start something, with Ferd, he was actually very shocked. But he could hardly say anything about it and Ferd is also married, so he can't suddenly run off with me.

The stereotyped judgements we make about each other. You have it easy, says the wife to the girlfriend. You get his beautiful romantic moments, dinners by candlelight while I look after the children at home. Yes, but you have him over the weekend says the girlfriend, you at least have the time just to talk to him, you share a past with him and children and breakfast. Great bargain, says the wives, the breakfast and the washing up, the children and his dirty socks and his filthy moods.

We allow ourselves to be played off against each other, we decide. It has nothing to do with all that beautiful progressive fun and games of allowing each other freedom. Because *we* aren't free. When I get angry because he has forgotten that *his* parents are coming to visit, he walks off complaining to *her* where he can let himself be stroked and can complain that his wife is so nagging lately. And the girlfriend says if I get angry because he promised he would stay a whole evening and he walks out again after an hour because his parents are coming to visit, then he runs back to his wife because I have no right to speak, I knew, didn't I, that he was married before we began.

We are played off against each other, are kept in a balance with each other. We become the stereotypes that are prescribed for us. The girlfriends, the smart, sexy girls with no problems. The wives, the caring understandable bosoms on which to rest their courageous heads. And neither of us dares to make demands.

How do you manage? we ask Sara and Willemien. Well, it is only partly successful, says Sara. We are friends too, that helps, and Willemien really doesn't mind when he is with me because then she has a little breathing space, but now and then it does get to me because I am very dependent on their family life. Even though I myself don't want to marry and have children.

We admire them, Sara and Willemein, that they manage not to allow themselves to be played off against each other, and are friends with each other. But a year later Sara is dead of an overdose of pain and sleeping pills.

Rita comes back from the Stedelijke Museum and says that she saw a film there just of cunts. The hall dead quiet, nobody even dared to giggle. Can't we show it, suggests someone, the blank place on the map of our bodies. How many women have seen another cunt, not their own, and how many women have ever looked at themselves properly? We meet, how much does it cost to fly the film over from America, and will it come in time, and how should it be organised. Until someone says, we must be stupid. So many thousand guilders for a film of American cunts while we ourselves all have one and are American cunts more aesthetically sound or more beautiful than ours or what?

We cook up a new plan, screaming with laughter. We can ask Hillie to make a film, we need a few rolls of colour film and a hired camera. Who dares? Everyone. Have we enough variation? Old and young cunts, cunts that have given birth and cunts that haven't.

We drum up a few more women, don't think too long about it otherwise we'll find reasons not to do it, now, in a few days time. Somebody should bring along a lot of wine to give us courage.

It was to go down in history as the cunt film or the film of the thirteen vaginas, as an editor of a women's magazine called it, who, it seems, *counted* and who afterwards refused to write a nice article about the conference. Giggling a little in Renee's room, how should we do it then, one by one? Once we have all taken off our clothes it won't seem so idiotic, says someone and in five minutes the room is full of shades of pink, flesh pink. A three hundred watt lamp on your cunt, very hot, nice, and Marjan can't sit still from laughing so that her cunt will go down in history as the laughing cunt. As there is film left over we do a row of breasts immediately afterwards, yet another complex overcome in one go. We are curious how it will look on the film,

188

even anxious perhaps of seeing ourselves magnified and enlarged on the wall, but it looks really friendly and companionable and pink, especially those with the blue and white tampax strings. That one is mine, says Chris enthusiastically.

Well, no, says Sara, surely that one is mine.

We are nervous as the conference opens. No idea how many women will come, but it is completely booked out. Two hundred women. We have never seen so many together in one place. The women in the workshop for triangular relationships stand on chairs, the women who act as wives with aprons on, the girlfriends with red roses. They scream the stereotypes at each other. Slut, you have the lust, I have the labour. Easy to talk, reply the girlfriends, who has him at easter and over the weekend? You don't have to wash his socks, bitch, the wives call back, you don't have to take his foul moods. We break cups in a storm of abuse.

Then workshops all over the place. No decisions are taken, no speeches made, there is no chairperson and no central committee and everything works. At night we dance. I am completely manic, all my friends are together. We sing raucously and out of tune and shout the battle songs which have been written the previous day by one of the workshops: I am no cunt, mr, your darling treasure, mr, no more, mr. And: liberty, equality, sisterhood, woman has once more got her finger in the pie.

At four in the morning a woman sits next to me, panting from the dancing. Between fifty and sixty. Did you ever think that it would be so good with women, she says to me. Girl, I haven't danced perhaps for twenty years. Because my husband didn't like it. Get up, she says, and pulls me with her by my arm. Just one more before we go to sleep.

The movement changes and grows. Etie phones me up from the adult education institution. She wants to start a course on feminism and socialism, do I want to participate. That depends, I say. Predict uncommitted lectures to which a pack of curious people will come to look at the monster. But when Etie and An and I talk it over, we agree on everything within half an hour.

189

Women only, begin with our own experiences, work from there, outwards to more theory.

The courses go like an express train. Twenty women together for a week, it's like a pressure cooker, the first two days they realise that they share almost all their problems with someone, then that it has to do with the whole of society. And on the third or fourth day if they read a piece by Engels in small groups, it is immediately no longer only a piece of men's thinking, but is also about them. How stupid the lefties are, we say, that they have never understood that women become socialist more quickly through their own experiences than through an appeal to their solidarity with others. At the end of the week the women stand with tears in their eyes as they say goodbye to each other, and they keep on coming back and starting their own groups. It seems like magic, we say. As if we have to do almost nothing to make it happen. Women have been ready for years to break out, break through, the only thing they still needed was the lifting of their isolation and a little support at their backs.

We call them Femsoc Groups, our feminist socialist groups, the chaotic network of autonomous women's groups with whom I study and celebrate, constant companions in the years of coming change. Women friends more faithful than a marriage partner: Truus and Trees and Ria and An and Mieke and Tillie and Lenie and Riemke and Marleen and Carolien.

Writing blows me onwards. I begin at *The Women's Newspaper*. Then Anneke asks if I will take over her column in *Sextant* magazine, just once. And that goes well and she asks for more. Then articles for other papers. And before I know what is happening I am writing regularly. While I always thought that you had to begin as an unimportant reporter for the women's page of a provincial newspaper. Have you never written before? asks someone. Never, I say. I had nothing to say. What should I write about then? Write in order to write?

But now the material is there in abundance, my own experiences, those of the women around me, bits of theory that we are slowly developing. I am in the middle of a wave of creativity that is bursting loose. And now and then I also earn something and don't have to be scared of the man in the black leather coat who comes to switch off the electricity and who is not moved when I tell him that after all we are both victims of the same capitalist system.

It still continues, my consciousness-raising. I am constantly noticing how I see things differently, things I used to take for granted. Like a fish who finally notices that she is swimming in water.

Back from an evening meeting I walk along the Wetering-schans, a main street. Warm weather, my coat hangs open. A man comes up to walk next to me, a foreigner, says something unintelligible in which fucking occurs. I pretend I don't see him, slowly wise to the fact that to begin a discussion is the last thing that helps to shake off someone. He begins pulling at my sleeve. I jerk myself free. Fuck off, I say to him. But he doesn't let go, says fuck, fuck, fuck and tries to grab my breasts. A wave of anger rises in me. All the unpleasant remarks and lip-smacking sounds are bad enough, but I become really furious if someone lays his hands on me unasked. Hit, I think. Not the charming tap on the cheek which I learned as a girl, but a strong blow with a fist, on his nose, that's what it is. He curses. Then begins to kick and spits at me. And walks away. So, I think, that succeeded. Until I feel a hard blow in my back and a brick narrowly misses my head and smashes on a parked car.

I could have been dead, I think, when I am sitting down at home and immediately begin to shake.

The rules, I had forgotten all the rules. You only have the right to protection if you behave helplessly. The people who were walking on the Weteringschans at the same time as me didn't lift a finger, only stared. It can happen to any woman who walks alone at night. The only way to avoid it is to put yourself at the service of *one* man who protects you against all other men. Or not go on the streets at night. And I was forgetting that a man struck by a woman no longer knows what he has learned from his mother, that you can't hit girls, and in his blind anger is capable of trampling you to pieces. There is nothing to be done except to hit harder next time, or otherwise to play helpless again, I think.

191

A segregated world. No signposts in black and white, therefore it isn't so obvious, until you start looking. The shops are for women, and the streets. At night they are for men, just like beaches, woods where you can go only if you are accompanied by a man. Pubs are full of men where you are protected only if you are a good chick and even then not really. Nothing has ever happened to me, says Veronique, but it is also clear that Veronique keeps to the rules and only goes out with her boyfriend and if she really has to go somewhere on her own after twelve she takes a taxi, which I can't afford.

Elli is raped when she accepts a lift from a truck driver, her own fault, a woman can't hitch on her own. A girl comes crying into the women's house. Raped by an Angolan with whom she had been talking in the pub about the liberation movement in the Third World and when he asked would you like to come home for coffee because we are having such a good talk she thought don't be paronoid there are some nice men. Own fault, she shouldn't have gone with him. Francine was attacked in a lift, threatened with a knife, abducted and raped, afterwards allowed to go. Own fault, you know that you mustn't stand in a lift at night alone with a man. Her woman friend, who thought rape only happened after twelve o'clock, had the same thing happen to her a week later during the day. I don't even dare talk about it, says Francine, it was a black man and there are all the disgusting things said about blacks that I always challenge when I hear them. I understand they don't have an easy time here and that they are discriminated against and that they must then take out their aggression somewhere, but why should it be taken out on women? What must you do, start a discussion about us both being oppressed?

While he has his hands in your pants.

While we talk we continually find more stories to tell. The usual stuff, pinching our tits as we walk past, hands on our cunt on the tram, being pulled off our bicycle, pushed against a wall by a gang of drunken adolescents. Normal experiences. And then, naturally, the remarks. Don't look so grim, otherwise I'll stuff a broomstick up your cunt. Now, girl, if your cunt is as sloppy as your tits you're in bad shape. Shall we get her, men?

I remember the opinions I held before. Women who don't want it aren't raped because he has only two hands. And: perhaps the woman to whom it happened asked for it a little. At least I haven't been raped really, I say in the group, and then immediately I realise it isn't true. Toni, I remember, wasn't that rape, he only stopped when I scratched his skin to draw blood. And afterwards the forced fucking to buy my freedom. Why didn't I see that, I say. You were married, says Francine, that doesn't count as rape, that's called normal. And then we investigate what that means for us, for all women, not only those to whom it happens. We don't walk alone along the street at night, if we do we look straight in front of us, big steps, hands balled into fists, and our buttocks tight. No strolling, no looking in shop windows, walking round groups of men, getting into a panic if you hear steps behind you, making a detour not to go through a dark street, being careful not to look anyone directly in his face because eye contact, by accident, is already an invitation.

Ordinary, daily fear. We don't even notice it any more, so ordinary. It's not about if it happens to you − it's about our living in a society where it *can* happen, we are all outlawed.

Karate lessons, twenty women in knickers and body stockings and overalls. Running, muscle exercises, I am in poor physical shape. Strong legs from walking a lot, but weak arms and lungs fit for nothing.

Harm teaches us, a man who is a head smaller than me. Kicking exercises, arm exercises. We try Japanese screams, but only civilised squeaks come out, and then giggles. We haven't learned to make a noise unless we are in a temper and forget that girls should behave themselves properly. Practise on each other. Harm stands in front of me. Hit me, he says, I'll defend myself. I can't do it. I have practised the blows endlessly but now that someone stands in front of me it isn't possible. Don't worry, he says. Nothing can happen, you couldn't touch me, even if you wanted to. I hit a half-hearted hole in the air, somewhere near his ear, he catches me by the wrist, taps his foot against my ankle and I lie on the floor.

It has nothing, nothing to do with muscle power. Everything to do with conditioning. And when I think over later about what stops me from hitting Harm when absolutely nothing can happen, instead of giggling nervously about it, I realise what it is. The man on the Weterinschans. The inbred anxiety, deeply hidden, that if you hit a man he has the right to beat you up, you are outlawed if you break the rules. A psychic barrier, much more than a physical one against using our strength. Which we do when we heave dustbins and shopping and children, dragging them behind us up to the third floor.

So I practise harder, now I know what the barrier is. I remember that I have so often dreamed that I wanted to hit someone and that I couldn't, my fist going through the air as if it were syrup, never reaching its goal. And now I dream suddenly that I smash up a huge fellow, all my aggression coming out, I kick him in his balls, bash at his skull. Thirty years of repressed aggression eventually coming out instead of being turned inward. The men who hear I am learning karate laugh sarcastically or a little uneasily. Helpless is more attractive.

Gordes 11

Not yet come on. My faithful ovaries, one a few days slower than the other, leave me in the lurch. A perfect cycle of twenty-seven to twenty-nine days. I listen uneasily to my belly.

No more smiling

Ton and Anna. A married couple.

I am visiting them. Petje doesn't stare so coldly at me any more. I have talked with Esther, their elder daughter. That I don't intend to take her father away, that she needn't be afraid of me. OK, she says.

A married couple, a family. The three of us sitting there. I feel like a visitor. Brandy makes it easier to talk in this situation. I look at Ton and Anna's wedding photographs. Photos of the 'Socialist Youth', Ton with ears sticking out and short pants. Their past, which looks so different now that Anna tells it from when I had only the image which Ton drew for me. Anna, born in a leftist home, who took Ton with her to meetings, brought him into contact with the left movement of the time. And then the children. Anna worked as a teacher to earn money and did the housework while Ton studied and became known as a left-wing activist. Gone is the picture of a dependent Anna, of Ton the strong man who takes care of her.

Where are the brandy glasses? Ton asks Anna. Where are the photographs? Where are the coffee filters? Anna looks at me and we smile. We think the same thing. Anna's house. Except for the study into which Ton can withdraw, can hide behind the paper, can stare out of the window without the children trying to catch his attention, only occasionally disturbed by Anna who brings coffee and then noiselessly vanishes. No, I think, if it ever occurred to me to take Anna's place, if in my dreams I saw myself as Ton's mate, working together, talking together, that dream is now gone for good. I see too clearly the price Anna pays for her security, how her own development has become subservient to his. I would never be satisfied with a writing table in the corner of the bedroom.

But Anna is also changing. Ton's relationship with me a starting signal for all her pent-up dissatisfaction to break out. Look, she says, I was willing to stay home for his political meetings, my contribution to the common good, but to stay at home because he needs to go to you? Only if he also sometimes stays home with the children when I want to go out. I agree with her. It doesn't make anything easier. When Ton brings me home and wants to come in with me to make love I am the one who reminds him that he promised Anna to go home at once. I can't manage to see Anna as a rival only. I like her too much.

I ring up, why hasn't he turned up. Oh, there we are again, says Anna. He promised me that he would stay at home with the children because I'm going to my women's group. He promised me that he would come round at eight, I say. We sigh. Men, I say. I'll ask him to go to you when the children are asleep, says Anna. Leave it, I reply. I didn't want it like that. He must just learn to make arrangements he can keep. I know all about that, says Anna, who regularly has to calm down angry people on the phone because Ton is once again somewhere other than he has arranged, or has three meetings at the same time.

Ton tries to get out of it, deviously, denies he had an arrangement, blames Anna who, he says, couldn't bear him to come to me. You lie, I say, I have just spoken to Anna and she didn't even know that you promised me. A complicated story, that he first wanted to . . . but then someone rang him . . . and Anna didn't understand properly and then he just . . . and he did try to phone me, but I wasn't there . . . and then he thought. . . Stop, I say, Ton, I'm not getting involved in this. Anna takes it from you because she is dependent on you. Not me. You can't hide behind Anna. You must not make arrangements you can't keep to. I'm damned if I am going to wait two hours for you. I didn't mean anything by it, says Ton, you read too much into it. I won't wait for you any more, I say. Good, says Ton, I'll come tomorrow at eleven after the meeting. You don't mean that, I say, because you know the meeting will drag on and that you won't be here before two. No, really, says Ton, whatever happens, if the meeting drags on or not, I'll be there at eleven.

At two thirty he still isn't here and I lock the door, write Ton a letter that I don't want to see him again and fall asleep. I feel sad and grey in the days that follow. But my ego is in one piece. Proud that I have kept to my own conditions.

Four days later Ton is sitting in my room when I come home. And crying. I can't bear men to cry, it catches me in my belly, in all my buried mother-conditioning. I can't live without you, says Ton. I am wrong, you are right, I must change my life. I must make room for you in my life. Will you try again once more?

But then Anna revolts. She could put up with the few stolen hours, but when Ton suggests that he stays a day a week with me, she pronounces her veto. We quarrel. Anna and I. You don't consider me, says Anna. You don't consider me, I say. She walks away, angry. Ton and I see each other secretly again. We must have patience with Anna, he says, she still has to get used to it. I am silent, sceptical. Back again in the old pattern which I have had enough of. If it doesn't work, we'll have to make a decision, says Ton. But I don't believe him any more. I know too well that I will never take over Anna's role, cooking for him, washing his clothes, keeping his house in order, keeping people away from him when he is too busy and reminding him of his appointments. And I see too clearly that he can't do without that. If a decision is made, I am the one who will go, I know.

Continuing problems about staying alive. An endless struggle to get enough money. A monthly battle, writing brings in very little and it is exhausting having to produce new articles all the time, never being able to rest. And I don't succeed in writing just for my living; if I don't have something I definitely want to say, I can't get a word down on paper.

A chance. I am asked to lecture in a social academy on social action. I am a marxist, I warn them. I won't give academic lessons that are value free and separate from action. They are pleased with that and anyway I am only a part-timer, paid

197

hourly, not permitted to make decisions on policy and easily sacked. A real wage, a place on the job market and this time not in spite of my political opinions, but because of them, I think. But I am wrong again.

Some students couldn't be bothered with talking about how capitalism fits together, they have this vague idea that, after all, we are all individuals and free to develop as we want and that we can't really determine whether workers are unhappy or not. To say nothing about women. But with other students it catches on and we begin to think about other ways of teaching. Not the unrelated lectures one after the next which have nothing to do with each other. From the working discussions that have taken the place of my lectures, criticism of other lecturers develops. What kind of contribution do you make to the problems of young working people? ask a couple of my students of the lecturer in developmental psychology. Are their problems really connected to puberty, are they not the result of their work situation, the life they have to lead?

I am whispered about. I am called disloyal because I am more often in the students' canteen than in the staff room where I don't feel at home. Indoctrination, I hear, dogmatism. I am hauled over the coals. I must not forget that I am hired to give lectures on social action, not to lead project teaching. I am told I am unqualified and, no, we would naturally like to follow your suggestions, but we can't justify your programme to the ministry. The students become angry and when they put on pressure it suddenly seems to be possible after all. I am allowed to lead a group which will study the position of young working people with my social action classes as an integrated part of the study.

But I feel isolated, driven into a corner. Must so often explain what I am doing that I tend to avoid conversations. Have had enough of people who grumble, and Russia then, are you in favour of that? And I think naively that nothing can go wrong as long as the students are satisfied, as long as I do my work well.

Join up with two other part-timers, also left-wing. No accident, we calculate, that even at this so-called progressive social academy, the most left-wing people are part-timers, only able to influence policy via the students and easily sacked.

One of them is called Jan. Jan, around thirty, slowly became left-wing through the student movement. He reads Marx while his wife Tine looks after their two small children and does the housework. I can talk to Jan about the women's movement and he reads my articles. Doesn't just say, 'interesting, but I don't agree with you', as other lecturers do, if they say anything at all, but talks about them seriously with me. And about his relationship with Tine which is not so easy. I have almost nothing in common with her, he says. She is so locked up in her house, so busy with the children, she just doesn't know what I am doing. Naturally, I say. How do you think there is time over for your development if you have to do the housework on your own with two small children? You wanted that, didn't you, a woman who looked after you, you wanted children didn't you? You are right, he says, it is my own fault, but what now, must I forever pay for the fact that I didn't understand?

I can talk to you, he says, and I feel flattered. Excited when he drops in, with an excuse, a paper he wants me to see. You don't have to make up reasons to visit me, I am pleased to see you, I say. You can come because you want to, without any other reasons. We look at each other. You don't make it easy for me, he says. Tine is jealous if I call on you, she has read your articles. . . She is scared that I will find you more interesting than her and the trouble is, that it is true.

Is this the first time? I ask. Ten years of marriage, never made love to another woman. What must I do, says Jan. I don't want to hurt Tine but jesus, how long can I keep on going. Your decision, your choice, your responsibility, I say. Why don't you talk it over with Tine. Which he does, courageously and Tine creates scenes, says she never wants to see him again if he starts anything with another woman. What must I do? he asks me. What do you want to do? I ask, I can't take your decisions for you. But the decision is made when we both lie on my bed talking and at last stretch out hands towards each other and our bodies no longer know their own boundaries.

Why is it so different with one man or with another. Why am I hooked, addicted after one time. Why do all outworn clichés immediately become true, the clichés about melting into each other, of feeling lost, past help. A man whom I would otherwise not have noticed, no love at first sight, but my body reacts strongly, has chosen for me and days later the image remains with me of his face when he yells as he comes.

Guilt. I must tell Ton; he, Tine.

I know that Ton was afraid of this, but he is not in a position to forbid me anything. Don't you do it too, I say reasonably, love two people? Why shouldn't I be able to do it?

But Ton isn't reasonable, he is enraged. In turn icy and distant, go ahead, I have nothing to say, and furious, raging. Tries to pin me down to an arrangement that I seem to have made with him. Ton, don't be an idiot, I say. You are angry because I have made love to another man, that has nothing to do with the arrangement. But Ton doesn't listen any more, rages and screams and wants to disappear with doors banging. I hold him back, lock the door, say, you can't go away like this.

Then he sits with hunched shoulders. Whispers, I know it is unreasonable, but I just can't take it. It is as if we are being defiled.

And when we try to make love it goes badly. It is as if I can see him making love to you, he says. And it is true, my body is still tuned to the experience with Jan and actually will not warm up for Ton. A pretty theory, loving two people at once, but if I really am with one person, like now with Jan – sad. Sadly we say goodbye to each other.

While I am talking to Jan the next day, Ton drops in. I am only coming to make a date, he says, when I tell him that Jan is there. A farce, it is as if it isn't really happening, they shake hands and introduce themselves. Jan, says Jan. Ton, says Ton. I want to laugh, have visions of duels, but after that they don't look at each other and Ton has taken out his diary and in a businesslike way makes a date with me. Thursday after the meeting, does that suit you? I'll be a bit later, I say, is that still all right? And Jan lies down on the bed. As if he belongs there.

A couple of days in Friesland with Jan. Cold outside, inside a fire. A farm with a fourposter bed and a red lamp. I can't get enough of his face when he makes love, his other face that is never seen at meetings. My blood on his belly because I menstruate, I draw flowers with it until we walk into the cold kitchen to wash each other.

I don't think I can go back to Tine any more, he says when we are in bed and have put out the light. I don't think I can go back to Ton, I say. After this. After at last having the feeling that it isn't about a quick fuck now and then for an hour or so. Such a different feeling, if you don't only share the bed, but also work with each other, the same politics. I know it, I know it, says Jan.

And the next day I write a letter to Ton, that I can't go on with him any more. That he has had more than enough chance to build something with me, but that it still only comes down to the hours in bed after a meeting, and now and then a conversation in a pub where we make plans we never carry out. I want to have the chance now to do more than that, I write.

And when we are back in Amsterdam, Tine is so overwrought that Jan doesn't know what to do and the next day stands at my front door, with his clothes. It looks as if I must choose, he says, and I can't give you up just like that. May I stay?

We talk. I don't want to live with him, he must look for a room, but he can stay with me in the meantime. And I tell him what I am afraid of: that he can't do it, break with his wife. That I am no wife and never want to be one. It is better if he lives somewhere else, or rents from someone else, so we have the space to find out what we want from each other. I have already chosen, he says. I can't go back to her any more. The only thing I have difficulty with is the children.

But it isn't true. Because when I go to my women's group he is jealous, sulky and silent when I come home. I have given everything up for you and you go on with your life as usual, he says. What do you want, I ask, driven into a corner. That I stay home for you? Then in a year's time I'll be just like Tine, exactly what you are running away from now. You can't want two things at the same time, an interesting independent woman and one who is your drudge and stays home for you. That's contradictory. You'll have to choose.

201

We find a room for him. Half the week he is there, the other half with me. He visits his children at the weekend. I am restless when he is away, don't quite understand why. We have another row when I go to my women's group. We argue when he is vague about going to his house, to his children.

Then suddenly while we are having breakfast, the doorbell rings. Tine comes up the stairs. Says to Jan, I saw your bike standing against the wall. I thought so. And to me: do you know what he said to me? That he has broken off with you, but that for half the week he is working in his room. That he only sees you at work now. I look at Jan, who has become red in the face. A pretty trick, says Tine. Pretending to her that you have broken off with me, pretending to me you don't see her any more. And she tells me how she found out, how she visited his room and noticed he had no pots and pans and no knives and forks. When he had told her he was learning to cook for himself. Jan is silent and red. Good, says Tine. This is it. You can choose, her or me. If you aren't back tonight you'll never set foot over the doorstep again.

I don't know what I should do, says Jan, when she is gone. You heard, I say: choose. I can't choose, he says. Then I go mad. And scream. That he expects Tine and me to adapt ourselves completely to his needs, that he plays us off against each other. That I won't take it either, no more than Tine. I throw a glass at his head and miss. Never learned to aim. He says, but what must I do? Choose, I say, just like we have to, goddammit. And when he still doesn't understand me I say, then I'll choose for you and grab all his papers and plastic files and throw them down the stairs. An extremely satisfactory noise. While he is picking up his things I throw his clothes down as well and lock the door.

And then drink a full bottle of wine at once and weep. And think I want to die. I am not suited for this world, these games. Stop the world, I want to get off.

Naturally, says one of the women, that's what you get when you are almost thirty and not yet married. And not married, she corrects herself hastily when she sees me spitting fire. Think of

202

all those men, in their thirties, ten years married, two children. Their wives earned the money when they studied, did the housework and stayed home with the children when they went to work and to their political meetings. And after ten years the men ask themselves if they haven't missed out on something when they notice they can't talk to their wives any more about their work, when their wives haven't had the same political development that they've had. And then they come to us, who haven't sat at home with the children and who aren't yet worn out and still have something to say. Leaving their wives embittered at home. It's such a cliché. But there aren't many who dare accept the consequences and really leave, walk out of their marriages. Unless we are prepared to take over their wives' roles.

And that we don't want to do, I say, because then in a few years' time we'll be in exactly the same position as their wives are in now and then the game begins all over again.

Poor men, says someone, who can't choose, who want everything at once, a wife to care for them, a woman for excitement.

We want that too, I say, we also want someone we can talk to, we also want to be cared for, we also want everything.

Except that we are never given the choice, says someone, we can't choose to have someone at home to look after our children and have a meal ready when we come home. Besides we'd burst with guilt. Let alone if we also had someone on the side because we wanted exciting sex and exciting discussions. We can only choose whether we want to be housewives and then only if we are picked before it is too late. Or the easy, free, fancy women, and then we know that it always goes wrong – the paradox is that it must stop as soon as it is going too well; that you are thrown away when you become really threatening.

Guilt. We sweep everything together and look at it carefully.

Guilt, we know all about that. Experts in guilt.

Guilt when we are the housewife and think it's our fault when we can't amuse him any more. Guilt when we are the girlfriend and are colluding in making his wife miserable. Guilt because of his children. That's it, we say, that's why we are so good at adjusting, why we are so pliable, take all the misery of the world on our shoulders. We understand everyone, we are killing ourselves with our understanding of others. We don't stick up for ourselves. And even then we are played off against other women. And then we feel guilty.

It doesn't make my work any easier that Jan and I have broken up. Tension not only between our group and the rest of the staff, but also now between Jan and me. The backbiting and plotting behind my back increases. When a replacement is needed, for a full-time lecturer which according to the agreement should be one of the part-timers, we are passed over. I go to London for a few days, to one of the conferences, to get away from the situation. When I come back Jan and the other part-timer have done a deal with the staff. Jan has publicly delivered an anti-Russian statement. Except for the group of students who keep on fighting for me, there is no one on my side any more. When I notice that I get stomach cramps each time I have to go into work I give myself the sack. To my students, who now feel left in the lurch, I explain that I can't fight any more, not as the only one on the staff.

Anyway, I am now supported by my women. It isn't just me, it isn't just that I'm not diplomatic enough so that everything always polarises around me wherever I go. I see it happening to other women who are outspoken in their attitudes. As a woman you are looked at mistrustfully when you don't behave like the stereotype. If you are also outspokenly left-wing that doesn't make it any easier. And then also a feminist. Who writes subversive pieces on sex. And makes love to a married colleague. And even once with one of her students. And doesn't even feel ashamed.

I see other feminists also have problems at work. There are no solutions, only survival strategies. You can do work which has nothing to do with feminism and then make a neat split between your work and your political opinions. Or continually make compromises, behave like other people want you to. Or be satisfied with a marginal existence, welfare, working without cards, earning on the side. Or become a taxi driver or a carpenter, like Jantien, and then work for other feminists. You can always marry, says Vera, who is a lesbian. As if I can still go back.

I begin to live with the fact that many people feel threatened by me. The colleague who, within five minutes of meeting me, delivered a story about his marriage, how he gave his wife a whole day off each week to go on a course. Barely disguised hatred from the other lecturers. An editor who picks an argument with me before I have even opened my mouth. When I ask why, he says: you came in so aggressively. I learn that men see my self-confidence as aggression, as an attack. As if they would automatically become a size smaller if I pulled myself up to my full height. It is true, I say to my women friends, we function as mirrors which reflect their egos twice as big as their real size. If we don't do that any longer, they experience us as castrating, plotting viragos.

That person Meuleveld isn't crossing this threshold again, otherwise I'll throw her down the stairs, says a friend's husband. When I see the black eye she got after visiting me, it is clear that he means it.

The university canteen. Two fellow students, the same ones with whom I was involved in political struggle in the first year. Ladies football, how ridiculous, mumbles one of them as he reads the paper. Yes, I say, football, how ridiculous. But he won't have that, becomes angry, tries to explain to me why women can't play football without being ridiculous and men can, but naturally he has no argument. The other men support him. Who made your sandwiches? I interrupt, pointing to the bags they have with them. Their wives and girlfriends, indeed. I am also oppressed, fumes one. When I want to cook my girlfriend won't let me. You must go and look in the countryside, there all the men are sat upon by their wives, says the other. And like the filling in a sandwich, the lecturer present produces the definitive argument, waving his forefinger in front of my nose. You are not an historical category he says.

And I notice I am slowly but surely becoming what I have for a long time been called. Frustrated, in any event. A strong dose of man-hate that grows every time some prick tells me how I should behave. And lesbian? In any event I like women more and more because they take me as I am, vulnerable and strong

205

at the same time. And I see how it happens to the women around me. Who had at first said, surely we can work with men if we try? When you really want to know how oppressed you are you have only to try to change the situation, stop walking around like a stereotyped female. Then it becomes crystal clear.

The smiling strike is a final proof. The vow to smile only if you are really happy. A shattering effect. People around you become uncertain. People quarrel with you for no reason. Men on the street say, you do look miserable. Men at work make a big detour around you. Only that, stopping smiling. And I notice how often we do it, how it has become a part of our uniform, how it is expected of us that we radiate decorative charm. How scared people become of us when we don't do it any more.

I don't understand what you're making such a fuss about, says a trim young newly married Mrs. My husband doesn't mind if I want to go out at night now and then, and he's quite willing to take an evening off occasionally too, then he takes me out to a meal in town. You demand too much of them, as if they didn't have a hard enough time earning the money to keep us. We should surely let them see we are grateful? All that dissatisfied grumbling from the feminists, she says. That's not for me.

Her husband, who sits next to her, nods happily.

Just you wait, I think, until you are stuck with two children in an isolated flat. Until your husband no longer notices when you have cooked something special. Until your children are out of the house and he doesn't look at you any more and you are too old to find a job. Until you find out he isn't doing overtime in the evenings, but has gone to his younger girlfriend who doesn't have red hands from washing up and who doesn't nag about the amount of her housekeeping money. But I don't say it out loud.

I'll meet her again, in a year or two.

Gordes 12

Farewell meal with An and Eric and Hanneke. I'm not looking forward to being alone with Hans and his son and mine. It feels safe to have a woman friend near even if we don't see each other very often.

The waitress in the restaurant looks more and more depressed as we try to decide about food, about wine. Once more, we say, how many omelettes and with what, how many salades niçoise. White or red wine or both.

I feel uncomfortable. The tension with Hans is not properly talked out, talked through. I drink too much and hear my voice becoming shrill, overconfident. I sit next to Eric whom I like, but we can't find the right tone. We react flirtatiously to each other, witty remarks, word-play, while we would probably both rather behave naturally. But I don't stop either, see myself merrily celebrating and laughing on one level, while on another I would rather cry softly, lean against someone and be patted on the head.

Eric and Hans deliberate who is fatter, An or I. Anja has narrower hips, says Hans. But she has more rolls on her stomach when she sits, says Eric. It is a belly that has been used, I say, almost indignant – so that doesn't count. And decide on the spot to go on a diet after the holiday while I spread my bread liberally with butter, the ham and butter which I have ordered, mainly because of the butter.

Hans talks about our last crisis. He is almost proud of it. I say how suffocated I sometimes feel when he walks around with his jesus face which says don't-bother-about-me. Do you get that too? says Hanneke, laughingly embracing me, so that you have to be miles away before you can get back your own peace of mind?

Eric and Hans are alike, almost brothers, have difficulty not living with one eye on the future.

And Eric says, it is like when we are drinking a good bottle of wine. An just thinks good wine and goes to sleep while I start to worry halfway through the bottle that it will be finished soon and where will I get another one from. Exactly, I say, but that's what makes it so difficult to be spontaneous. Because when I see Hans looking frightened at what he will lose, then I'm almost unable to be loving towards him any more. Because whatever I do, there is always that moment when I stop caressing or want to be alone again and then I see his face cloud over.

It is as if I have to fill up a deep hole with a toy bucket, there is never enough. The Eyore complex, I call it, from which I suffered so much in the past. Eyore from *Winnie the Pooh* who never believed someone loved him when he was being caressed and when they stopped stroking him said, you see, they don't love me.

And An and I tell each other how difficult it is to say no, to stay true to our own feelings. How we sometimes think we are hard and yet don't want to pretend to be loving when we don't feel it. And we ask Hans and Eric why they want us quarrelsome women and not one of the thirty thousand other women who would really love to walk hand in hand with them in the moonlight.

Hans and Eric grimace rather sheepishly at each other. Difficult. Masochism? No, says Eric, because I know for sure that what I get is real. Which makes the struggle worth while.

Shall we go to therapy together? says Hans to Eric. I can see it already, I say, with a man who will tell you within five minutes that you had a dominating mother and that you therefore always fall for castrating women like us.

But I will naturally look for a feminist therapist, says Hans. As if there are dozens of them in the telephone book.

I wish we still had a few days here without the boys, then we could sit together in a sidewalk café, says Hans. Don't you see, do you see it now, I say. Because we *are* sitting in a sidewalk

208

café without the boys. You are again forgetting to take pleasure in what you are doing now, you are already reserving the next bottle of wine.

I feel empty. Finished. Not in a state to give anything. Scared of the moment when Hans will ask me what I feel for him. Because I feel nothing at this moment, absolutely nothing. Nothing left to comfort him with, I don't even feel guilty.

I don't even feel like writing, such is my emptiness.

All women are lesbian except those who don't know it yet

Lesbian? Me? With my past populated by men? Fire under my skin and flames in my cunt with Shaun and David? Lesbian? Me?

The women around me who have always been faithful heterosexuals are now, one after the other, not so sure any more. Fashion, say a few straight feminists.

I talk about it with Ankie in France, in the Dordogne, how strange it is that I am so emotionally involved with women, much closer to them, but in one way or another don't see myself in love with them.

No earlier worship of your teacher? asks Ankie interested. Ankie lives with another woman and has a beautiful long slim body such as I would like to have, with thumb-tack breasts, very aesthetic. I also love sitting cosily close to women, walking arm in arm and kissing often, but really, with butterflies in my belly and not being able to sleep and being totally obsessed, staring into the distance and imagining female lusts?

Have you tried? asks Ankie. Oh yes, I say, that's why I don't think that I can.

Josje and Carla, fellow students – women friends to go with to the pub. Again in de Pieter, where each time I go full of expectations and when I'm there can't remember why I came. I don't meet new people, I never make contact, we stand drinking a little while we look around out of the corners of our eyes. Carla does sometimes meet someone whom she fancies, but Carla is miles more cynical than I and noticeably less particular in her bed-partners. Bahasj is also there and Josje stands chatting up a sweet boy, but much too young. A strange atmosphere tonight. We are laughing and flirtatious towards each other. Who began it? Where did the idea first surface? On the way home it was clear that we were going to do something with each other, but I can't remember that anyone said anything. We weren't even drunk. The boy with whom Josje was talking walking behind us like a little dog. He wanted to come, says Josje, I didn't ask him. Home, bed, my bed. Josje has a very small strong body and Carla is big. Four arms around me and four breasts next to mine in my bed. Two cunts. Strange, but also snug, all that roundness. We giggle and laugh and stroke each other. Josje curls her tongue in my ear. Group sex and, in addition, with women. I think, and actually it remains completely innocent, a game. Bahasj sits next to the bed smoking roll-ups and eating an orange. The boy – I had forgotten that he was also there – had sat for a while fumbling with the zip of his trousers and then understood that he was completely unnecessary. He disappears to the kitchen where he fries eggs. When we have had enough lovemaking, we eat up his fried eggs. Sitting naked in a row on my bed, six breasts above three plates. Bahasj goes to bed. To the boy we say that he is a good cook, but that he really must go now and we fall asleep. Before I fall asleep I am again afraid that we will be ashamed the next morning, that we won't dare look at each other, but everything is quite ordinary. That was good fun, we say. And no one thinks of repeating it. Josje never talks about it again, except when she's pissed and has had a row with one of her boyfriends she cuddles me and whispers in my ear. Josje comes to cry on my shoulder when one of the scientific colleagues with whom she is making love treats her badly, plays her off against his proper girlfriend who cooks for him. Carla is too cynical to attach much meaning to it.

What else? asks Ankie.

Deirdre. Deirdre is quite a different story. There was the women's camp in Callantsoog. Not as big as Femø. Tents in a circle and the women's flag which someone has put up. Deirdre is big and has lots of red curls and comes from Ireland and lives in France or the other way round. She mourns a lost woman friend and I mourn a lost man – when you have lost them the sexes don't matter any more – and we feel solidarity for each other and talk about pain. I will have to cling to you a little, says Deirdre, because I don't know anyone here and I feel I do know you, and I think that's a good idea. Deirdre drinks too much and I hold her tight when she first throws up and then cries, her big body shaking from the sobs. The others dance in the big tent, Janis Joplin just as in Femø, and Deirdre and I sit like witches outside under the full moon and she drinks still more and cries some more. May I sleep with you, she asks. I hesitate and then think don't be so stingy with your warmth, the woman needs it, and say, yes.

Five women in a two-persons tent. My contact lenses are out and I see almost nothing and it is a warm ball in which I caress an arm which suddenly doesn't appear to belong to Deirdre.

Deirdre wants all of me. For herself alone. And says it's such a pity we aren't alone because then she would be able to make love to me better. Better, I think, scared. Jesus. And Deirdre mumbles endearments in my ear. That she dreamed she would meet her great love in the Netherlands. Great love? Who? Me? Oh jesus. Help. That is completely not the intention. Panic. Deirdre, Deirdre. Because I want to cry with you under the moon and bemoan our sad women's fate, but Deirdre, Deirdre I am not your great love, or I should know about it.

I escape, cowardly, say I'm going back to my own tent because I can't sleep like that, which is true, but it isn't the reason and

211

Deirdre sadly lets me go. And sits waiting for me the next morning, big, misty cow eyes bent on me. I try to escape, but it isn't going to be so easy. Guilt, guilt. What have I done, while I thought that I was only comforting in a sisterly way, sharing our sadness?

She follows me all day. Sits in my line of vision when I am talking to someone else, stands in the opening of the tent so I can't get out to piss without touching her as I pass. Finally I flee when she rears up each time in my path wherever I go like a great sad animal. It has begun to rain and it is cold and my kidney infection which I can feel coming is an excellent excuse. And so I miss Anna, who arrives a few hours after I am gone, when the sun is shining again.

Lesbian, I am not a lesbian, I have decided. I feel a lot for women, I feel it with my body, not only with my head, and if I have to choose between living with women or living with men, then I choose women, but in love – no. I am completely sure when once again I am dancing with a group of women at a gay club and one of the women strokes me under the chin and says, this one is a darling too. Not me.

Oh Anna.

I haven't seen Ton for months, or Anna. Anna rings up. She would like to see me, it isn't good when we feminists keep away from each other, avoid each other. We had nearly bumped into each other at the women's camp at Callantsoog. We sit in the Women's House, I crochet squares for my bedspread to do something with my hands, self-conscious. Anna tells me she was at the women's conference to which I didn't go, half not to make it more difficult for her, half so I could spend the weekend with Ton. There suddenly she had had, as happens to so many women, a sort of breakthrough. In a fit of crying in the car on the way back, her bitterness towards me disappeared. I nod, recognise the peak experiences which you can only describe in religious terms: revelation, conversion. She wanted to talk to me, tell me she didn't mind so much any more that I had a relationship with Ton, that she had discovered something else, herself

212

as an independent person, other women with whom she could feel physical solidarity. But nothing came of it, and shortly afterwards Ton and I broke up and she could do nothing more with her feeling of solidarity with me. It is late. She must go home, to Ton. It hurts. She tells me she has talked a lot about me, that Ton often still thinks about me, is sorry it's over just when she had overcome her anxiety. I don't mind if you want to see him again, she says. And then she says she wants to go to the feminist socialist study week in August. I will also be there. The fifth or sixth course for me, the first for her. It seems to me to be a good idea, to work together as women, feminists. Not as Ton's wife and Ton's ex-girlfriend, as we have been before. We arrange that at any event we shall still see each other then, if we can't manage to do so before.

I see Ton again. A little of the old feeling rekindles. Mixed with mistrust. He asks if he can visit me in France when he will be in the Vancluse with a group of people and I in the Dordogne with my new commune. Sympathy overcomes mistrust. We write beautiful letters to each other again.

When Ton comes he gives me an envelope. From Anna. In it there is a blue bangle with three big blue beads. A note: I bought this for you in Avignon, have fun, no guilt feelings, writes Anna. When I put on the bangle one of the beads breaks. If that is symbolic I am scared which one of us three it will be, I say to Ton. As if I didn't know.

My body is not yet used to him, an absence which has been too long. We don't quite know what we should say to each other, it is all too much or too little. We swim, I see him in the water for the first time. We have known each other for a year and a half, but there are whole areas in his life which are unknown territory. We have never had a holiday together, always short hours, at most a stolen weekend. Crammed emotions, no time for everyday things. Slowly I get used to it. In a fake castle we can laugh again. The next morning we are familiar with each other again. You still smell the same, he says. You too, I answer. We can now chat together. The next day he has to return, it's the Fourteenth of July. I am a bit disappointed he didn't set aside more than two days for me if it was so important to him. But don't say it. He takes me back to the Dordogne, wants to see the farm before he drives home. I am sad on the way back. Memories of always waiting, always having to take his family into consideration, always having to be satisfied with a few hours. For the first time in a while it is overcast and cold when we get to Thenon. The farm looks inhospitable and grey. My little room, even with the crocheted squares of all the colours of the rainbow which I have pinned to the wall, looks poverty stricken. The glass of wine we drink is sour and too cold. I sink slowly into a leaden depression that won't lift, stays around for days after he has gone and I have crept into bed.

Oisterwijk. My sixth feminist socialist course. And now with Anna. Sun. We sit naked on the grass and study Engels. I feel Anna's presence, know it's her when I hear footsteps in the passage, a tension which disappears when she isn't in the same room. A strange tension. Only because of Ton? On the third evening I sense something is about to happen. I am in my room and hear Anna's footsteps in the passage, I know they will stop in front of my door. She knocks, shyly, sits next to me on my bed. I don't know what it is, she says, I feel so peculiar. Yes, I say, me too. But I can't give it a name, what I am feeling. I caress her back clumsily. We are turning in circles around each other, I say. We should meet more often. Luckily we still have two days before we have to go home to sort out what it is we want with each other.

When Anna disappears to her room I am confused, can't sleep. See her face in front of me constantly. And I don't know if I like it, this tension in her presence. I am scared. And at the same time, excited.

The following day the circles in which we turn around each other are smaller, we smile at each other when we go out the door at the same time, my heart beats when I meet her in the passage. The last evening. We talk about relationships. I talk about my doubt about my relationship with Ton, now while Anna is present. My feeling of always being the gooseberry, having to be satisfied with left-overs, always dependent. I don't know if I want to go on in such an unequal situation. But I also

214

don't know if I can manage to break it. It presses down on me as heavy as lead. I say I expect it will always be like this for me. Always having to choose between being alone and the kind of relationship where I am dependent, in the weakest position.

And then I talk to Anna who has come to sit next to me and puts her arms around me. And I cry, suddenly all the sorrow of years that I have bitten back so bravely, that I have rationalised away, analysed. So busy trying to understand why it couldn't be otherwise, that I, the woman that I am, must choose, that there are so few alternatives for women like me, that I have forgotten it is so painful. Anna strokes me, gives me a hanky to blow my nose. I'll never stop, I say to Anna, I am just a leak. Go on, cry, says Anna. I understand everything. And I love you. But I don't really hear it and continue to cry on her shoulder.

Hardly notice that everyone has gone to bed and Anna and I are alone in the room. Do you hear me, says Anna, I love you. Slowly it gets through to me, I hear what she says. I peer carefully at her through my tears. Naturally, I say, luckily there is the women's movement, women who support each other, it certainly helps. I don't mean it like that, says Anna, and I suddenly see that she swallows and is white and shaky. I mean I love you, she says. And then I understand it for the first time. The tension I felt over the past days. Which I would immediately have recognised if it was connected with a man.

We look at each other. Really, really? I ask. Really, truly? I can't help it, says Anna. I didn't expect it either. And suddenly we are laughing, while we hold each other and I hide myself in her dark hair and the smell of her neck, sorrow transformed into a wave of warmth. I am still leaking, I say when I feel the tears fall over my face even while I am laughing, dripping on Anna's shoulder.

I'll sleep with you tonight, says Anna bravely, and I feel an explosion of fear and happiness and excitement in my belly. We tiptoe giggling up the passage to drag her mattress to my room. Build a nest into which we creep, hand in hand, my head on her shoulder and I fall asleep exhausted while Anna caresses me carefully and looks at me and wants to make love and doesn't sleep all night.

I wake up next to her dark head on the pillow, she looks at me. Goodmorning, I say and stroke her breasts with the tips of my fingers, carefully, carefully. Goodmorning she says and kisses my shoulder. Did you ever think a year ago that we were . . . like this. . . .

The other women see our radiant faces when we sit on the lawn to finish the course. We don't circle round each other any more, but sit close to each other, a hand touching her hair, or her knee against mine. We hardly talk about it, about what is happening to us, about what we want. We just radiate like little fires and can't stop looking at each other. Sit close to each other on the ride back. Will we tell Ton? we consult. Decide to ring him up together from a café, to put off the parting for a while. Ton. We had almost forgotten him. Do you want to see him first? asks Anna. No, I say, you go to him. I would rather be alone to think about what has happened, not have to explain it straight away. Good, says Anna, we'll see each other again really soon. And we walk hand in hand across the street and onto the tram. Suddenly realise that people are looking at us and then just laugh. We are invincible.

When I print the photographs at home which I have taken during the week it appears that she is everywhere, Anna. I cover a whole wall with pin-ups.

Ton thinks it is really creepy. Had hoped that we would like each other, but so much. . . . He enquires 'how far have we already gone' and is pacified when it appears we haven't yet made 'real' love. But what is 'real'? Anna and I get nervous when we think about it, as if we have to prove something. When I haven't seen her for two days I become uncertain, worry whether we only felt something when we were with that group of women in Oisterwijk which will evaporate in 'normal' society, which doesn't really exist. In the interaction between men and women the codes are so clear. A relationship. You have that with a man if you go to bed with him, that is to say, if the sexual act is performed. Penetration. Otherwise it is friendship. Another

216

category. It feels as if our vulnerable, tender emotions are being put under a magnifying glass, analysed in terms of the norms that belong to the heterosexual code. And found wanting. Not real. Only a friendship between women. A little elevated perhaps.

Clammy caressing, an angry *Sextant* reader calls my description of my celebratory feeling with other women. You are scared of 'real' sex. Sex with men, therefore.

And before Ton goes off to Besançon for a few days because of a workers' occupation of the LIP factory, he gives both Anna and me a good go. As if then nothing will happen while he is away.

Anna and I eat Chinese food, with Petje, her daughter. The usual life, I almost leave it at that, think that perhaps it is just an ordinary experience, a deep friendship between women. Nothing more. In the restaurant we can't get the mood back. Petje is listless and fussy. Over her head we hardly have a chance to talk properly with each other. I say nothing when she has to go home to put Petje to bed. Kiss her on her cheek. I'll phone you tomorrow, says Anna. I go home, restless. Walk around in circles. Think, this is crazy. We are letting something slip through our fingers which has barely had the chance to live. But I also think about Ton, who will come back from France and will ask what went on. I don't like the feeling we have to prove something, don't want to give in to it. But I want to go to Anna, be with her, get back the feeling we had in Oisterwijk.

Around eleven I can't bear it any more. Ring up. Anna, I say, is it all right if I come to you? I want to be with you. Yes, she says, yes. I've been walking up and down here in the house for hours, restless, considering whether I should phone you.

When she opens the door and I see her warm open face, it is back again. She is wearing an unfamiliar blue shirt, her legs bare. Janis Joplin is on the record player. Freedom's just another word for nothin' left to lose. My memories of Femø, hers of the women's conferences which I didn't attend. She has put out two glasses of cognac, I taste cognac on her lips, which are soft.

217

Lucky you rang, she says. I don't know whether I would have dared. It was my turn to be brave, I say, you began.

The marriage bed in which I now lie for the first time. Anna's skin is soft and she smells like newly-born kittens. Suddenly it isn't so important what is real and what isn't only what we feel. Skin and skin. She is big and soft and round, round soft mother breasts against mine. I dive into her, into the dark of her hair, into her eyes, the wet of her cunt. It is so natural, so natural, as if I have done it for years. Her body nearly as familiar as mine. I know what she wants because I know what I want. She comes proudly, shamelessly, loudly. And then it is my turn. Anna, Anna, I say, why did we wait so long for this?

We can't stop caressing each other. After all, women do it so much better, we say to each other, satisfied, when we are almost falling asleep. How good it is to get back everything that you give. What a full feeling. What riches. Janis Joplin sings *Summertime*, the sounds and the warmth of Anna's body merge into each other until I feel I am fluid. I am overflowing, I say, when I again feel tears on my cheeks, feel them land on Anna's belly, on her neck. Sweat, cunt, tears. Wet, wet, we are streaming. Anna, I'm tripping, I whisper.

Now that we are over the barriers we don't understand what we were so tense about. It is so natural, so natural, what we do with each other, that I can't ever describe it. We forget it isn't allowed, are amazed over and over again at the looks people give us when we walk hand in hand to socialist party conferences, stand in bars against each other with our arms round each other's waist.

Warmth from working together, warmth which we take with us to bed. Together we set up a new group, socialist women who want to work on the relationship between feminism and socialism. Opposition from the leaders of the party – quibbles over space for meetings and that they don't want to pay for stamps because we aren't an 'open' group, that is to say we won't allow men – only persuade more women to join us. The women in the group aren't surprised Anna and I are lovers, that we sleep in the same bed when we are away with the group for the weekend.

218

Other people are. I had always thought that lesbians were no longer discriminated against in progressive circles, but now I notice the subtle differences that are less apparent to you if you have always been heterosexual. I write articles about it in magazines, because I am proud of Anna and me and because I want to share our warmth, want to say how ordinary it is. Furious letters from men. A few anxious ones from women. Advice about not being so open about it, that it hurts the women's movement, imagine if everyone started thinking that it is made up only of lesbians? I didn't say that, I am describing *my* experiences which have something to do with feminism, because without the women's movement it would never have been possible. If you wish, I reply to them, you can write a declaration about the pure heterosexuality of the majority of the women in the movement. Quickly, before it ceases to be true.

People like you shouldn't be allowed to write about contraception and sexuality, say the letters to me. You are one-sided – as if heterosexuals aren't. When I write something about my difficulty with motherhood I get letters saying, naturally, lesbians can't be good mothers. When I write about men's liberation I hear I'm not allowed to write about that because am I not a lesbian and therefore a man-hater? And I explain again and again that being a lesbian is not the same as hating men but is about choosing for women. Heterosexual women have far more reason to hate men because they are still dependent on them.

When I notice how pacified people are when I say I still make love to Ton too, I don't say it any more. Refuse to be approved because I also have a relationship with a man. And see them thinking: as long as it is just an excursion, a variation, this making love to a woman, it is progressive. The aggression comes only after you let it be seen that you no longer need men. A direct attack on male privileges, all their unconscious fears now realised, precisely what they were afraid of. Their own superfluousness demonstrated. And they have no other choice but to look for those women who haven't yet made that discovery, or to take care they offer us just as much as women do and become equally worthy partners.

And over and over I explain. That what Anna and I experience

219

with each other is not an accidental preference, because we find cunt nicer, but that it has to do with emotions, with recognising each other, with living in the same world and speaking the same language. Ordinary, as ordinary as bread.

And I see, looking back, where my own fear of homosexuality came from. The fear of not being approved of, not being considered nice, not able to join in any more. I have to defend myself against the suspicions of the people around me that I make love to Anna because I am frustrated, or too ugly to get a man. That it is a second choice because of a chance bad marriage that didn't turn out well.

A bad case of fear of lust, the We-Want-to-Know doctor calls me, who, without having seen me, refuses to debate openly with me. *What* asks my friend Herma angrily. Fear of lust? I can hear Anja's orgasms right over on the Keisersgracht! I can't be bothered to defend myself anymore.

A party. Couples dancing loose, not holding each other. I dance with Anna. A tall man keeps on dancing between us. I push him away, but he comes back. Then I understand what he is thinking: Anna and I are dancing *alone*.

And Ton is jealous. He sees how much more easily Anna and I get on together than we ever did with him. Not only the hours of celebratory fucking in the middle of the night, but working together. I don't have to explain to Anna what I am doing. And I move more easily into her life, shop with her in the shopping centre with Petje on the back of the bike, go with her to buy Esther a pair of trousers. Esther who asked us not to hold each other when her friends are around. That her father had a girlfriend she could defend, but her mother. . . . We cook a meal together, exchange recipes. And Armin belongs with us now, while he felt completely outside the relationship with Ton.

I sleep at Ton and Anna's house. But Ton can't sleep on the sofa if Anna and I are lying in the marriage bed, he feels excluded. We take him maternally into the bed which is actually not big enough for three people, let alone when Petje also sneaks in the next morning and the fat cat jumps off the cupboard onto it.

220

The three of us make love. it works on one occasion when Ton and Anna celebrate their wedding anniversary while I babysit and the three of us continue the celebration when they return. My new room in the commune, my mattress with the green sheets, between the boxes and piles of books and tins of paint. Moonlight and street light and reflections of the Amstel on our bodies, the electricity isn't switched on yet. Ton makes love to Anna and I make love to Ton and Anna and I make love. I am touched to see them, to be close to them. Ton is pacified; it isn't something mystical between Anna and me, but ordinary, ordinary.

But we don't do it often, the three of us making love together. Not only because of all the arms and legs in bed, or because Ton has to divide his exhaustible attention so neatly between the two of us, but because I have such a different relationship with Ton than with Anna and when he is present I can't talk to her like we do in our way.

At Christmas we rent a farmhouse and sit peacefully with all our children round the fire sewing and reading. In turn Ton and I sleep in the double bed, or Anna and I, or Anna and Ton. The third one gets the children up and makes breakfast. Who are you going to sleep with, says Petje, who is not surprised at anything, with Ton or with Anna? Or with the cat? Or by yourself?

A socialist feminist conference in London. Anna and I go there together for the first time. Ton is jealous and we arrange that afterwards I will go with him to London for a weekend.

London, where so many pieces of my past lie. My first big women's conference, two thousand women, I am dazzled by it. Touched by emotion when I see how the Free Women from the Spanish civil war who live in exile in London come into contact for the first time with the newly-formed illegal group of Spanish feminists. The grey-haired woman next to me wipes away her tears and tells me what it means to her. That now, after years, the work which she began at that time is again continuing. Consternation when photographs are taken. Spanish women protest because they could be put in prison if it became known that they were at a feminist conference.

And at night one of the women with whom we are staying makes a suicide attempt. She weeps, broken hearted because a woman has left her. And suddenly we notice that she is quiet, that she has swallowed a whole bottle of pills. Lemme sleep, she mumbles, and won't answer when we ask her if she wants to die or not. We lift her unwilling body up, make her vomit with salt water, and, a spoon down her throat. Her slippery body is threatening to evade us when we stop for a moment and she passes out again. We'll have to ring a hospital, says Sue, with whom we are staying. And she tells us what it will mean. Police and an investigation. The woman is lesbian and has a child whom she will surely lose if it becomes known that she has made a suicide attempt. But we can't let her lie there, take the risk that she hasn't vomited up all the pills. At four in the morning they come to fetch her with an ambulance. We stay up, waiting for the police, phoning the hospital every hour to hear if she is still alive; the doctors don't want to tell us because we aren't relatives.

Dominique went with us to the conference, the singer who, with her dark, deep voice, sang for us at the first Netherlands women's conference. There I sat close to Sara and looked at the white face of the women around us, pale with emotion and the feeling that something very important was happening at that moment, the beginning of something – Dominique sings now in the drab kitchen at Sue's house while we sit waiting for the police, the same songs.

And suddenly I get a flash of Sara who has been dead some time, died completely alone after she had tidied her room, put on clean clothes and written a farewell letter to tell us it wasn't our fault. That she just couldn't go on, could not endure the same pain over again. That she just didn't want to. And while Dominique sings, I mourn for Sara, which I couldn't do at the sterile cremation her parents had organised. They hadn't invited us and denied that Sara had chosen her own death. Saw us as the guilty parties. Why is Sara dead and not I?

The woman lives.

I can now give London as a present to Anna. I show her my old haunts, the theatres, the moving toy animals in the magic shop in Tottenham Court Road, which have been in the window for ten years getting dustier and dirtier. Buying presents for Ton and Petje and Esther and Armin. Wandering through the city. Forgetting once more that it is madness to walk hand in hand. And making love quietly in the dark on a blanket on the bare wooden floor between sleeping women. A relationship so ordinary that I almost forget it's unusual. Is that why I don't notice that Anna sometimes has difficulty, feeling I am theoretically ahead of her, that my English is better, that I have studied while she postponed her own development so she could look after Ton and the children?

A few weeks later when I am with Ton it is quite different, so much less relaxed. I can't wander hand in hand without asking myself what we are doing. We don't have the women's movement in common. We make plans. My haunts in London suddenly look banal, not interesting enough to let him see them. We sleep in an hotel instead of with an English woman friend.

We drive in a rented car through the docklands, extended re-development areas, empty storage depots, abandoned, derelict houses, then suddenly blocks of new loveless flats, stuck in the emptiness. And then again miles of nothing, hoardings, broken-down houses. Another world, desolate, and I see no reason to be cheerful. The pubs in the area are empty, or full of broken, drunk old people. On the boat back Ton, for the first time, can't make love and I cry, feeling we are at the end of something, that we have lost each other somewhere on the way.

Gordes 13

Not yet come on. For days I have felt my belly rumble, but I am paying so much attention to *whether* I feel anything that it could just as well be imagination.

Again the age-old panic, pregnant. I think of the time when I was almost about to leave Toni and thought that I was pregnant. The certainty that then I couldn't leave him. I didn't even know at that time how to get an abortion.

The panic is irrational. I don't have to have a child if I don't want to. Abortion is one of the few experiences I haven't had. It is not as difficult as it once was, and I have worked with others to make this so. I shouldn't be afraid.

The abortion demonstration was the biggest women's demonstration since the contemporary women's movement began. It is pouring with rain the whole time of the march, but everyone is happy. Thousands of women, hands linked, singing. I feel so much more at home than at all the demonstrations where I just got to tag along. This one is ours. We have succeeded in getting the communist women to participate and the lesbians. Men have joined us. I recognise one from gay liberation. There are women in smart coats who have never been on a demonstration before. They listen, unfamiliar with the abortion song – 'There is a murderous conspiracy of church and capital' – then join in hesitantly. Liberal party women walk with us, but don't sing. I constantly see more women friends. A great reunion. An and Eric and Hanneke, arm in arm. We pass the Right to Life people with their filthy pictures of pieces of foetus. As if anyone on the march would dream of having an abortion for her own pleasure. As if it isn't always terrible when it's necessary.

Selma is beautiful and strong – how can you be anything but

a feminist when you see how those fat men decided about our wombs. Lenie screams behind the microphone, so much more self-confident than on the mornings when she haltingly practised her long Social Academy sentences. She is from Brabant, the Catholic South, with her soft 'g'. Her eyes shine under her wet hair, the rain dripping down her face, she screams about the knitting needles and being tied onto the back of a motor bike and driven over the cobbled streets. About the hypocrisy of the catholic gentlemen who will never know what it is for a girl to give up her future because of an unwanted child.

In the distance, Anna, in an unfamiliar blue cap. Far away. I can hardly imagine she is the Anna over whom I had so much pain. That strange unfamiliar woman with her round face.

At night in the tent I dream I am pregnant, not by Hans, but by the last man who still wanted to marry me. A colleague of Ton's, but not a friend. I found him attractive although we would clearly have got into arguments as soon as we talked about politics. Too much of a social democrat. He wanted a child and knew me from the time when Armin was little and he was married. And one way or another had it in his head that he would have liked to be a father to Armin, to make a child with me. Amazed when I tell him about Ton – I thought there was so much gossip in the political world that he would surely know. I told him I was by definition unmarriageable. That I never wanted to be a housewife again. Never want to be a wife of a politician, look at Anna. And that having children was out for me. Not that whole thing over again, the leaden responsiblity which I would have to bear whether I was married or unmarried.

But I dream of him at night. A deal which seems so simple. I have a child for him. I walk out of the taxi, the baby, a girl who is called Sara, wrapped in a yellow blanket and I ring his doorbell. He is not surprised but I see tears in his eyes and I arrange with him that I will live with him for one day a week to see my daughter. It was simple in my dream. A good feeling to make a child for someone who wanted one so badly.

And when I am awake I think about it and it doesn't even seem absurd. Why shouldn't it be possible? Why must people live in

225

sets of two with each other? Why should I have to give up half of my self for fifteen years in order to have a child? Why should I live with someone with whom I would surely fight?

But it is a dream. I would still like to have a child. I become warm when I see new-born babies. I get broody when the cat has kittens – but I know only too well what it means, and Armin is nearly grown up. So much guilt about how I have failed him. And on top of that the man was politically on the wrong side. I don't see myself getting out of a car with such a present for him now, even if it were possible.

Then it will have to be an abortion, even though I know I will find it sad. No guilt feelings. Guilt feelings are what you experience when you have a child and constantly feel inadequate.

After the euphoria

After the euphoria of so much solidarity among women, disillusion must surely follow.

Andreas Burnier, once the mother of the movement, becomes more and more publicly right-wing. It is increasingly difficult to feel we are in the same movement. When we are both asked to speak at a forum, she refuses to speak on the same platform with me because she has heard that I am a socialist. And therefore not feminist. On the same morning on which I receive a copy of her letter, there is another letter from a communist party member who is waging a campaign to kick me off of the *Sextant* magazine. Because I am a feminist. And therefore not a socialist.

Arguments over demonstrations. Differences come to the surface. One of the women suggests street demos on Mother's Day. I don't believe in them so strongly, only find them useful to attract attention and Dolle Mina did that long ago. I argue that we should work inside unions and socialist groups, inside the work places. Liberal take-over, shouts Helmi. You are participating in the system, you should keep outside it. As if we aren't outside it already, I say, as if anyone notices if we don't participate.

That is just a rationalisation because you don't dare go on the streets, Helmi accuses me. I become angry because I *am* scared, remember too well the aggression when I carried a placard for the Black Panther party across the Rokin and men hissed at me that I obviously wanted to be fucked by blacks. But it is not because of my fear, which I would gladly overcome if it were necessary. Helmi calls anything theoretical that isn't action. I can't explain what my alternative is, we aren't yet far enough ahead, the difficult, much less spectacular, work inside unions and universities and in courses with housewives is hardly off the ground. We do not agree. And then the distrust in my second women's group. Why do you write for the paper, I am asked. Because I reach women that way who don't read *The Women's Paper*. Do you get money for it? asks someone severely. Yes, I say, it's work. As long as I find it so hard to stay alive, I think they should pay me. And *The Women's Paper* then? someone asks, the women on that work too and they don't get paid. I am condemned. Corrupt. You use the ideas of the movement, it is said. You make a career on the backs of women.

I lie sleepless in bed and fret. Hold long debates in my head in order to defend myself. I am not paid for the ideas because the ideas belong to no one. I am paid for the technical work of putting ideas into language, setting words down in a line, typing. The voices in my head argue against me. If an unknown journalist suddenly became famous because of some book or other on feminism, would I not then be angry? But I am an active feminist, not a journalist. What is the difference?

And next time the discussion group meets I come back to it, where are the boundaries of corruption? Annegien earns a lot of money by assisting at abortions, isn't that corrupt? Helena has a good job in education where she anxiously keeps her mouth shut about feminism and writes fierce pieces anonymously for *The Women's Paper* in her free time, but doesn't get paid for them, isn't that corrupt? Am I corrupt because I have at last succeeded in combining my work and my politics just a little? We can't agree. I go home fed up, feel betrayed, bitter. If the women's movement oppresses me so much in my attempts to become big and strong and to earn a living in a way that is also useful, what is it worth to me? Women from the Women's House react coldly towards me when I am with them. Because I put myself too much in the limelight. I say they are right and that I won't give any more interviews, or lectures, won't pretend to represent the whole movement. Then, a few days later, I am invited by those same women to give a lecture in the Women's House because someone has dropped out and they know I talk easily. No, I say crossly, I am not supposed to be so much in the limelight, remember? And do it anyway.

The time of Purple September. The lesbian separatists. Confusion and anger. Divisive, they would be called by the left, but in the women's movement you don't say such things. Purple September women put up sensible subjects for discussion like our heterosexual conditioning and how far it is used to keep our oppression going. I recognise much of what they say. I know only too well my own fear of losing society's approval, the fear of having to live without a man which for years kept me from standing up for myself and other women. And now?

But the alternative, a hierarchy where women who only make love to women are *more* feminist than their sisters? The inquisition, the need to prove that we have nothing to do with the patriarchy in any way? And I see how one of them radiantly embraces an old male friend when no one is around, then suddenly snubs him when she comes into the pub with her women friends. As if women become feminists by having a pistol shoved at them. As if we aren't struggling against women having to comply with prescribed roles, stereotypes.

. And the anger towards me comes from both sides, because in their eyes I belong to the despicable type who experiment with women but don't dare accept the consequences because I don't want to cut off contact with the men I still like.

I don't count because I am a junior. I do make love to one woman, but I'm not yet a senior: I still make love to one man.

I can't be a teacher. I can't convert others by preaching the gospel.

One day I walk unsuspectingly into the Women's House and am confronted with about twenty to thirty black men who stand in the passage and hiss things at me like baby, you want it too?

What's going on? I ask, upset. But one of the women pulls me into the room next to the passage where a group of women stand, talking anxiously and loudly, some of them staring white-faced in front of them. A trick played on us by the council, who have always been against us because they think the house we squatted is too big for us. And one of the officials, from the department dealing with young people, a woman goddammit, who hates us for some inexplicable reason, has sent a group of black men from Suriname to us. When one of the women talks to the men the picture becomes clearer. For months they have been promised a place where they can start a club for Surinamers, and while they become angrier they keep on hearing over and over that there is nothing available for them. Until they threaten to riot and the woman from the Youth Department thought of this nice plan to house the group in the upper story of the Women's House and said to them, go and talk to the women. They want a house, send two Suriname women to us who, once they are inside, open the door for the men who are waiting round the corner and then quickly take to their heels.

We try to talk to them, but there is nothing to talk about, in their eyes we are yet another club of whites trying to do them down and when one of the women generously tries to explain that women don't have an easy time in this society either, raucous laughter breaks out. Women do nothing but lie on their backs, says one. Women ought only to lie on their backs, says another, and the women who need to go to the toilet have to run the gauntlet of hands that want to pinch their bums, and get obscene remarks whispered in their ears.

We telephone the council and the official says innocently that she thought the two groups would be able to get used to each other. But they are men, shouts someone from the Women's House, and this is a women's house, that's what it's all about. They are Suriname men though, says the official, aren't they also oppressed, just like you? Doesn't that give you something in common?

Confusion. We have telephoned a lot of women and around one hundred have come in dribs and drabs. Must we fight and put them out? we ask each other. Have they got knives? We have seen one of them playing threateningly with a knife. Telephone the police? Can we do that, set the police onto a group whom we believe are right to be angry, although not, as it happens, with us?

But when the police are called they do nothing, they say they have to wait for orders from the mayor, and he says it's nothing to do with him. We ring Lammers a high official, who is ultimately responsible, and threaten an enormous fight. Lammers comes. I phone Ton, who is also an official, ask if he will come round because I don't trust the kind of double-dealing that Lammers gets into to save himself from difficult situations. We need to negotiate. Three representatives from the Surinamers and three from the Women's House, says Lammers, I can't talk to a hundred women. Who is in charge? No one is in charge, we say. Oh yes, says Lammers, this is a listed organisation and so you must have a management committee. We look at each other. Then the women who have already negotiated with the council should talk. The women from Purple September are furious. We join in their power games, they shout, we are not represented by a set of women who negotiate with the council. What do you want then? we ask. Let Lammers piss off or talk with all of us. He won't do that, we say, and we may have the men in the house for weeks if we don't. Negotiations take place. The police arrive, grinning men who think it is beautiful, who hate black men just as much as the lesbians they expect to meet here. They stand grinning in the passage and make filthy remarks.

The Surinamers say they won't leave the house until they are given another place. Ton intervenes and suggests another place is found that same night, it should be possible. Lammers gives in. Ton comes to where I stand waiting in the passage. It will be all right, he says. Who has brought that sickening little man here? asks one of the Purple September women. Oh I'm going, says Ton, with all his hackles rising. I asked him, I say, I consulted with a few women and if you get Lammers here you

230

need to take care there is someone present who will see he keeps his promises. But no one is listening any more. I am one of the deviants who has brought a man into the Women's House and I will hear a lot about it in the future.

Then Lammers produces a place and we are only waiting for a key. Lammers now behaves like the big saviour of the Women's House, as if he couldn't have given the Surinamers the place long ago. They have already waited nine months.

After the last men have left, the fight starts in earnest. The handful of Purple September women accuse the rest of corruption and male power trips. How would you have solved it? I ask, but they don't have an answer to that and that isn't what it's about, they say, it's a matter of principle. Whether you participate in the system, they say.

We all participate in the system, I say. What do you live on? Welfare or wage? Where do you buy your bread? At a feminist baker? If that is corruption then surely we are all corrupt, you just as much as us? And an older woman begins to cry and says she doesn't even know if she is lesbian because her husband has been dead for twenty years and ought she not to have murdered him with her own hands, would she then have been less corrupt. I feel sick at the performance. These women accuse others of power trips while they terrorise everyone present. Which they can do because there isn't a single structure in the Women's House, all meetings are open and decisions are taken by everyone who wants to be involved. I go home, disturbed at gut level, and hide myself in Anna's breasts.

But when Anna and I attend a conference of the Women's Association and hear that a satirical song has been made up about the Purple September with verses ridiculing lesbians we become angry. Walk up to Hedy to warn her that it isn't on, that you can't use an open conference to poke fun at other feminist groups. That it is a cheap way to make yourself popular, putting yourself up against the most extreme group. But Hedy refuses to take the song out of the cabaret and says she doesn't agree with the words either, but thinks the tune is sexy. And so Anna and I and a handful of women boo the song and some men also present give way, embarrassed. They think there are a whole

231

lot of Purple September women here, instead of just three or four, I whisper to Anna, and we walk satisfied and giggling through the pack of progressive ladies and gentlemen who try stiffly to look tolerantly at us.

The Purple September women entrench themselves in the upstairs rooms of the Women's House and conspire. They use their energy to write angry letters about other feminists. Divisions form right across friendship groups. Sisters won't talk to each other because one is 'from above' the other 'from below'. One group goes backwards and forwards between them. I don't go in during this time, don't want to attend senseless discussions which use up the energy for all the work that needs to be done. I wait until the Purple September women, as expected, have thinned out their own membership by accusing each other of corruption, because they are not clear themselves who the enemy is. One after the other the women come down again, leaving the hard core behind them without anything to do. Slowly the Women's House becomes the Women's House once again, as it was meant to be. Open to all women, gay women and socialist women and non-aligned women who come to take courses there.

I have learned *one* thing through all this trouble with my men. That the way I live isn't good, that the way I live with Armin depends too much on all my experiments. Division of property is too traumatic to repeat too often. When I have broken up with someone is the precise time I need warmth and friends around me. And Armin is too vulnerable, too dependent on the amount of attention I can give him, because he has only me.

So, after six years, I move out of the one and a half rooms in the Pijp, the working-class district. I need stability and more people around me.

Yet it was no solution to rent a house with four other women. Armin was the only child, if someone looked after him on the weekend I still had to say thank you over and over again. We lived past each other, did not succeed in forming some kind of community, in the house. There was jealousy, people waited until you came to them, bitterness which I didn't share. I got on best with Carla, but she lived so differently from me, came pedalling in at eight in the morning, fetched her last bottle of beer from the grocer who was just opening when I stood on the doorstep waiting to go to work.

This was the group of women with whom I had been on holiday, four women and seven children. What we could do in the holidays ought to be possible in our ordinary lives, we said, and shortly after Armin and I joined them we found a house.

Messy meals with lots of screaming children, Sunday breakfasts. So much organisation needed to get all the children to bed on time, away from the television. House-meetings about the never-ending alterations and repairs. I felt at home in the beginning, in spite of the difficulty I had with all the children I didn't know and who all had different needs.

Fights, most of the children were boys, their powpowpow was never out of the atmosphere.

We decided that everyone had a day a week to collect the children, do the washing, cook the meal. Except for the children's meeting and the house-meeting the rest of the time is your own, we said. But in reality nothing happened like that. Fighting children had to be separated. After a month or so I noticed I felt guilty if a week passed and I hadn't eaten at home. Felt dreadful if Armin excitedly pulled down a washing line while I wasn't there, or refused to shower. But I think, persevere. Armin has been an only child for so long, I have been an independent woman for ages, we still need to get used to living with other people, it will turn out all right. And with Marianne, who joins us later, I can drink endless cups of coffee and gossip, with Truis I can hide in front of the television and chat while we pour each other sherry. Truis is the only one in the house who also likes good food and now and then we escape from the mashed potatoes and endives and meat balls – almost the only food the children like – and go out to eat, return home arm in arm, laughing from too much wine. The first argument in the house. It isn't easy to agree about a reasonable level of dirt-tolerance. I'm aware that I am the only one without the years of training as a housewife which the others, married women of long standing, have behind them. I am used to tidying up the mess in spurts. Not used to remembering to wipe down the gas cooker after every wash-up

233

really unmistakeable. Marianne is not a good housewife either, but she isn't blamed as much as me because I am a mother and she isn't.

It was such a fine ideal, living with women so different from each other in age, in background. But so much more difficult than I had thought when we knew each other only in the women's group and on holiday. There is a large part of my life I can't share with anyone in the house. If I want to succeed in the house I have to invest so much of myself there will be little left over to give to other people. And I will never lose the label of house slob. But for the first year I carry on trying. I want to carry on, and there are always times when I feel the experiment is succeeding. The Santa Claus evening with all the children. A peaceful afternoon drinking lemonade in the garden. One of the children with whom I unexpectedly make contact. Honest conversations where we tell each other what we find difficult.

Ton drowns in the world of politics. Now and then I still see him for an hour. And then he promises remorsefully, after his games have been found out, that the time for his relationships must come out of his political life. There is nothing now for him to hide behind, Anna doesn't hold him back.

Ton is jealous that Anna and I have much more time for each other. But he does nothing about it. Makes plans to work with me, for us to write articles together. Tries to trap me into working with him in the party, but I am wary of being an assistant in a party which will see me only as Ton's mistress, and I would have to neglect work with women. Nothing comes of the other plans.

I don't wait for him any more if he is hours late, but go to sleep. Don't even hear when he turns the key in the front door. Don't argue, but just refuse to wake up.

Don't you love me any more? asks Ton, who knew he was important to me as long as I created loud scenes.

I've had enough of this I say. There isn't any room for me next to that idiotic work you do. There isn't any place for Anna either, but she takes it because she hasn't any choice. What do you know about Anna's and my relationship, says Ton, stupidly forgetting that I am the one who regularly comforts Anna.

Ton, I say for the twenty-third or thirty-eighth time, you promise things you don't do. You keep me on a string. You want me to be available to you when it suits you, but you aren't prepared to be available when I need you. Therefore I don't need you any more.

Do you want just to throw away all the good things we have built up over the years? asks Ton. Just? I ask, for the forty-third time, just?

You are right, says Ton – also not for the first time. I must change my life, make more time for you two and for myself. But the party makes it so difficult for me, they want me to take up an important position. Why don't you just say no when you can't manage it, when you are torn? But who will do it then? asks Ton, if the party wants it. . . . It's up to you, Ton, I say. You know that you are losing me like this and if you don't look out you will lose Anna as well. You are right, darling, he says. Thank you for helping me make up my mind. I am now quite decided. I'll write a letter tomorrow that I can't take the position.

And the next day I read in the paper that he has made a statement about another party which he suddenly calls an ally, when six months ago he had strongly criticised them, and I understand that he is busy sucking up to them because he wants the job.

Anna and I sit on a step close to the Central Station, between her house and mine. I'll not leave you, says Anna, even if it is more difficult now that you have broken with Ton. And don't think I will accept the fact that he is trying to make a career, says Anna, daughter of a left-wing father, granddaughter of a left-wing grandfather. He will lose me too if he really does it, and I'll tell him too.

But I am sad, sad, almost inconsolable. Not about Ton, but for Anna, my friend, my sister. I am scared Ton won't give you the chance, I say softly. You can count on me, says Anna.

But I am proved right.

I'm not allowed to go to their house any more because Ton won't have it. When Anna comes to me and he has to look after the children, he disappears at night and comes home blind drunk at seven in the morning when the children are already awake. Anna is white and thinner than I have ever seen her. I feel pulled in all directions, she says. I can hardly go on, Ton with his scenes and Esther has difficulties at school and Petje whines, she is also feeling the tension. And in a week I have to do my entrance exams. Sometimes I think I am going crazy.

I try to comfort her. Arrange to go away with her with the women's group, so we can again be together peacefully, working and sleeping, Anna having time for herself.

Then she lets us know, just before we are about to leave, that she is staying at home. That she is too tired, the house needs cleaning, she has to study.

I feel dismayed and when I am home again I write her a letter. It can't go on like this. She can't go on always having to ask Ton's permission to go away. He will never make it easy for her because he simply doesn't want it, our relationship. He can't forbid it directly, considering all the girlfriends he himself has had behind her back, and therefore is finding other ways of sabotaging it.

Anna retreats for a few days, hides herself even from Ton. I sit at home and am sad and lonely. But at least have the feeling I have made a decision myself. Rather be without Anna than see our relationship go slowly through a mincing machine. I can't do all the work for Anna, I think. If she can't stand up to Ton then it won't succeed anyway.

But Anna returns, stronger and more determined, and says she wants to go on, that she will fight for our relationship. That she won't ask Ton's permission, but will do what she wants. And while we are talking she tells me of the other things she has been thinking about which she has never told me. How she is sometimes bothered by the feeling that we come from different worlds. How hurt she was by a remark I once made about the packet of bread she took to her work which I called proletarian. Sometimes she feels I look down on her because she is a housewife, because I am not one. As if I think I am better than her.

I am startled that I have noticed so little. It's stupid too that I haven't dared say anything to you, she says, because you can't know how you hurt me.

And I say it's true I sometimes find it hard to watch her make herself insignificant in front of Ton, that it annoys me she stays home for him, doesn't demand that he look after the children when we want to go away together.

You must accept, says Anna, that I am tired of fighting. Perhaps you are right, you are probably right, but it doesn't mean I can get it together to do something about it. You must leave me to fight it out with Ton on my own. I think I could, I say, if you didn't give me the feeling that you allow Ton to decide whether we can see each other. Because if you make us dependent on him, we will lose. He won't give us permission. And Anna says she will try, that she doesn't want to lose me, that I belong in her life. We celebrate our new happiness in the Women's House which is celebrating her first birthday with hundreds of women.

I feel we have come a whole lot further, more honest with each other now than when everything was still rose-coloured and idyllic.

We have survived the first scratch on the new car.

I love Anna.

I dare to trust her.

We had an arrangement to go on holiday together in France, my whole commune and Ton and Anna with the children. Now Ton won't go. Anna says bravely that she will go anyway, even if Ton doesn't want to. I look forward to it, a few weeks with Anna, without Ton always keeping an eye on us. But a week before we leave Anna says Ton is going with us after all.

Why, I say, scared.

I don't know, says Anna, but I can hardly forbid him, can I?

A difficult conversation with Ton in the pub. I can't break through his façade any more. Why are you coming with us to France? I ask. Because Anna and the children are going. I'm going with them, naturally, says Ton coldly. But I will be there too, I say. What do you have to do with it, says Ton, I'm just going on holiday with my family.

You are going to try to break up the relationship between Anna and me, I say. I don't need to break anything, says Ton. It will be clear that it isn't possible. Next to Anna's and my marriage there is no room for any other relationship, that was obviously why our relationship failed also.

I almost choke from suppressed anger, can't get a word out, speechless from so much hypocrisy. Ton always had his mistresses concurrent with his marriage, always left it to Anna to adapt herself. Ton now calls on holy matrimony when Anna, for the first time in her life, is the one who is having another relationship. I hate him as he sits there, gambling on his power position. The power he has to force Anna to choose between him and me, between two ways of living.

While Anna never made him choose.

I'm going, I say. I can't talk to you any more.

And I ring Anna, depressed and sick with anxious forebodings. Whatever happens in France, however fucked up it becomes, however difficult he makes it for us, we will in any event be together afterwards for ten days, just the two of us, in Femø without the children. Women among women. To recover, have time for each other without all these tensions. Not always having to talk about Ton and the situation. Be able to work out peacefully what we want to do with each other next.

I am a little pacified. Think that whatever happens in France, we'll find each other again in Femø.

Truis and I and a few of the children in France. Peaceful days while we wait for the others to come, until Anna and Ton arrive in the car. Truis and I are having a good time with each other. I like cooking, she likes eating well and she doesn't mind washing up while I hate it. In the commune there is a strict rule: everyone does everything, whether you like it or not, so that one person doesn't get all the plum jobs which get all the praise, another all the invisible work. My pleasure in cooking is almost lost in the commune, criticism when I buy too expensive food, the children

238

– unlike Armin who is used to eating everything – won't swallow anything with an unusual taste. But now we are having a good time, Truis and I, and I sigh and say I wish it could stay like this. I'm not looking forward to all the people in the tiny house which has no doors and where you can literally hear every conversation. Too many children. And when I think that Ton and Anna will soon be here, I get a pain in my stomach. The worst idea we have had for a long time, I say to Truis. The most stupid thing I could have done.

When they eventually come I am weepy and scratchy. Anna is too, after the drive. An argument on the first day when I lie on my bed upstairs and don't want to come down to celebrate the arrival of the family. Anna attacks me. Everyone in the whole house can hear and when I go downstairs I see Ton looking triumphant behind a straight face. And become even more depressed.

Anna and Ton settle into the house opposite, which is empty. Two stretchers next to each other and a camping table with two chairs. It annoys me. Now at last they have the chance to behave in the commune like two independent people. Anna always said she wanted that. And at the first opportunity they again play at being married, fall back on their established patterns.

Anna tries to divide her attention. Sleeps for one night in the big bed upstairs with me, the next with Ton in their little family place opposite. But Ton isn't about to make it easy for us. Stays sitting downstairs until twelve when Anna and I have gone up, knowing that every squeak can be heard and that we can hardly exchange a word without him hearing us. Sits behind us when we sit by the river. Walks behind us. Or walks around with such a long face that Anna can't help but go to pacify him.

Now and then we escape for a little. Take the car to Anduze where we shop, buy a bottle of cognac for the two of us. Buy old pictures in a dark little shop. We walk hand in hand, again forgetting that it is unusual. Eat pizza. After a little relaxation I can now eat again. But around one o'clock Anna becomes nervous and wants to go back.

At night we drink cognac in my bed upstairs, giggling like girls at boarding school, whispering and making love under the blankets, forgetting after a while that the lawful husband is sitting downstairs. You smell so lovely, I whisper to Anna. You are so soft, Anna whispers back.

Anna, my sister. I love her rounded shoulders, her mother's belly, even the blue veins on the backs of her knees.

Petje-petje. Anna's daughter. One of the few children I truly love. A little witch who knocks over tables to get exactly what she wants. With a radar for the weaknesses in the people around her. Looks inside one of the men's swimming trunks. My father's is bigger, she says, waits with shining eyes for his reaction.

Petje, my little sister. Her small naked body against my back when I swim across the river with her to pick flowers on the other side and to look for caterpillars. An easy eroticism, not yet destroyed by society. She grunts happily when I bend her little body to fit into mine in the water, shameless and yielding. Kiss, she says suddenly. I kiss her fragrant cheeks. No really kiss, she says, looking passionately into my eyes while she holds my head and her lips press on mine. Who is she imitating, Anna and me, Ton and me, Ton and Anna?

Ton won't leave us alone and one day everything explodes. I am sombre, hardly able to be cheerful. Tell me what's wrong, says Anna. And I say, I daren't be honest with you any more. I daren't say how difficult it is for me. I'm too scared that you will feel even more under pressure. Tell me anyway, says Anna. We must be able to stay honest with each other, otherwise what we have isn't worth having.

Then I burst out, the pent-up frustrations of the past days, why does she let herself be defined by Ton. Why doesn't she ever say to him that she wants to be alone with me. How can she stand it that he is phoning Amsterdam daily to save his career which is now at risk because the majority of the party have said that they don't want him in any leadership position. You said you wouldn't stand for it, I say, and yet you allow it all the same, and sit and listen. Is that the man you want to rule your life? I ask. Anna how can you stand it?

Anna sits with bowed head. I expected this, she says. I think that we should go away.

Which 'we' I burst out earnestly. 'We'? Naturally you mean the couple, the family. Do you remember that you came here because you wanted to be with *me?* Doesn't it occur to you that you could let Ton bear it for a change instead of me? Is it so obvious that I must suffer when it gets difficult. Anna, don't you differ even by a hair from all the men who dropped me when their wives didn't like it any more? Am I that for you too, a throwaway girlfriend for your free time? Don't you see that you are doing exactly what Ton wants?

And then Anna says softly and decidedly, then we should break with each other completely and I feel my whole body getting cold and everything becomes black in front of my eyes. Ton bangs on the door. He wants to come in. I'm coming, calls Anna.

I weep, I weep against Anna and say, Anna I can't let this happen. You can't leave me alone like this, Anna, not like this. Not like all the other times. Not you too. Anna you must help me. Even if it can't happen, even if we can't go on with each other, you can't leave me alone like this. Not you Anna. Please Anna, not like this. I fall asleep exhausted, next to her. Wake up in the grey morning light and look at her sleeping face and cry all over again.

I can't do anything more about it, says Anna. There is no solution. I can't let her go, such black abysmal panic at the thought that she will go away.

You must help me, Anna. If you leave me like this I'll hate you so much, we will never be able to do anything with each other again. Can't you help me? Can't you stay one day without Ton? You are the only one who can help me now.

OK, she says. I'll stay another day. I'll tell Ton to go ahead with the children.

But Ton doesn't approve, is much too scared that she will go back on her decision now that he has won, and she obeys and comes to tell me that she will leave the same afternoon. You see, I say, you see how you let him live your life, how you let him make your decisions?

The last few hours. The hottest time of the day. We wade through the river, help each other over rocks. Take off our clothes in Mialet and swim naked in a deep pool of cold water right next to the road. Siesta, no one passes by. My whole body aches now, it is as if I am tripping on pain. Everything I see engraves itself on my memory, the details of every rock, Anna's wet hair, the sun reflecting on the water. A few little fish shoot out ahead of us as we wade to the bank to fetch our clothes.

Pain. We sit in the shade of a chestnut tree. Ear-splitting cicadas. I am almost peaceful now. I am inside the pain of which I was so afraid. Nothing else can happen to me. It has happened already. And I tell her that I can't believe she will stay with Ton for long. That I can't believe she can so suddenly cut off her emotions.

I don't dare go on, whispers Anna. I have become scared of all the emotions. I am scared I won't be able to go back if I go on.

Scared of the depths, I say.

Yes, says Anna.

Right next to the corner where the car is waiting to take her, we say goodbye. Anna is suddenly in tears, sobs, doesn't want to let me go. I am, surprisingly, the one who comforts her, helps her.

Go then, go then, I say.

Gordes 14

We have used up our money. We have eaten too much, drunk too much. In a day or two we will have to go home. I don't mind.

The experiment, a holiday together, has failed. Or rather, it has succeeded: we now know exactly what we can't do with each other. The differences between us are as clear as daylight now, while they were not so clear in Amsterdam where we were diverted by our work, by other people.

We talk it over again. Hans, please stop trying so hard to do your best, I say to him. Let's stop trying so madly to be the perfect couple. Hans is depressed. He had, has so many expectations. I am much more accustomed by now to live without high expectations. What do you want then? he asks. I want to be one of your friends, I say. Not *the* woman friend, but *a* woman friend. One of the people you live with, like Marjan. That is worth so much, is so valuable.

Do you prefer never to have any long-standing relationship with men, asks Hans masochistically, ready to define my decision as ideological. How do I know that, I say. I don't know anything about relationships any more. I only know that I feel sucked dry. That there isn't enough space in it for me. But I left you alone yesterday for the whole day, and you were glad when I came back, you said so.

How difficult it is to make it clear. That this responsibility is just too heavy for me. That I can't bear being the cause of his depression. I am irritated if he asks how I liked the film when we are out. Asks where we should eat, what we should do tomorrow, should we go for a walk. But I can learn to be independent of you, protests Hans. But I don't want you to do your best to fit in with me, I reply. It won't be what you need. It isn't what I need.

The new breed of men. Men who feel attracted to feminists, who catch a glimpse of what we are doing, the warmth, the vitality of the women's movement, a new way of being together. I can understand it, but what are we to do with them. Men who look at us with a look which says, am I doing it right? Mirror image of myself fifteen years ago, looking up at a man, am I doing it right, I'm leaving you free, see, look, I'm not possessive, and meanwhile I put the whole responsibility for my happiness in his hands.

The new men who try so hard, who don't want to dominate, who can wait, who dare to be soft and to cry, I don't want to be responsible for them. Don't want their weight round my neck, next to the ballast of my own life which I can only just manage to carry. Don't want to put myself second again, direct all my energy to understanding someone else. I feel hard and severe when I tell Hans. Terribly unkind to let men who are doing their very best stand in the cold like this. But I can't go on any more. Being dependent myself is just as painful as having someone now dependent on me. Hans, I say, we are too unequal. We have such different histories. I can't take an unequal relationship any more. I can only have relationships with people from whom I can get as much as I give to them. I feel so old when I see where you are.

I am only two years younger than you, protests Hans.

Young man, I could be your mother, I say.

Once it is said, we are relieved. We are suddenly in a festive mood. Without the leaden pressure of sexual roles we can once again like each other a little, the old sympathy returns.

Let's let Armin and Manuel stuff themselves with French bread and coke and treat ourselves for the last time to an expensive meal, says Hans.

We drive to Apt. It is almost dinner time. Walking in the street we can hear subdued eating sounds, forks on plates, talking. A woman with a French loaf under her arm hurries home. After we have rejected two restaurants which are too touristy, we find the ideal place. White tablecloths on wobbly tables on a terrace between big pots with real and plastic flowers. Decayed bourgeoisie. No tourists, French people sitting chewing with an inward looking gaze, burping discreetly. A menu on which we understand nothing. We order with our fingers crossed.

Hans is suddenly cheerful, can't stop talking. His childhood, his parents, his marriage, his girlfriend. About how he just thought I was nice when we first began to make love, nothing very special. Then the warnings. Are you having a scene with Anja, well then, you'd better look out. And Marjan said, be careful, Anja is ahead of everyone. And then Hans thought, jesus I'd better watch it, will she find me interesting enough, she'll be bored with me soon. The spirals of uncertainty, the old ones, his parents always taught him he was inadequate, however hard he tried. Calvinism. Mother isn't angry, mother is sad and it is for your own good. He could never live up to their expectations.

244

While I kept on saying, be natural, I'm not looking for stimulation, I'm over-stimulated already. I don't need to be amused. I'm looking for peace, something simple. I'm not the myth I'm made out to be.

While Hans sits chatting something of the old feeling returns. He lets his steak grow cold, while I have been given a piece of toast on my plate and on it a little bird which seems to have been grilled in the middle of its death agony. Deliberate whether I can eat it. Decide that it isn't worse than the square unrecognisable pieces of meat that after all once grazed, coupled. I slide the head and feet under a piece of lettuce, the same as I do with trout if they look at me from my plate.

You see, says Hans, when we aren't acting like idiots, we get on very well.

I still have to wash my prick, says Hans at night when we begin to make love. The time is past when we are ashamed of the prosaic side of our bodies. I don't slide my diaphragm into my cunt secretly in the bathroom any more. Have stopped worrying whether he thinks my body is beautiful enough. Tracks across each other's bodies, familiar, we don't need to ask any more, do you like it like this, or like this. With Hans I felt at home immediately. I didn't have to swallow three times before I could make it clear to him what my favourite way of making love is. Hans, already broken in by his last girlfriend, also a feminist, who never faked orgasm. Mouth on my cunt, I always come more quickly than he does, then his turn when I don't have to concentrate on the waves that ebb away so easily when I have to think too much about someone else's pleasure. I feel him full inside me, all attention now on him, almost a second orgasm when I wave with him.

Cold turkey

Kicking the habit. Waves of pain that keep on coming back. Deceptive calm in between, waiting for a new attack that can suddenly set in. During which I am defenceless, paralysed, carried away in a whirlpool, can't even scream or cry. Come up again, gasp for breath as if I have nearly drowned. Think only in minutes then in hours. If I can live through this day, hour by hour, just manage that after the first attack. I am concentrating only on survival, not giving in to all my instincts which tell me that it has been enough, that I want to die. The wrong movie, the same movie, I want to get out. But I force myself to live, first in hours later through days. Make the gestures that belong with living. I eat, talk mechanically, try to deaden the pain in the hot sun until I am dizzy, burnt, reduced to a body.

There is a glass wall between me and the other people. Truis strokes my head and says, that's life. Paulien says, you just make too high demands on a relationship. Marie says, you want too much, and then switches to the housekeeping, that I should pull my weight more in the commune, that I leave the cups dirty too often, that I haven't put the children to bed lately. Peter says nothing.

I try to behave normally. To remember to wash up often enough. Overcome my fear of doing the shopping in the town where every shop reminds me of Anna, behind each corner a fresh attack lies in wait for me. I talk with the other people who visit, even hear myself laughing. Take part in the children's party on the roof where I keep myself busy with the salads and with painting the children's faces and bodies.

Only Armin occasionally penetrates the glass wall when he

brings me a glass of wine when I am paralysed, nailed down, not able to move, lying on my bed.

Selma and Jeanne visit. I fall relieved into their arms. Women friends with whom I can talk, who will encourage me to talk, with whom I don't need to pretend. When they come in I am washing up. I'll do it later, I say to the others, I want to go outside with them. See the poisonous look from Paulien, the confirmation that again it is me who will leave the dishes.

Pain, always recurring, when I see Petje's toys which she has forgotten. I read Anna's superficial holiday letter with trembling, with shaking hands. The first attack of anger. It betrays what we had.

And just before we leave I write her the letter which has to be the last. That I hate her. Not Ton, with whom I have finished. For whom I still feel only a mixture of sympathy and pity when I see how he destroys himself in spite of his frantic politicking. Hate for Anna who fled like a coward, who deprived me of the chance to fight it out with her.

I write to her that I don't want to see her ever again, to work with her ever again.

I receive her reply, when I am back in Amsterdam and have tried once to talk with her, tried to find a way not to leave each other completely in the lurch. We make an agreement to see each other once more when I have returned from the femsoc course. But in the meantime she gets my last furious letter from France, which I hadn't warned her about emphatically enough, and she doesn't dare to see me any more. Too scared of my fierceness.

Femø, where I come to recover. To find answers to all the questions I'm stuck with. Feminism, which suddenly seems to me impossible, abstract. The reality is that women can destroy each other too. What are we doing it for then, all that work? What does it mean then, solidarity?

But what other alternative is there to live for?

I can talk and cry with the women on Femø. Better than with the women in the commune. There are more women like me, who walk around with old wounds, with pain which will never again quite disappear.

247

Relationships with women are so much more vulnerable, so much more under pressure from society.

Surely it doesn't surprise you that Anna didn't choose you, say my women friends. Surely it wasn't a choice between Ton and you, it was a choice between two completely different ways of life. If she had chosen you, what then? Would you have lived together? No, I say. No, I could never have taken Ton's place. Wouldn't have wanted to. And what would that have meant for Anna, alone with her children, earning her own money, without protection?

And I see, slowly, how unequal our relationship was. Anna, who was for me a warm place, someone who was always there even though I might not see her for a week. A fixed point in my life which is otherwise such a turmoil, with so many uncertainties and changes. She was almost a mother to me. I trusted her because she was a woman, because I didn't think that women would be able to hurt each other as men hurt women. Because I trusted her so much, the pain was so much worse. And I feel the anger flare up in me again when I tell the women around me how it began. How she comforted me in my loneliness, how indignant she was at all the vile experiences I had already had with men and now she herself . . . I feel so betrayed, I say.

And what was I for Anna? Anna who lived securely for years, the unchangeable nature of her existence frightening. For her I was a new life. When we walked hand in hand she was young again, she was Anna, not just the mother of her children, the wife of her husband. She gained strength from me, stuck up for herself again. Bought a real desk for herself instead of the little table in the corner of the bedroom. Demanded that Ton be with the children more, do more of the housework. Looked for work, began a new training.

I was something new for her, something exciting. Until she was at last set on her new course and didn't need me any more. Ballast. One too many duties, next to all her other duties.

I understand it better now, but the rage is there still, stays.

Femø. I recover slowly. Open up again to the women around me. Two women lovers sleep next to me. In the morning I wake to the sound of soft kisses and soft whispering. Now and then a caress in my direction, they have enough to share, they have more than enough. The women from my femsoc group, with whom I celebrate, dance, run into the water. The arguments in which, slowly, I feel myself involved.

Two hundred and fifty women are a lot. There is disagreement about the desired degree of anarchy. Every day big pots of food are cooked and put outside where the women press around them with their plates. Sometimes latecomers find empty pots. We talk about how the meal should be distributed. Can't the women who cooked it divide it up and make sure there is enough for everyone. But there is another group of women who don't agree, who think women should be able to see for themselves that they shouldn't take too much, and that others have enough food, without it being necessary to have leaders to ensure that will happen.

The Italian women have an argument in the middle of the night when a couple of them plan to cook a big pot of spaghetti for all the women who haven't had enough to eat that day, whereupon other women become angry and say that the contradictions are disguised by such an action, instead of being argued out.

The German women put on a beautiful play. A lecture on heterosexuality. That heterosexual people can't help it that they are like that. That it isn't a sickness but a normal variation. That we should therefore accept heterosexuals. One question from the audience at the end of the lecture. Can you perhaps explain its cause, heterosexuality? And is it curable? And is it really just as nice as when women make love? And how do they *do* it actually?

Discussions on what it means to love women. The women who were already lesbian, the women who have become so because the dividing line between working with each other and loving each other becomes steadily less defined, steadily more absurd. The first women who were brave enough to come out. They now feel let down by women who will experiment with other women but still don't dare take up a public position. The more there are who are not ashamed, the easier it becomes for all of us, they say, and I believe they are right.

But that still isn't everything, I say. Feminism isn't only making love with women. I can dare to be publicly lesbian. But that isn't something you can *demand* from women. And it is easy to say the personal is political, therefore if we want to have a pure feminist life we have done our political duty. Capitalism isn't only a male conspiracy. It won't disappear by itself, by shrugging your shoulders and pretending that you have nothing to do with it. And where is your solidarity with the women with children and without education who can't afford to go and sit on an island?

Nilde, beautiful, big, strong Nilde, who on the evening the Italian women were to come with a discussion programme says she has prepared nothing, has had enough of talking, talking, talking and she says in broken English, I came here for affection, I want to have affection. I want to have affection, I want to give affection, I don't want it that our headz are for womenz and our bodies for the menz. I want bodypractice with womenz, and she calls up the women whom she has wanted to touch all day and didn't dare and they embrace each other in the middle of the big circle while the other women rejoicing, hugging each other, begin to make love to each other. Something snaps inside me, a wave of warmth with which I overflow. I can feel again. Filled with emotion, I grab the two women sitting next to me and don't mind it when after that a massive argument breaks out. Women shout that this is exactly the way men solve problems, fuck it away, and then other women get angry and scream that it is exactly a male way always to have to discuss things and other women shout that they didn't come to a fucking women's camp to be told they are like men goddammit. Chaos, it is no longer possible to draw a line. Two hundred and fifty screaming women, exactly what everyone thinks that women do together when there are no men there to give leadership. But I am still happy and when half of the women stamp off to continue the discussion in another tent, there is enough room to dance. The music starts. Janis Joplin. Freedom's just another word for nothin' left to lose.

Make love or war? asks the high priestess of the lesbian front. We dance. On Femø we are two women, not two feminists of different persuasions, she a radical lesbian, I a feminist socialist. And the next day she sends a woman to me who says that I must

250

lie on the grass and pretend I am ill and then the high priestess comes across wailing like an ambulance with a bottle of gin and a bunch of flowers, to visit.

Surely I still belong here, I think, in spite of political contradictions. I need islands to become strong, to recover, but they can never be solutions on their own. In the self-help health group I ask for my coil to be taken out. For the past six months I have made love only to a woman and I can't get pregnant from that. And I don't think I will easily start something with a man. Nancy from the self-help group takes it out, ceremonially. The women around me rejoice. That's good says the high priestess. Are you sure? asks one of my friends, that you don't ever want to sleep with men again? No, I say, I know today for sure, but tomorrow is tomorrow. How can I predict the future? When I remember everything that has happened to me which I never expected.

Jill Johnston is on the island. A meeting with all the women writers and feminist journalists. About problems we all have and for which none of us has solutions. Sophie doesn't want to write independently any more about the movement, as if she doesn't belong there. But if she writes showing her involvement, she knows that she will no longer be allowed to write any other political articles. Let alone if she writes that she has become a lesbian. I do write showing my involvement, but at the same time notice that it is still threatening to many women. Jill wrote articles for nothing for years, living below the breadline until she became famous and now can pay her way with her writing, but knows she won't get any other work. A Danish woman who, like me, lives in a minority language area, knows that you can never live off it unless you write best sellers, and why should you? There are conflicts within the movement, some women say you shouldn't get paid for your work, which means that in addition to a lousy job you have to work in your free time and can never do all you want to. And I let myself be paid, but feel guilty.

The rage is still there. Every morning I wake, tossing in my bed, thinking bitch, dirty traitor, but I have my feminism back. I want to go back home, to work.

251

A busy year. Selma and Joyce and I work nights through on our book of marxist/feminist articles. We leave rows of bottles, empty of the white wine which we needed to help us through. Harvest from two years' research. Slowly a theory emerges which says something. My excitement when, in lucid moments, I suddenly see connections. Understand that the split between political and personal is a symptom of capitalism also. That the division between man and woman has to do with the division between production and reproduction. And our emotional qualities are linked to our economic position. Housework the missing link between the economy and private life. A framework of a theory which is directly related to my private life. A theory which is still a bit thin, a bit shaky on its legs, but I still have years to work on it and I can develop it in many different ways.

The work is healing, therapeutic, part of our alienation is lifted now that we make the connections visible for ourselves between what is happening to us personally and the times in which we live, the economic order, our social class.

It is good to work with women who are not suspicious of me, who think as I do. The direction we want to go is the same, criticism is support.

But in the meantime, I have been so busy writing articles, being in groups, giving introductory talks, that I get a fright when I realise how much of a phenomenon I have already become. The Meulenbelt institute. An authority. You probably won't have time for me, says one woman humbly over the telephone and it annoys me that indeed I don't have time, but I get so sick at the sound of her voice, the, you won't find me important enough, that I am silent – guilt. Trouble from other women who are learning from the women's movement not to let themselves be put down and to kick back, and who then promptly kick *my* shins. I get the feeling that they first nominate me as an authority so they can blame me afterwards because I am one. I'm being put on a pedestal unwillingly so that it is almost impossible to look others properly in the eyes. Image-making, so that I first have to penetrate walls of prejudice before I can really meet someone.

252

I become afraid. Begin to behave more diffidently than I really am. So scared to be thought dominant that I apologise before I have opened my mouth. I begin to make myself small again, while I had been so happy to be big at last. Hardly dare to be proud of my work, still the result of hard slog. Strong. I begin to hate the word. But you are so strong, women around me say, amazed when I am hurt by criticism which I find unreasonable. The dilemmas of the women's movement, its contradictory demands. On the one hand, collectivity, not competing with each other, not joining in with the hierarchical idea that writing is more important than typing. On the other hand the ideology of personal growth. Women must also be strong individuals if they want to survive. And becoming strong also means for me work in which I am visible, an independent income. I am always balancing on the edge of what is good for me and what is good for the movement. I sometimes work anonymously, sometimes under my own name. Refuse honorary posts. Sometimes do paid work, sometimes unpaid. I blush when I meet a woman who says, are you Anja Meulenbelt, do you know how much you have helped me with your articles? Do you know that for months I have gone to bed with *Sextant* magazine because of what you write? Do you know that through you I have had the courage to leave my husband? I stutter, feel just as uncomfortable as with the criticism. Then read Fanon who describes how groups emancipating themselves have the tendency first to take out their suppressed agression on each other. Women are easier victims. I don't after all hit back, I only feel guilty.

Arguments with Paulien in the commune. I come back from Femø convinced that if I want to stay on living there I must indeed put more into the house. I talk it over with Paulien. That we don't have the same ideas about housework, but that I agree I should fit in more with what the majority in the house want. Paulien doesn't understand me. We do the absolute minimum here, she says. We only expect you to take your turn, to be here at meetings, to finish your jobs. But five minutes later she accuses me of being too little at home. Listen, I say, I want to do my best. I think you are mostly right with your criticism of my

253

untidiness. But I will never be like you. If you want to criticise there will always be something I do wrong. I have the feeling there is something else. You are not irritated only because I forget to wash the tea towels or sweep the floors two days late. Paulien begins to cry. Then it comes out that she feels I don't care about her. She had actually expected she would be able to talk to me about her work more easily than with anyone else in the house. Why don't you come to me then? I ask. Because you are busy. Because I think you find your women friends outside the house more interesting than me. You don't ever come to me either, she says. And she is right. I avoid her because I expect to be scolded for not cleaning the cat box, or to get a cross look the minute I come through the door. We will have to try again, I say, while we hug each other tearfully. I'll try not to be so untidy. And if you would be a bit less critical and if we talked more with each other . . .

For a while it is better, but not for long. I realise that I am quite unable to manage to do anything with the whole group of children. Am happy if I even make contact with Armin now and then. The feeling continues that I can't succeed whatever I do, that I can't do anything right. I continue to look for warmth outside the house. Marie tells me she is occasionally obsessively jealous of me. At least that is honest, but it doesn't make our communication any easier. Armin does badly at school, one of the reasons is that he often comes home late and doesn't do his homework. Rows about bedtime and television. I begin from the premise that Armin has learned to go to bed when he is tired. I don't mind if sometimes he exhausts himself with a rubbishy programme. I myself often watch Peyton Place or Colombo and don't notice any deterioration in my brain cells.

And then I must admit things aren't any better between Paulien and me. That her sullen face still annoys me. And, if I am honest, that I really don't want to talk to her because she doesn't interest me. When Marianne leaves the house, it is the last straw. As soon as I have expressed my own decision to leave, I become calmer, the pressure is off me. Marie and Paulien are angry. Say that I am letting everyone down. But, I think, eighteen months is long enough to find out that I'm not suited to this. It isn't a question of misunderstandings or getting used to one another. If

I want to stay on here I'll have to make many more adjustments than I have so far and I don't want to do that. I learned in France that when I am in a crisis, overwhelmed by a life in ruins, no one in the commune can help me. I don't really like them very much, these people. Truis is the only one I'll miss when I go. I warn the commune that I am looking for a house, that I could be gone in a few months, that they should look for another person because I will not pay two rents. When I get a two-roomed flat quite quickly through the student accommodation bureau Paulien is angry, demands that I continue to pay rent. This is just like a divorce, I think. I am the guilty party, having to pay alimony.

I've no regrets. I know better now what I want, that I don't want to live alone, but also not in a group with so many children and living so much on top of each other. Armin and I are getting on much better than before. Happy in our little house. As if Armin has looked critically at all kinds of mothers and decided that I am certainly not the worst. As if we now have room again to like each other.

Work. Classes at the university with Hans, work where I can at last use my feminism. I like it, working with groups, with women who are changing. I stop giving lectures. The last one I let myself be trapped into is for a mixed audience from women's and gay organisations. When I arrive they tell me cheerfully they have invited me because the members' evenings have been so badly attended lately and, yes, look, it works, the hall is full of people who have come to see what the vampire really looks like.

I always have to answer the same stereotyped questions. Isn't it dangerous to cut yourself off from men in this way? asks one man. Dangerous for whom? I ask in reply. Not for me. For men perhaps? Abstract wordy arguments which disguise the simpler emotions underneath. The way men are threatened when we don't need them any more, because they don't have anything to offer which we can't get from other women, and better.

But you isolate yourselves, they say. And I ask in reply why no one accused me of that when I was shut in a house with a man and a child and felt truly isolated. While now I am available to tens, hundreds, thousands of women. Have never felt myself to be less isolated.

But why are you so against men? one man asks. Am I? I ask. If I choose for women does it then follow that I am against men? I just don't bother so much about them any more. Make my own rules. Become angry if they get in my way, hold me back, demand my attention. Is that being against them? The man hesitates. He can't put it into words, the rage which lies close behind his eyes. A strong taboo on saying that you don't need men. That they should first demonstrate what they have to offer. A stream of abuse to get me back into harness: manhater, unnatural, unfeminine, frustrated.

Yes, but we should work together, calls another man. What do you mean together? I ask. Where were you at the establishment of the first liberation groups, which were still open to men. Were you there? Did you march in the abortion demonstration, do you do half the housework? What do you mean by together? Is it chance that men are interested in feminism now, when we no longer wait for them, don't try to remain reasonable, to convince them, to take them with us?

As if it is a football match where only one side can win. It is exactly the same people who always talk about 'together' who have this idea in their heads that men will deteriorate if women gain anything for themselves. Don't see how they unconsciously start from the premise that there is a conflict of interests. Would they ever tell me that I hate old people because I choose to work in youth programmes? Or that I hated whites when I worked with the Black Panthers?

And then the soft man, the new generation. Who wants to throw himself into my arms so that he can personally be saved by me. But I *agree* with you, he calls, when I explain that I can't solve his problems for him. Almost walk into the same trap as before, guilt, responsibility. A mother of the soft men who sympathise with the women's movement and are now hurt because they can't join in. I have given my energy to the preservation of men for almost thirty years. Now I don't want anyone round my neck any more. But I *agree* with you, the dear soft man calls again. If you really want to do something, I say, tell that to your own kind who won't listen to us, not to me. When you learn to be kind to each other, then I'll have one thing less to worry about.

Do you really enjoy that, just being with women? asks a fat man at the exit, smiling suggestively and spitefully at me. Oh yes, I poisonously spit back, they are really just like people, you know.

My last lecture. I don't want to work again ever for such uncommitted mixed groups. The men always succeed in drawing all the attention to themselves. The women, caught in their double loyalty, no longer like me when they see me react too quickly to their men's stupidity. We need a different climate to allow our solidarity to grow. From now on I make my own conditions.

At the bookshop I see a book for sale: *The Mixed Marriage*. What is that then? I think stupidly. Until I realise what it is about. I thought all marriages were mixed, by definition.

London, a few days away from everything, the half yearly feminist socialist conference as excuse. I need to get material for my article on domestic labour, to talk with a few women there about publishing their articles, about their participation in the seminar. On the boat there are other feminists, a few from the group to which Anna and I belonged. Rita is on board, I still need to talk through an argument with her. It is clear that this must happen in London. At the last moment Paulien comes on board, when I see her I want to murder her. Then Barbara says: I didn't tell you before, but Ton and Anna are going to London for a few days with the children, Anna is even coming to the conference.

Christ, I groan, I wanted to get away but this is beginning to look like trouble.

And then I start to work myself up. Bloody hell, I think, your second honeymoon in London, London that I gave to you as a present. And on top of that a visit to the conference. Phoney feminist. When she knows I'll be there too. When she knows that I hate her.

London, always the same excitement when I am there, I ride on

257

the bus, smell the underground. The conference, unstructured as usual, in an old school building or hall. Four to five hundred women, how many are there this time? I embrace my friends, Jill is too busy with the revolution to talk, rushing around with notices and stencils. I descend on the tables, laid out with material neatly divided into trotskyist, leninist and radical feminist, third world, abortion, community politics. I see that this year the maoists have come inside with their stall. Last year they stood outside shouting that we shouldn't join the middle-class women inside who betray the class struggle. Perhaps it is too cold outside for them, the same pamphlets are still for sale. I become manic from so many words, upset piles of books, find discussions on housework which I don't have. New books. I already know that when I go to London I have to take a half-empty suitcase. Last time a woman gave me a friendly tap on the shoulder: are you a compulsive buyer? she asked, ready to help me.

I keep one eye on the door to avoid Anna if she comes in. There is a big hall where the discussion proceeds in a disciplined and civilised manner. The first time I was very impressed with the English women who were so articulate, seemed to have so little difficulty in standing up and giving their opinions, hardly ever interrupting each other. Now I feel at home, but I am tense, because Anna is coming.

She doesn't arrive. I become happy and calm again. At night we talk with the women with whom we are staying. We share a bottle of wine. Talk about sexuality. What am I? Practising heterosexual, but only recently once again. Political lesbian. Should you call that bisexual? What do you call that? I ask. If I say bisexual I hear feminists say that I am scared to lose approval, that I don't dare take the final step. If I say I am a lesbian, they blame me because I make love to a man. If I say I am heterosexual they blame me for betraying my relationship with women. What should I do? Sometimes I don't make love. Then I can say I am celibate and am only accused by men of frustration. We should stop using words which define our sexuality in terms of its object, says one of the women. *My* sexuality is *my* sexuality, whether I make love to a man or to a woman. I talk about sex with Sandra who is in a relationship that has lasted a long time. Do you feel guilty? I ask, when you don't feel like making love? In the beginning I did, she replies. You always get something like, isn't our relationship good any more. Don't I deprive Paul of something? I find it difficult.

A second bottle of wine has also been drained. Caroline and Ria together in one bed. I am alone, in a cold English room with Russian posters and the collected New Left Review on the bookshelf.

The next day she is suddenly there, Anna, when I no longer expect her. I walk away, my stomach in knots, look for Rita and Ria to cling on to. They take me to the almost-empty canteen for watery English coffee. Suddenly there is a break, the discussion groups dissolve and women stream into the canteen. I see Anna come in with a few women from her group, she stands close to me. I sweat, tremble, almost crush my cup. Bitch, I mumble. What would you really like to do? asks Rita therapeutically. Smash her face in, I say irrationally. Why don't you do that, says Rita, who believes in living out your emotions. My heart beats loudly, all my muscles are tense. My anger conquers my fear of misbehaving. I stand up, go to her, without knowing what I am going to do until I stand in front of her. Hello Anja, she says, white-faced. Bugger off, I scream. Get out. Stay away from my place. Bitch, you don't belong here. I see her shake too. I have just as much right to be here as you, she says. But naturally it isn't about rights, but about anger. Before I can think I hit her in the face as hard as I can. She hits back, but I hardly feel it. She says again that she has just as much right to be here. I go back to my table. Ria is crying. The women around us pretend they haven't seen anything, very British. I get a fright when I see the tears on Ria's face, but she takes my hand, isn't angry with me. I still tremble, enough aggression to beat Anna into little pieces, the blow only a hundredth part of the wave of anger. But when the trembling stops I notice that it helped. I am almost proud that I dared, instead of always talking. At last I have expressed the anger which I have always turned inwards, tossing in bed, thinking as I wake in the morning, rotten traitor, bourgeois frump with your family.

I am happy the next day. I eat at Sandra's house, she has also invited the 'Political Economy of Women' group. We exchange

259

information. I dance with them. Make a date with Pauline together with her friend. The following day buy books, wander through the city with changing groups of women. Pick up Pauline after her karate class, with her friend who was once a soldier and is now in the men against sexism group, the group which always looks after the crêches when there is a conference. A pub, subdued lighting, dusty dark colours. Pauline becomes more beautiful the longer you know her. Richard radiates warmth. He explains the self-hatred which made him take the first career which would take him abroad. This is a man who can talk about himself in the same way women do. Tells me about Pauline and himself, how difficult he finds it that she continues to live with her husband, that they can see each other only a few times a week. He makes jokes. About how sexist language is. That we should replace the words 'man' and 'miss' with 'person'. That chairman and madam chair should be 'chairperson'. And that the word 'mismanagement' should therefore be changed to 'personpersonagepeopled'.

Pauline laughs, happier than I have ever seen her. She says on the way to the bus, one hand in mine, the other in his, that she feels she has just discovered what making love is. And she has three grown-up children.

I am under the spell of their happiness. And exhausted. I am not looking forward to another day in London. Send a telegram that I am coming home. I miss Hans, my own bed. When I leave Richard yells his final battle cry after me: the land for the farmers, the factories for the workers, the breweries for the alcoholics.

And always I return to my femsoc group. Weekends together, weeks, dancing after studying. My body is supple, When I see myself dance past the reflections in the window I think that I am beautiful, my body does what I want, fluid movements, and I follow the rhythm of my hips. I dare to do silly things, stamp around with Marleen doing the bouncing bunny, follow Lenie's movements, who dances manically inward-looking, in a trance, and then, with an embarrassed laugh, with me.

I dance parodies, the seductive siren, Meulendyke femme fatale. Parodies on how we used to dance, I grab Mieke, with one hand on her bum I push her backwards across the floor while I look over her shoulder at the other women. The trick of the young men who look glassily unmoved above you while they grind their hips against you and you never know to which messages you should react, those from above or those from below. We try them out, all the sexist ways of dancing and how we defended ourselves subtly in order not to be called aggressive.

Flopping against each other, screaming with laughter, stomach cramps from laughing. And then I dance again on my own. Janis Joplin, freedom's just another word for nothin' left to lose.

On the wall of the toilet in the women's house in Berlin I read: a woman without a man is like a fish without a bicycle.

Epilogue

'And what is the next stage?'

'The next stage is, surely, that I leave the safety of myth and Anna Wulf walks forward alone.'

'Alone?' she said, and added dryly, 'You're a communist, or so you say, but you want to go alone. Isn't that what you'd call a contradiction?'

And so we laughed, and it might have ended there, but I went on ... 'But now I can feel. I'm open to everything. But no sooner do you accomplish that, when you say quickly – put it away where it can't hurt, turn it into a story or into history. But I don't want to put it away. Yes, I know what you want me to say – that because I've rescued so much private pain-material – because I'm damned if I'll call it anything else, and "worked through it" and accepted it and made it general, because of that I'm free and strong. Well all right, I'll accept it and say it. And what now? I'm tired of the wolves and the castles and the forests and the priests. I can cope with them in any form they choose to present themselves. But I've told you, I want to walk off, by myself, Anna Freeman.'

'By yourself?' she said again.

'Because I'm convinced that there are whole areas of me made by the kind of experience women haven't had before ...'

Doris Lessing, *The Golden Notebook*

Gordes 15

There is definitely no money left. We can make the border only if we just eat bread and cheese on the way.

An unexpected queue. Burning heat in the car. We are packed tightly against the luggage now that Manuel is also with us. Move only a meter at a time. Everyone is irritable. It is impossible to eat the cheese, the mineral water is finished and the wine is luke-warm in the bottle.

The previous day I felt it suddenly come on before I could see it. The first drop of blood. Relieved that I don't have to go through the experience of an abortion. The need for a child is so close to the surface that I couldn't have gone through with it without feeling bad. All the toilets on the road are closed. I struggle behind a bush with tampax. Can't wash my hands, lick the blood off my fingers. Cleaner than tap water after all. My body no longer consists of two parts like when I had one flannel for below and one for above.

One body, my body.

Fret over my book, the two notebooks in the bag next to me. I'll have to leave out so much. I don't say enough about Armin and me. I don't say enough about the content of my feminism, much more about how I live it. It should be a unity, but again . . . I can think it in my most lucid moments, I can dream it, but where is the language in which I can express it? I leave out jobs in my book. Scrap relationships, houses, communes. Write little about my parents, who remain colourless. Write little about the political background to Ton and me, Anna and me. Tell myself that it is impossible to write a book with everything in it.

I am delighted to be back in Amsterdam. Can already see my cats rubbing themselves against my legs, crying reproachfully. Excitement when I look through the pile of letters, journals. My own house, the dark brown walls, the books. Put on a record. Sleep gently under my coverlet, with all the colours of the rainbow.

The next day I'll go to Van Gennep, the bookshop, to see if there is anything new in the women's section in the basement. Open the rest of the mail in an espresso bar. A roll with mince and onions. And perhaps, if I feel like it, unpack my red typewriter and see if it is possible to turn the black scribbled letters into proper legible type.

On the crest of the wave

Slowly I emerge from sleep, float for a while just below the surface. I don't know which bed I am lying in. Noise of people above and below me. Friendly movements. Marjan is walking up and down above me, below me I can hear Jantien and Gerdien laughing. These are the noises of the commune on the Prinsengracht. Not the noises of the Noordermarkt: women passing by on their way to the market to do their shopping, garbage vans, lorries which can't make the corner.

I have been sleeping in Boukje's room for the last couple of days because I am finishing my book. My hands are stiff from last night's fly-posting. Abortion posters. I still have a stupid fear when I go fly-posting, even though I know that nothing worse can happen than a few hours in a police station and a small fine, which anyway will be paid by the abortion committee. But we weren't caught, the other team was. Released at once because they weren't 'political' posters. The women ask, almost insulted, what is political then? Well, if you were from one of the communist groups you wouldn't get off so easily. Protection because we aren't taken seriously. In Germany the first feminists are already banned from state employment, under the *Berufsverbot* laws. There they realise that abortion is a political issue.

The final chapter. I have taken nine months to type this pile of paper, two hundred and seventy-one pages.

Nine chaste months during which I have made love to no one and lost a stone in weight. All my energy has gone into my work, all my emotions into the book. New friendships, but no overwhelming new loves. Nine months reflection, rest. An evaluation of my life, finding in dark corners what I had forgotten, old emotions which I had swept under the carpet with other rubbish and which now come to light. An ego trip in which there was no place for relationships which would demand too much from me. A therapy in which I could at last mourn for those people I had not yet mourned. Too busy keeping myself on my feet. Been brave too long.

How could you endure all that? asks someone who read the first chapters. I did not endure it, I say. I survived those three years. Because I had to. You can't afford to break down if you have a child. I wanted to kill myself, but I couldn't, my responsibility was more important than my need to leave the movie. And now I'm glad that Armin kept me in harness, held me tight, gave me no chance to escape. Until I came into the women's movement and now live, not more easily, but more clearly. I don't endure my life any more as if it were a natural disaster. I do something with what has happened to me.

I still have no solutions, but perhaps the fact that I have learned to live with that is the solution.

A declining relationship with Hans. It look a lot of effort to turn what we had into friendship. To stay working with each other and to meet each other in the commune without falling back into the old irritations which belong at the end of a marriage. Difficult, perhaps too difficult. Perhaps we will hate each other.

For a year and a half we have been busy splitting up, trying again and again to keep the pieces of our relationship that were valuable to us, trying to be honest, but not to destroy each other. There are few models. Friendship with men hardly exists. So much easier to slam the door behind you and say, I don't want to see you any more. So difficult to find a shape for what remains, appreciation for each other and work in which we can find each other. An excellent eating relationship.

Armin almost grown up. Just a few more years, in a month or so he is fourteen. But still the uncertainty, that I don't do it properly.

The telephone rings. Anja speaking, I say, because I can't get my surname over my lips any more. The institute Meulenbelt, the phenomenon. My first name is still the closest to me. A polite cough on the other end of the line. Am I speaking to the mother of the pupil Armin from Class 2B?

I immediately begin to sweat. Images flash by of all the things he could have done. Truanted, fought, stolen. Insulted a teacher. Made a girl pregnant. Smoked hash in break. Locked up the headmaster. Discovered making love with a friend. I already feel guilty.

I have done it wrong, I want to confess everything before the man says why he rang. Mrs Meulenbelt, says the man, we have looked through the accounts and it appears that you have not yet given your money for the parents' fund.

I stammer something about sending it at once, that I had forgotten, and hang up with damp hands. Immediately put Armin's clothes in the washing machine. I never learn to be self assured when they touch my weak spot, my motherhood.

Solutions, I don't have any solutions. There aren't any. But I survive, see women around me waking up. My world becomes more and more habitable. The women's movement has long since outgrown me. I have retreated from the organisation of the femsoc groups because I felt that others should do it, because it isn't good always to have my finger in every pie. And now I look on, like a mother hen to see if things are going well.

Actually I want to be everywhere, always have the feeling that I want to be where things are happening.

But that isn't possible any more. The cells of the movement have grown unnoticed, are no longer eradicable. They can't measure our strength by the demonstrations on the streets, we have been working. Women's groups in neighbourhoods, in political parties, in unions. I do my part of the work, concrete work, visible. Working with women who don't call themselves feminists, but who are whether they want to be or not.

I still get waves of anxiety about my livelihood even if I believe in my work. Panic if the management threatens to interfere if we overstep the limits of what the ministry thinks the college ought to be doing. I have nightmares about being sacked. Become uncertain because of the suspicion of some of my colleagues. Hear a student from another group call women's groups racist and fascist because they don't allow men in. Get visions of the German *Berufsverbot* slowly creeping over the border so that the politically committed can't get state employment. See myself unemployed again, driven into isolation. Above my desk is stuck a piece of paper: Just because you're paranoid doesn't mean they're *not* out to get you.

The dream I had on my return from Femø, high on women, radiant on women. The dream of a huge group of women running somewhere. Suddenly I look round and I am the only one running. The others have disappeared.

Sometimes I envy the women who have gone voluntarily into isolation. I can't do that, and mustn't, the feminism which says withdraw from society is not effective. There is work to do and I must learn to struggle, to fight, to be considered a threat, unpleasant.

Uncertainty about where I live. I can't stay at the Prinsengracht commune now that Hans and I no longer want to share one room any more, not even for a few days in the week. There is no space there for me. I retreat to my temporary flat in the Noordermarkt. I miss the people in the commune, the talk on the stairs or at mealtimes. I miss Marjan whom I now see less, both of us always busy and not the sort of people to spend an afternoon visiting.

269

My new commune group has just started. We still haven't got a house and that can take months or a year or more.

I walk backwards and forwards between houses with my plastic case. Have to plan in advance which clothes I'll put on, which books I'll read in the next three days. Too difficult. I'm too old for this, for this wandering, for moving each time and painting new walls brown, once again sawing up my bookcases to fit.

Relationships, I don't know any more what happens in them. Perhaps we still ask too much? suggests Marjan. Partial relationships seem to be the only alternative. Someone with whom you share a bit of politics, but from whom you don't get the same recognition as you get from women. Someone with whom you can identify within the movement, but with whom you have arguments over politics. We are too peculiar, says Marjan. Socialist and feminist and demanding. Too threatening. How often do we need to scold each other, comfort each other, say isn't it ridiculous this vision of a great love, the one person with whom we shall share everything, who is still waiting for us somewhere? Remember Andreas Burnier who knew exactly how many women in the Netherlands were her type, lesbian, her age, academically trained, and she had had all of them.

Marjan chooses to try now and again. I choose to have no more relationships just out of need for warmth or sex. No polonaise over my body.

Are you too good to fuck now and then just for pleasure? asks a man sarcastically. Exactly, I say, for that I am too good. Everyone is too good for that, for bloodless, emotionless gymnastic exercises. It bores me as well. There are limits to the number of ways that you can fit two bodies into each other. I have done them all, experimented for ten years. Don't tell me what I need. I know what I need. I'd rather sleep alone in my bed with my nest of books built around it, a little sad, but whole, than let myself be seduced again into relationships which don't touch my source, which stay outside me.

Shall we make a deal, says Marjan to me, when we are around fifty let's begin a relationship with each other? You don't mean it, I say when I see her face. That's true, she says, and we'd have arguments about the cat box.

Relationships. I don't know what happens in them.

I see long hands with narrow nails. We talk, I haven't had such a good talk with a man for a long time. Almost always I get the feeling that I have to explain everything, that I am pushed into a defensive position, must descend to the emotional level of the nursery.

But I talk to him and I notice that he *really* listens.

Long hands which roll a cigarette from my pouch of tobacco. I hide myself behind a curtain of smoke. I am embarrassed by how I feel.

Black hair falls into his eyes. He pushes it away with a stereotyped gesture. I almost have to sit on my hands to stop myself doing it, smoothing the hair off his forehead. Instead of which I roll another cigarette. How idiotic, I think, when I walk home warm and confused. If I have a good talk with a man who doesn't immediately make a pass at me, then I am the one who wants to drag him to my nest. And I don't even know him. Have only seen him a few times from a distance. A lecturer. It is striking that he is one of the few who don't interrupt an older woman who is asking a question, but listens to her, answers with a soft voice. That is all, and I walk around my room like a tortured animal, like a tiger in the zoo before feeding time. Can't concentrate and lie tossing in my bed.

Long hands, a gold ring. A warning: possession, don't touch. A reason for not walking bravely up to him and saying listen I can't keep my hands off you, do you mind? May I look for the soft places on your body and exchange them for mine?

Probably he won't want to, father of a family with responsibilities. And perhaps he beats his wife, wipes his feet on her.

Quiet, quiet, I say to myself. These are all projected fantasies. It will pass, this sickness. Just wait. Afterwards you can never make out what you saw in someone. Then I meet him again in the street. Sidle past him, while all I say is hello. Knees of cooked spaghetti, an aquarium with zigzagging sticklebacks in my belly. Help.

Quiet, quiet. You know that it isn't good for you, I say to myself to calm the beast in my belly. Eat something sweet. Pour

271

yourself a glass of wine. Put on a sad record. Go to sleep, dream sweetly. Tomorrow just get on with the work.

The feeling is there still, but no one forces you to do something about it.

'Do you believe in love at first sight?', asks a woman in an old Paul Newman film. No, he says, 'but I believe in confusion.'

Work. Satisfaction in allowing bits of theory to grow. All investments now appear to be valuable: all the books I have read, work-groups, conversations. All my experiences are material. The lines become clearer, I begin to see connections. The links between all the individual emotions and the economic structure in which we live. A year ago we made a joke about holding a lecture on love under late capitalist relations of production. But we aren't laughing any more.

There is still a split between most of our political work and most of our experiences. I still write in two languages. Zwei Seelen wohnen, ach, in meine Brust, but that is dialectic, and the synthesis is growing. The different areas in my life begin to overlap more. We work while we make love. We live politics. And now and then we succeed in lifting a little of the alienation which is laid on us. A vision of the society that is to come. We women already live on the boundary between the personal and the political. Relationships are our work, we are closer to our emotions, the understanding we had for others – the slave mentality – is a weapon we use to support each other while we make the private life public once more.

I receive a parcel in the morning post. From the ministry. When I open it curiously, it appears that I am one of the fifty Dutch women who are honoured in International Woman's Year. The dreadful UNO bird with the woman's symbol on it and an equal sign, mounted on a block of marble. Honoured, god forbid, while I have done my best as a semi-subversive element to sabotage the year. Aren't you ashamed, asks Marjan, when I just sit laughing at this ridiculous object, this dead sparrow which is, at this moment, also rotting on the queen's bedside table, which is useful only to smash windows with. I must send it back, I say crossly, can you imagine if they publish my name as one of the

272

women in the Netherlands who have participated in this farce? Netherlands? where they don't even notice when you try to bring the revolution nearer home. Where you are patted on the head by the authorities when you try to saw the legs off their thrones.

All the uncertainties in my life. I don't know how my future will look. I have no image in my head when I think ahead two or three years.

A celebration in the Women's House, the lesbian front. When I come in the High Priestess greets me, surprised. Yes, I say, you didn't expect me here. Frump, she says, that's your own guilt trip. I am glad you are here.

She's right, I think. She doesn't decide if I belong here, among the women who have chosen for women. I decide. I see women friends dancing with each other, also see women I didn't expect to see here, and am intensely happy.

I dance in the crowd to the witch music. *Lavender Jane loves Women*. Or just look, at women whom I have begun to find so beautiful, who dance close together in couples, who dance in groups, with swinging hair and shining eyes, proud of what they are. Grown-up and now stronger than those people who had no need to fight oppression. I am in love, I think, with a species. It could be her, or the woman there on the other side. I dance with old friends and new ones, my body supple, the warmth of their breasts against mine, their smell. I see other women look at me, but I don't feel watched.

I feel beautiful among women, am beautiful. No longer afraid to grow old.

It is as if I have come home, I say to Jantien. Back in mother's arms. Everyone comes back, says Jantien, everyone.

I live on the crest of a wave. Vulnerable in all my uncertainties. How can you hold tight to a river? Indestructible and strong in my feeling that I can only go forward this way. There is no way back.

Return to GO

I meet her again in the supermarket, the young woman with the inward-looking gaze. Myself, but no longer who I am. She blushes as she drops her money. I smile encouragingly at her when she has picked up her purse and stands fumbling at the cash desk. She doesn't accept the eye contact I am offering her. Perhaps she is ashamed. Perhaps she thinks I am laughing at her, patronising her. Perhaps it escapes her, she has closed herself off. I should like to put my arms around her, warm her cold breasts in my hands. Mouth to mouth resuscitation. But I am afraid to offer her more than the eye contact which she is refusing. She would be afraid if she knew what I am thinking. Would call me one of those dirty lesbians, unnatural women, fanatical man-haters. She is scared of me and I understand too well why.

She will have to take the first steps herself. I can do nothing more than wait on the sidelines until she bursts out of her cage. I can stretch a hand for her if she wants. Can give her a shoulder to cry on if she can't go on.

As long as her face is closed and mistrustful, I am not free. As long as she is ashamed and bends her shoulders instead of drawing herself up to her full height, I am not free. As long as she accepts her life as it is, the daily walk to the supermarket, the accounting to make sure she will balance her housekeeping allowance, the chops cost more than last week and her husband doesn't like mince the way she makes it, I am not free.

I need her just as much as she needs me, but she doesn't know it yet. She looks shyly around at me when she leaves the shop with her two heavy bags. Myself, but no longer who I am.

Whoever thinks that this is all, *one* woman who wrestled with her shame, *one* unique herstory separate from all the others, has not understood.

If friendship is so simple then I have said too little.

SHULAMITH FIRESTONE
The Dialectic of Sex
The Case for Feminist Revolution
Introduced by Rosalind Delmar

'The most readable, persuasive and still provocative attempt to develop "radical feminism", which, when taken as a whole is inadequate as a social theory but which brilliantly homes in on the moment-to-moment "sex-war" which anti-feminists deem to have been ended either by the vote or by an appeal to biology which claims sex difference as merely biological, discounting history and social structure'

Michelene Wandor, Books & Bookmen (sic)

'An extraordinarily rich and all-embracing book, taking on the whole of history, the whole of politics and the whole of culture in order to emphasise the different but consonant ways in which women have been labelled over history and in our own times as different and therefore weaker and inferior'

Michèle Roberts, Gay News

'It is very radical, very intelligent and a pleasure to read'

The Scotsman (sic)

'We all have a long way to go. That's why it was very good to read this book again. A sober experience. Don't miss it'

Women Speaking

Politics   £2.50

The Women's Press is a feminist publishing house. We aim to publish a wide range of lively, provocative books by women, chiefly in the areas of fiction, literary history, art history, physical and mental health and politics.

We can supply books direct (please add 35 pence for postage and packing) but please support our efforts to have our books available in all bookshops, libraries and educational institutes. To receive our complete list of titles please send a large stamped addressed envelope. We welcome suggestions and comments.

If you have enjoyed *The Shame is Over* you will be interested to know that we have published another journey of self-discovery.

VERENA STEFAN
Shedding

'There's honesty, artistry and humanity leaping out of every page of Verena Stefan's book *Shedding* . . . The way she has written about her personal growth means a triumphant leap forward for feminist literature'   *Aberdeen Evening Express*

'Her book is a lucid, witty and honest account of a political and emotional journey . . . The "shedding" of the title refers to layers of insecurity and self-dislike; the dependency that leads women to confuse the need for male approval with love or even desire for men's bodies . . . It's not a very militant book; just an infectiously joyous one'   *Spare Rib*

'Deserves to be a basic text of the movement'
                                                        Woman's Place Newsletter

Politics/Autobiography   £1.50

MICHELE ROBERTS
A Piece of the Night

'Uncompromising in its feminism and confident and original in its style . . . a landmark in the British Women's Movement and in women's writing. Its language is our own – angry, analytic, harsh and poetic'   *Women Speaking*

'A new writer of talent and energy'   *The Guardian*

'Her prose is rich and sinewy and invigorating and her ideas are stimulating and thought provoking'   *The Sunday Press*, Dublin

'The writing has quality and vigour'   *The Times*

'Ms Roberts' prose has the distinction of Colette' *The Sunday Times*

Joint winner of the *Gay News* Book Award, 1979

Fiction

£2.95